AMERICA: WHAT WENT WRONG?

DONALD L. BARLETT and **JAMES B. STEELE**
of the Philadelphia Inquirer

Andrews and McMeel
A Universal Press Syndicate Company
Kansas City

Designed by Barrie Maguire.

Library of Congress Cataloging-in-Publication Data

Barlett, Donald L.
    America : what went wrong? / Donald L. Barlett, James B. Steele.
      p. cm.
    Includes index.
    ISBN 0-8362-7001-0 : $6.95
      1. United States—Economic conditions—1981-   2. United States—Economic policy—1981-   I. Steele, James B. II. Title.
    HC106.8.B373   1992
    338.973—dc20   92-6026
                                                  CIP

First Printing, March 1992
Fifth Printing, August 1992

CONTENTS

ACKNOWLEDGMENTS

America: What Went Wrong? is an expanded version of a nine-part series originally published by the *Philadelphia Inquirer* in October 1991. The series generated the largest response from readers in the newspaper's history—some 20,000 letters, notes, telephone calls, and requests for reprints.

Of all the debts we incurred in researching and writing this project, the largest is to the institution where we have worked for the last twenty-one years—the *Philadelphia Inquirer*. In an age in which many newspapers are advocating short news stories, the *Inquirer* continues to swim vigorously and successfully against the tide, believing, as we do, that readers want detailed information they can get nowhere else, that they will read long stories if the material is interestingly written and appropriately presented.

"America: What Went Wrong?" filled twenty-five pages and was typical of what readers have come to expect from the newspaper. It is a tradition that began for us in 1971 under John McMullan, who brought us together in a temporary partnership that is now in its twenty-second year. It continued under his successor, Gene Roberts, who expanded the horizons of investigative reporting and made the newspaper's name synonymous with the best of the investigative genre. And it flourishes under Roberts's successor, Maxwell King, who became Editor of the *Inquirer* when Roberts retired in 1990. King not only brought enthusiasm and commitment to this project, but he also helped shape the research into some of the broad themes that have had a powerful impact on readers. To all of them, we are deeply appreciative of their support and belief in us.

In addition, we would also like to thank all those we interviewed, many of whom are quoted in the book, as well as many others who are not yet whose observations and insights were of equal value to us in understanding the nuances of everything from defined-benefit pension plans to junk bonds.

We would also like to express our appreciation to employees of state, local and federal agencies and of state and federal courts throughout the country who patiently assisted in the difficult task of locating records and documents. A special word of thanks must go to Lela Young, in the public reading room of the Securities and Exchange Commission in Washington. An island of serenity in the most chaotic workplace imaginable, Mrs. Young has been a help for many years and this is a small way to say thanks.

As always, we are indebted to librarians at public, private and university libraries across the country, including those at Lippincott Library of the University of Pennsylvania, in the government-publications room of the Free Library of Philadelphia and at the Niles (Michigan) Community Library. We owe special thanks to the library staff of the *Inquirer* for hours spent assisting us in ferreting out information from electronic data bases.

We would also like to thank all those who edited the original *Inquirer* series on which this book is based. They are an exceptional group who did much to make this subject come alive for readers: Managing Editor Steve Lovelady, with whom we have enjoyed what may be the longest, and certainly for us, the most rewarding editing-reporting association in newspapers. That association is now in its twentieth year. We also profited greatly from the editing skills of Assistant Managing Editor Lois Wark, and Deputy Features Editor Marietta Dunn. We also had the benefit of the expert copy-editing skills of Julie Stoiber and Hope Keller. We also want to thank *Inquirer* graphic artist Bill Marsh for the splendid graphics that grace each chapter and the guidance of David Milne, the newspaper's talented graphic-arts director. A special note of thanks is also due Bing Mark, an *Inquirer* editorial assistant, who performed invaluable research for us in the final moments of the project. Finally, we are indebted to Rick Bowmer, an extraordinarily gifted *Inquirer* photographer who accompanied us on many of the reporting trips and shared many of the experiences that are recounted in the book.

At Andrews and McMeel, we want to thank Editorial Director Donna Martin, whose enthusiasm and support for this book were so helpful from the start; Barrie Maguire for his outstanding design; Tom Stites, whose careful reading of the original articles helped us immeasurably in converting the material to book form; and Bill Robbins, whose gifted editing skills made this a better book.

PROLOGUE
THE CHANGING FACE OF AMERICA

WHAT WENT WRONG

The wage and salary structure of American business, encouraged by federal tax policies, is pushing the nation toward a two-class society. The top 4% make as much as the bottom half of U.S. workers.

In 1959 (each symbol=1 million workers):

 ◀ **The top 4%**
(2.1 million individuals and families) earned $31 billion in wages and salaries — the same as

the bottom 35% ▶
(18.3 million individuals and families).

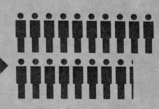

In 1989:

◀ **The top 4%**
(3.8 million individuals and families) earned $452 billion in wages and salaries — the same as

the bottom 51% ▶
(49.2 million individuals and families).

SOURCE: Internal Revenue Service

Where Are the Referees?

Listen to the people in charge of the American economy tell how well the recovery was going in 1991.

Listen to them explain, month after month, how economic conditions were improving for you.

On Dec. 16, 1990, Nicholas Brady, secretary of the United States Treasury, told a television audience: "I have great conviction the American economy is strong. We're in a cyclical downturn. It'll return to a good strong level sometime in 1991. . . . We'll be back on the growth path, jobs, investment, during that year."

On Feb. 4, 1991, the Council of Economic Advisers, headed by Michael J. Boskin, reported: "The downturn in the U.S. economy in the latter part of 1990 does not signal any decline in its long-run underlying health or basic vitality. . . . Several factors suggest that the economic downturn is not likely to last long and that a recovery will begin by the middle of 1991."

On June 11, 1991, President Bush told the National Advertising Federation: "If I can borrow a term from Wall Street, I am bullish on the economy. . . . While some sectors are still sluggish, on the whole, a turnaround in the economy appears to be in the making. . . . Things are beginning to move forward. And as far as your industry is concerned, I'm optimistic that it, too, will pick up as the rest of the economy gathers steam."

On July, 10, 1991, Alan Greenspan, chairman of the Federal Reserve Board, told a news conference: "I think the evidence is increasing week by week that the bottom is passed and the economy is beginning to move up. . . . I think it's a pretty safe bet at this stage to conclude that the decline is behind us and the outlook is continuing to improve."

On Oct., 4, 1991, President Bush told a news conference: "I think the economy is recovering. I think it will be more robust as we go along here. Job creation is fast."

Job creation fast?

You might have a different view. Especially if you were one of the 74,000 workers destined to lose their jobs at General Motors Corporation, the world's largest car manufacturer.

Or one of the 2,500 workers whose jobs were eliminated at TRW Inc., the space and defense contractor with interests in information services and automotive equipment.

Or one of the 8,000 workers whose jobs were eliminated at GTE Corporation, the telephone operations and telecommunications company.

Or one of the 4,000 workers whose jobs were eliminated at Westinghouse Electric Corporation, the diversified broadcasting, energy and electronic systems company.

Or one of the 5,000 workers whose jobs were eliminated at Allied-Signal Inc., the aerospace, automotive and engineered-materials (synthetic fibers and plastics) company.

Or one of the 1,000 workers whose jobs were eliminated at First Chicago Corporation, the global corporate bank.

Or one of the 4,000 workers whose jobs were eliminated at J.I. Case, the construction and farm-equipment maker.

Or one of the 20,000 workers destined to lose their jobs at International Business Machines Corporation, the computer company with a decades-old reputation of guaranteeing job security.

You also might have a different view if you are one of the millions of workers competing for a shrinking number of manufacturing jobs. Preliminary figures show that in 1991 about 18.4 million men and women were employed in manufacturing, earning middle-class wages. Ten years earlier, in 1981, there were 20.2 million men and women at work in manufacturing. Between 1981 and 1991, a total of 1.8 million manufacturing jobs vanished in the United States—a decline of 9 percent.

This at the same time the population 16 and older rose from 171.8 million to 191.2 million—an increase of 11 percent. In other words, while the potential work force grew by 19.4 million persons, the number of manufacturing jobs shrank by 1.8 million.

You also might have a different view if you are a member of America's disappearing middle class—whether blue-collar, white-collar, middle-level manager or professional.

And you especially might have a different view if you are one of the millions of Americans seeking to attain a middle-class status that you now find beyond your reach. But that's because you have a skewed vision. You are on the bottom looking up.

Those in charge, on the other hand, are on the top looking down. They see things differently. Call it the view from Washington and Wall Street.

It is a view that can be documented by a mountain of statistics. Such as the amount of money you receive in your weekly paycheck, contrasted with the paychecks of more affluent citizens.

Take 1989, the latest year for which complete data, as compiled from federal income tax returns, are available. That year, the top 4 percent of all wage earners in the country collected as much in wages and salaries as the bottom 51 percent of the population. Mull over the numbers carefully: The top 4 percent of America's work force earned as much as the bottom 51 percent. That is in wages and salaries alone. In more precise numbers, 3.8 million individuals and families at the top earned as much from their jobs as did 49.2 million individuals and families at the bottom.

The view from Washington and Wall Street was not always so distorted. In 1970, the top 4 percent earned as much on the job as the bottom 38 percent. And in 1959, they earned as much as the bottom 35 percent.

Now put the numbers in order, as viewed from the bottom: In 1959—a time of growing middle-class prosperity—the bottom 35 percent of the work force earned as much as the top 4 percent. By 1970, it took the wages of the bottom 38 percent of the work force to match the top 4 percent.

By 1989—a time of middle-class decline—it took the wages and salaries of the lowest 51 percent of the workers to equal the wages and salaries of the 4 percent at the top.

If the trend continues, sometime early in the next century the top 4 percent of individuals and families drawing paychecks will earn as much on the job as 60 percent of the rest of American workers.

Keep in mind these numbers deal only with wages and salaries. They do not include interest and dividends; gains from the sale of stocks, bonds and other capital assets; or income from other investments, indeed, from any other sources. This income, too, flows overwhelmingly to the top 4 percent.

For a growing number of individuals and families, the exploding difference in wages and salaries among the people at the top and everyone else means the end of the American dream. Call it the relentless shrinking of the middle class.

Not to worry. The people in Washington want to help. Democrats, for example, have proposed both tax cuts and tax credits for the middle class. But lest you believe Democrats at work in the nation's capital have an edge over Republicans—who through most of 1991 insisted all was well—in dealing with the economy, ponder the words of one party leader. In a speech to his colleagues in October 1991, Richard A. Gephardt, the Missouri Democrat who is the majority leader of the House of Representatives, criticized President Bush and other Republicans for their tax policies of the last decade.

Gephardt zeroed in on the generous tax cuts that were handed out to the wealthy in the 1980s at the expense of those in the middle: "For the last ten years, Democrats have warned of a day of reckoning. We warned that excessive tax cuts for the rich, wasteful military spending, and neglect of the middle class would someday combine to dampen our abundance and diminish our prospects."

Five years earlier, Gephardt delivered quite a different message to lawmakers while urging them to approve the Tax Reform Act of 1986, the legislation that provided hefty tax cuts for the wealthy. Said Gephardt in September 1986: "[This bill] does give a tax cut . . . to ordinary, average taxpayers. It does not give the lion's share to people at the top. It helps people at the bottom . . . [and] people in the middle, the people we are supposed to be worrying so much about."

It didn't. But that's another matter.

Everyone, to be sure, has a definition of middle class. It is a term that conjures up varying images for sociologists and economists, politicians and ordinary folks. In Washington, for example, it is often said that the top of the middle class is whatever salary is earned by members of Congress. That is $125,100 a year in 1992. But that is more money than 97 percent of the households in America earn. Similarly, many families that earn $80,000 in wages and salaries a year consider themselves middle class. But that income actually puts them in the top 6 percent of American households that file income tax returns.

For these reasons we have defined the heart of the middle class as those wage-earners who reported incomes between $20,000 and $50,000 on their tax returns in 1989. Median family income that year was $34,213, meaning half of all Americans earned more and half earned less. All told, just under thirty-four million individuals and families filed tax returns reporting incomes between $20,000 and $50,000. They accounted for 35 percent of all tax returns.

A definition of an extended middle class might include all households with reported income between $15,000 and $75,000. While individuals or families in New York would be living in poverty if they earned $15,000, the same individuals or families could well achieve a middle-class lifestyle in, say, Sedalia, Missouri.

Slightly under ten million tax returns were filed by the $15,000-to-$20,000 income group. That represented 10 percent of all returns. At the other end of the extended middle class are people earning $50,000 to $75,000. A total of 9.2 million returns were filed by that income group, accounting for 10 percent of all returns.

Overall, 53.2 million individuals and families in the extended middle class—with income between $15,000 and $75,000—filed tax returns. They accounted for 55 percent of all returns. That put 37.3 million individuals and families at the bottom, with incomes below $15,000. They represented 39 percent of total returns. While this figure includes returns filed by teenagers working part-time, the overwhelming majority are married couples, single persons and single parents who represent the working poor.

In fact, the fastest-growing group of persons filing tax returns is made up of heads of households. They include a single parent caring for a child and a person who provides support for a relative, often an aging parent. Their numbers have shot up 1,100 percent over the last three decades, rising from one million in 1960 to an estimated twelve million in 1989.

They represent part of the changing face of America. In 1960, a majority of all tax returns filed—62 percent—were submitted by married couples. By 1989, that figure had fallen to an estimated 44 percent or less. During the same period, returns filed by single persons rose from 33 percent to an estimated 44 percent of the total.

Now consider the incomes of these different groups: 94 percent of all returns filed by heads of households and married persons living separately reported incomes of less than $40,000 in 1988, the latest year for which there is a detailed accounting.

As for married couples, keep in mind that the government statistics on median family income exaggerate the financial condition of families, especially when looked at in historical terms. In the 1950s, median family income was derived largely from the wages and salaries of one working spouse. In the 1990s, median family income represents, in a majority of cases, the wages and salaries of a husband and wife who both work. Thus, goods and services that once could be purchased with a single income now require two incomes.

Whatever your status—a married couple with children, a single person, a married couple without children, a single parent with children—if you work for a living and if you are in the middle-class income range defined here, the chances are that your standard of living is falling or will do so in the coming years. If you are striving to join the middle class, you are working against long odds.

None of this, it must be emphasized, is related to the recession, which, depending upon your economist of choice, began in July 1991 and ended, or will end, on a date uncertain.

In the early days of the recession, Treasury Secretary Brady dismissed the seriousness of what he then labeled an "economic slowdown" by saying: "I don't think it's the end of the world even if we have a recession. We'll pull back out of it again. No big deal."

That is true—recessions do end. But when that day comes, your standard of living—over the long term—will continue to decline. That is because the plight of America's middle class is rooted in serious structural problems within both the economy and society that go beyond the recession.

To correct those problems will require comprehensive changes in government laws and regulations on a scale of the sweeping legislative revisions of the 1930s. In the absence of such action, the future will remain bleak for the middle class.

This is especially true for the generation now entering the work force. For those at the lower end of the middle class clinging to a lifestyle once promised to everyone. For those at the bottom struggling to move up. And for those who will be retiring early in the next century.

This is one reason why the stories you read in newspapers and magazines, the reports you watch on television, and those you listen to on radio seem disconnected from your personal situation. For the fact is you are adrift in uncharted economic waters.

The experts—the economists, Wall Street analysts, the politicians—talk in traditional terms, use traditional navigational measures to pinpoint the economy's location. Like interest rates.

On Feb. 21, 1991, the *Washington Post,* relating the testimony of Alan Greenspan, the Federal Reserve Board chairman, before a congressional committee, reported: "Greenspan did note that interest rate cuts engineered by the Fed over the past three months are finally bearing fruit, but he carefully sidestepped questions about whether future rate cuts are needed."

On Mar. 9, 1991, the *Chicago Tribune* reported: "The Federal Reserve moved to lower a key interest rate Friday just hours after the government reported that the nation's jobless rate jumped unexpectedly last month to 6.5 percent, the highest rate in four years. . . . Since October the Fed has pushed the rate 2.25 percentage points lower in an effort to encourage borrowing and stimulate growth."

On May 1, 1991, the *Boston Globe* reported: "The Federal Reserve yesterday gave up all hope that post–Persian Gulf War euphoria will lift the nation from recession and cut the discount rate it charges banks by half a point to 5.5 percent in an effort to reverse the economic slide. . . . The rate cut signals the Fed has returned to its pre-war strategy of cautiously cutting the cost of borrowing to jump start the economy back to growth."

On June 6, 1991, the *Washington Post* reported: "Federal Reserve Board Chairman Alan Greenspan said today that recent evidence suggests the U.S. economy has begun to recover from recession, a prospect that makes unlikely further cuts in interest rates by the central bank to spur growth."

On Nov. 7, 1991, the *Los Angeles Times* reported: "Acting for the second time in as many weeks to pump more money and confidence into a faltering economy, the Federal Reserve moved decisively Wednesday to reduce interest rates by lowering its benchmark discount rate to an 18-year low of 4.5 percent. The half-point reduction . . . was clearly designed to force down interest rates paid by business and consumers in an effort to stimulate more borrowing and to breathe new life into the apparently faltering recovery."

And on Dec. 21, 1991, the *New York Times* reported: "In a bold move to revive the slumping economy, the Federal Reserve chopped its bedrock discount rate by a full point, to 3½ percent, the lowest level since 1964. The surprisingly big cut was seen as part of a broad effort to stimulate borrowing and perk up an economy whose signs of recovery from recession have all but vanished."

Label it the interest-rate obsession.

But for a different view, listen to an exchange between Richard Ford, a reporter with KSDK-TV in St. Louis, Missouri, and President Bush, that took place on Nov. 13, 1991:

President Bush—"Interest rates are down, and today yet there's—another very important credit card company came down on their rates. At some point when those rates are, people see the rates are where they are, I believe you're going to see confidence start back in housing or in consumer buying. And that's what the economy needs."

Ford—"But people don't have jobs, sir. They don't have any income. They don't care what the interest rate is. They can't spend any money. They can't borrow any money."

Indeed so. Nonetheless, the experts continue to talk of interest rates and gross national product and gross domestic product and savings rates.

Once upon a time, the measures served a purpose. Their usefulness today, in assessing the current and future state of Americans at work in a global economy, operating without restraints, is doubtful.

For the middle class, there are more relevant measures. For example: What is the rate at which new jobs that pay middle-class wages—upwards of $20,000 a year—are being created? What is the rate at which such jobs are being eliminated?

How much of your weekly paycheck is being transferred to wealthy investors in the form of interest payments on the national debt? What percentage of your paycheck do you have left over after deductions for Social Security and federal, state, and local taxes? How does that percentage compare with, say, the percentage retained by persons earning more than $100,000 a year? What is the rate of job loss attributable to unrestrained imports?

How much of your paycheck is going for health-care costs? What is the percentage of the work force that will receive a guaranteed annual pension?

In the pages that follow, you will find the answers, or at least partial answers, to these and many other questions. But mostly you will find a disturbing picture of American economic life at the close of the twentieth century.

You might think of what is happening in the economy—and thereby to you and your family—in terms of a professional hockey game, a sport renowned for its physical violence. Imagine how the game would be played if the old rules were repealed, if the referees were removed.

That, in essence, is what is happening to the American economy. Someone changed the rules. And there is no referee. Which means there is no one looking after the interests of the middle class.

They are the forgotten Americans.

CHAPTER ONE

DISMANTLING THE MIDDLE CLASS

Increase in total salaries of people
earning more than $1 million:

2,184%

WHAT WENT WRONG

The total amount of dollars in
salaries funneled to the rich soared
in the 1980s — as did the number
of rich themselves. Meanwhile, the
total dollars in wages that went to
the middle class increased an
average of just 4 percent a year,
or 44 percent over the decade.

It was a phenomenon
unlike any America had
seen in this century.

Increase in total
salaries of people
earning $20,000
to $50,000:

44%

Increase in
total salaries of
people earning
$200,000 to $1
million:

697%

SOURCE: Internal Revenue Service

Rigging the Game

Worried that you are falling behind, not living as well as you once did? Or expected to?

That you are going to have to work extra hours, or take a second job, just to stay even with your bills?

That the company you have worked for all these years may dump you for a younger person?

Or that the pension you have been promised may not be there when you retire?

Worried, if you are on the bottom rung of the economic ladder, that you will never see a middle-class lifestyle?

Or, if you are a single parent or part of a young working family, that you will never be able to save enough to buy a home?

That you are paying more than your fair share of taxes?

Worried that the people who represent you in Congress are taking care of themselves and their friends at your expense?

You are right. Keep worrying.

For those people in Washington who write the complex tangle of rules by which the economy operates have, over the last twenty years, rigged the game—by design and default—to favor the privileged, the powerful and the influential. At the expense of everyone else.

Seizing on that opportunity, an army of business buccaneers began buying, selling and trading companies the way most Americans buy, sell and trade knickknacks at a yard sale. They borrowed money to destroy, not to build. They constructed financial houses of cards, then vanished before they collapsed.

Caught between the lawmakers in Washington and the dealmakers on Wall Street have been millions of American workers forced to move from jobs that once paid $15 an hour into jobs that now pay $7. If, that is, they aren't already the victims of mass layoffs, production halts, shuttered factories and owners who enrich themselves by doing that damage and then walking away.

As a result, the already rich are richer than ever; there has been an explosion in overnight new rich; life for the working class is deteriorating, and those at the bottom are trapped. For the first time in this century, members of a generation entering adulthood will find it impossible to achieve a better lifestyle than their parents. Most will be unable even to match their parents' middle-class status.

Indeed, the growth of the middle class—one of the underpinnings of democracy in this country—has been reversed. By government action.

Taken as a whole, these are results of the rules that govern the game:

- They have created a tax system that is firmly weighted against the middle class.
- They have enabled companies to trim or cancel health-care and pension benefits for employees.
- They have granted subsidies to businesses that create low-wage jobs that are eroding living standards.
- They have undermined longtime stable businesses and communities.
- They have rewarded companies that transfer jobs abroad and eliminate jobs in this country.
- They have placed home ownership out of reach of a growing number of Americans and made the financing of a college education impossible without incurring a hefty debt.

Look upon it as the dismantling of the middle class. And understand that, barring some unexpected intervention by the federal government, the worst is yet to come. For we are in the midst of the largest transfer of wealth in the nation's history. It is a transfer from the middle class to the rich, and from the middle class to the poor—courtesy of the people in Washington who rewrote the rules.

Those who have taken advantage of the changed rules are beneficiaries of the transfer. People like Andrew G. Galef, an art collector, millionaire investor and resident of one of the nation's wealthiest enclaves, Bel Air, California. Meanwhile, those who have played by the old rules are victims of the transfer, people like Mollie James, a sixty-year-old factory worker, mother of four, grandmother of six, who lives in a working-class neighborhood in Paterson, New Jersey.

Andrew Galef never met Mollie James, but a decision he made in 1989 had a profound effect on her life. Galef eliminated Mollie James's job.

For more than three decades, James worked at the Universal Manufacturing Company in Paterson, rising from assembly-line worker to become the only female operator of a large metal-stamping machine. In the process, she gained a wage of $7.91 an hour, or more than $16,000 a year.

On June 30, 1989, MagneTek Inc., a Galef company that had bought Universal, halted manufacturing in New Jersey—terminating James's job, along with the jobs of 500 others. The manufacturing operation was transferred to Blytheville, Arkansas, where wages were lower, and part of the existing manufacturing operation in Blytheville was moved to Mexico, where the wages were even lower—less than $1.50 an hour.

For her thirty-three years of service, Mollie James received a severance check that, after deductions, came to $3,171.66—or a little less than $100 for each year she had worked. When she reaches age sixty-five in 1996, she will qualify for a monthly pension of $101.76. That is about half the $2,400 that Andrew Galef spent in a single year to feed, groom and care for the family dog, according to his second of three wives.

The extreme differences between the lifestyles of the rich and those of ordinary working people have existed always. But there is a notable difference today: The ranks of the Andrew Galefs are growing by the thousands. The ranks of the Mollie Jameses are swelling by the millions. And the ranks of those in between are shrinking.

Once upon a time, membership in the middle class was open to everyone. Now it is severely restricted. And existing memberships are being revoked. A few statistics, drawn from an analysis of a half-century of tax and economic data, tell part of the story.

Shrinking Middle Class. Nearly thirty-four million individuals and families who earned salaries filed federal tax returns for 1989 reporting adjusted gross incomes between $20,000 and $50,000. They represented the heart of America's working middle class. Median family income that year amounted to $34,213—meaning half of all families earned more and half earned less.

But the middle is shrinking when measured against comparable income groups of earlier years. The middle-income group accounted for 35 percent of all tax returns showing income from a job in 1989. That was down from 39 percent in 1980.

The Great Salary Gap. Between 1980 and 1989, the combined salaries of people in the $20,000-to-$50,000 income group increased 44 percent. During the same period, the combined salaries of people earning $1 million or more a year increased 2,184 percent.

Viewed more broadly, the total wages of all people who earned less than $50,000 a year—85 percent of all Americans—increased an average of just 2 percent a year over those ten years. At the same time, the total wages of all millionaires shot up 243 percent a year. Those figures are not adjusted for inflation, which cuts across all income groups but hits the lower and middle classes hardest.

The Bulging Ranks of the Rich. Between 1980 and 1989, the number of people reporting incomes of more than a half-million dollars rocketed from 16,881 to 183,240—an increase of 985 percent. That represented the largest percentage increase in this century. It even exceeded America's other era of excess, the 1920s.

During that decade, the number of people reporting incomes of more than a half-million dollars rose from 156 in 1920 to 1,489 in 1929—a jump of 854 percent. The 1920s, like the 1980s, were marked by an uncontrolled financial frenzy on Wall Street and a government responsive to special interests.

More significant for most people is a comparison with the 1950s, the decade that saw the largest expansion of the country's middle class. It was a time when ever more Americans climbed the economic ladder and substantially improved their living standard. It was also a time when the number of people reporting more than a half-million dollars in income barely rose, from 842 in 1950 to 1,002 in 1959, a gain of 19 percent.

The decade began and ended with fewer people reporting such incomes than had during the 1920s, even though the population had increased by more than 50 percent and a 1950s dollar did not have as much buying power as a 1920s dollar. One reason for the slow growth: In the 1950s, taxable income above $400,000 was taxed at a rate of 91 percent. In 1991, the maximum tax rate for individuals was 31 percent. That was a tax-rate reduction of 66 percent. In both the 1920s and the 1980s, Congress enacted large tax cuts for the wealthy.

Because of the dramatic increase in their numbers, the over-$500,000 group is accounting for a larger share of overall income tax collections at a time when their individual payments have fallen off sharply. In 1980, they paid $8.1 billion in taxes, or 3 percent of total individual income taxes. In 1989, they paid $59.4 billion, or 14 percent of the total.

If this trend continues, those at the top will pay an ever-mounting share of the taxes. But that is because everyone else will be falling further behind. Consequently, they will have less income to be taxed.

Rising Taxes of Middle Class. In 1970, a Philadelphia family with an income of $9,000 to $10,000—median family income that year was $9,867— paid a total of $1,689 in combined local, state and federal income and Social Security taxes.

In 1989, a Philadelphia family with an income of $30,000 to $40,000— the median family income that year was $34,213—paid $8,491 in combined local, state and federal income and Social Security taxes. Thus, while these taxes consumed 17.8 percent of a middle-class family's earnings in 1970, by 1989 they took 24.3 percent of the family's income. And when real estate taxes, sales taxes, gasoline taxes and other excise taxes and local levies that have gone up are added in, the middle-class family's overall tax burden rises to about one-third of family income.

Illusory Tax on the Wealthy. When Congress enacted the Tax Reform Act of 1986, lawmakers hailed its alternative minimum tax provision as the most stringent ever, guaranteeing that nobody would escape paying at least some tax. Financial publications sounded warnings to their readers. The *Wall Street Journal* said the new law "would toughen the alternative minimum tax" and *Fortune* magazine predicted that "a lot more taxpayers are likely to be hit."

Congress's Joint Committee on Taxation, declaring the alternative minimum tax was necessary "to ensure that no taxpayer with substantial economic income can avoid significant tax liability," estimated the amended provision would generate an additional $8.2 billion in revenue from 1987 to 1991.

Representative Marty Russo, the Illinois Democrat who was a member of the tax-writing House Ways and Means Committee and an architect of the alternative minimum tax, said during debate on the bill: "I take particular pride when I hear my colleagues . . . say that this bill has the toughest minimum tax they have ever seen. It makes sure everybody pays a fair share."

Tax 'reform': Small break for you, big breaks for the rich

The Tax Reform Act of 1986 cut everyone's taxes. But three years later, some fared much better than others:

INCOME BRACKET	SIZE OF TAX CUT	AVERAGE 1989 TAX SAVINGS PER RETURN
UP TO $10,000	11%	$37
$10,000 – $20,000	6%	$69
$20,000 – $30,000	11%	$300
$30,000 – $40,000	11%	$467
$40,000 – $50,000	16%	$1,000
$50,000 – $75,000	16%	$1,523
$75,000 – $100,000	18%	$3,034
$100,000 – $200,000	22%	$7,203
$200,000 – $500,000	26%	$24,603
$500,000 – $1,000,000	34%	$86,084
$1,000,000 OR MORE	31%	$281,033

SOURCE: Internal Revenue Service

It did not. Under the existing law that year, 198,688 individuals and families with incomes over $100,000 paid alternative minimum taxes totaling $4.6 billion. Three years later, in 1989, under the new law praised by Russo and his colleagues, 49,844 individuals and families with incomes over $100,000 paid alternative minimum taxes totaling $476 million.

Passage of "the toughest minimum tax ever" resulted in a 75 percent drop in the number of people who paid the tax, and a 90 percent drop in the amount they paid. On average, a millionaire in 1986 paid an alternative minimum tax of $116,395. Three years later the average millionaire paid $54,758. That amounted to a 53 percent tax cut.

At first glance, the dropoff in alternative minimum tax collections might seem to suggest that the system was working as planned. After all, the 1986 law eliminated many tax shelter schemes that had triggered the alternative minimum tax in the past. Thus, it would appear that those at the top were paying more in taxes at the regular rate and were not subject to the stricter alternative minimum tax.

This was certainly true in some individual cases. But for millionaires and other upper-income people as a group, it was not.

From 1986 to 1989, the average tax bill of millionaires—exclusive of the alternative minimum tax—fell 27 percent, dropping from $864,068 to $634,196. At the regular tax rates, that represented a tax savings of $229,873.

A comparison with individuals and families who reported incomes of more than $1 million in 1980 is even more stark. From 1980 to 1989, their average tax bill—again exclusive of the alternative minimum tax—plunged from $980,869 to $634,196. That amounted to a 35 percent tax cut, giving those people $346,673 extra in spending money.

During that same period, the average alternative minimum tax payments of the same income group fell from $144,474 to $54,758. That amounted to a 62 percent tax cut, giving those people an increase of $89,716 in spending money.

Trapped at the Bottom. Almost half of all Americans who had jobs and filed income tax returns in 1989 earned less than $20,000. Of the 95.9 million tax returns filed that year by people reporting income from a job, 47.2 million came from people in that income group. They represented 49 percent of all such tax filers.

Between 1980 and 1989, the average wage earned by those in the under-$20,000 income category rose $123—from $8,528 to $8,651. That was an increase of 1.4 percent. Over the decade, the average salaries of people with incomes of more than $1 million rose $255,088—from $515,499 to $770,587—an increase of 49.5 percent. That, it should be stressed, was their increase in wages and salaries alone.

The figure does not include other types of income, such as dividends and interest, or profits from the sale of stocks, bonds, real estate or other capital assets. For those at the top, such income far exceeds salaries. In

Fewer rich are paying the minimum tax, contrary to reformers' promises

To keep people from erasing all their taxes with shelters and deductions, the "alternative minimum tax" was devised so everyone would pay some tax. It was supposedly strengthened in the Tax Reform Act of 1986.
But collections dropped 90 percent.

Before tax reform

1986 alternative minimum tax collections:

$6.7 billion

After tax reform

1989 alternative minimum tax collections:

$0.7 billion

Fewer rich pay the minimum tax...

Income bracket	Taxpayers in 1986	Taxpayers in 1989	
$100,000-$200,000	126,127	29,195	— **down 77%**
$200,000-$500,000	46,874	14,112	— **down 70%**
$500,000-$1,000,000	10,428	4,176	— **down 60%**
$1,000,000 or more	15,259	2,361	— **down 85%**

...And those who do pay less

Income bracket	Avg. tax paid in 1986	Avg. tax paid in 1989	
$100,000-$200,000	$ 10,295	$ 4,561	— **down 56%**
$200,000-$500,000	$ 23,237	$ 9,037	— **down 61%**
$500,000-$1,000,000	$ 45,218	$20,694	— **down 54%**
$1,000,000 or more	$116,395	$54,758	— **down 53%**

SOURCE: Internal Revenue Service

1989, salaries on average amounted to just 29 percent of the total income received by persons earning more than $1 million. In the case of individuals and families in the $500,000–to–$1 million bracket, salaries amounted to 50 percent of their overall income.

The story is different for members of the middle class and lower-income groups. They are dependent on their paychecks to meet daily living expenses. Take individuals and families who earned between $30,000 and $40,000 in 1989. Of their total income, 88 percent came from wages and salaries. It was 86 percent for those in the $50,000-to-$75,000 income class, as well as for the $10,000-to-$20,000 income group.

The Good Life—Tax Free. During 1989, some 37,000 millionaires supplemented their other income with tax-free checks averaging nearly $2,607 a week. That was $135,548 for the year. No tax owed.

The money came from the return on their investment in bonds issued by local and state governments. The interest on those bonds is exempt from federal income taxes. All together, some 800,000 persons with income over $100,000 picked up $20.1 billion from their exempt-bond holdings, thereby escaping payment of $5.6 billion in federal income taxes.

That lost revenue, as you might guess, was made up by other taxpayers—among them the 26.5 million persons with income under $20,000 a year who paid taxes on the interest earned from their savings accounts. All together, these persons paid about $7.1 billion in federal income taxes on savings account interest that averaged $1,782 for the year. Many of the same millionaires escaped payment of billions of dollars in state income taxes as a result of their investment in United States government securities, which are exempt from state and local taxes.

Subsidizing the Affluent. If you earned $20,000 in 1990, you paid $1,530 in Social Security taxes. Of that figure, $1,240 was earmarked for Old Age and Survivors' Insurance; the remaining $290 for Medicare.

So where, exactly, did your $1,240 go?

Most people think it goes into a special fund that is set aside for their own future retirement. It does not. In effect, some of it goes to people like Alan Cranston, the three-term Democratic senator from California now best known for his close association with executives at a failed savings and loan association. It took your $1,240—and the $1,240 of fifteen other people in your income group—to cover the $19,034 in Social Security payments that Cranston collected.

Like most members of the United States Senate, Cranston ranks in the top 1 percent of all income earners. His total income in 1990 was about $300,000. That included $19,034 in Social Security payments, according to his financial disclosure report filed with the secretary of the Senate. Of course, your $1,240 didn't necessarily go to Cranston. It could have gone to some other wealthy American receiving Social Security benefits.

Cranston, in fact, was among more than 400,000 individuals and families with incomes above $100,000 who also received Social Security. In

1989 those high-income beneficiaries—four-tenths of one percent of all tax-return filers—collected a total of $4.9 billion in Social Security payments. That sum exceeded the Social Security tax withheld from the paychecks of about two million workers in Massachusetts earning less than $30,000 a year. Plus more than one million workers in South Carolina in the same income category. Plus more than three million workers in Illinois. And about one million workers in Oregon. Think of it as a simple transfer of money.

Of course, the wealthy paid into Social Security, too. But the $4.9 billion they received is more than the Social Security taxes paid by about seven million workers who earned less than $30,000 in 1989. And it was turned over to 400,000 people who earned more than $100,000 in 1989. Only 14 percent of the over-$100,000 set is collecting Social Security now. But in coming years that number will grow. That means ever more workers in the under-$30,000 set will be tapped to pay the bill.

For all this, you can thank a succession of Congresses and presidents who set the rules for the American economy. Congress does so when it enacts new laws and amends or rescinds outdated ones, and then provides the resources that determine whether the laws will be enforced. The president does so through the various departments and regulatory agencies that implement new regulations and amend or rescind outdated ones—and then either enforce or ignore the regulations.

Both Congress and the president do so when they succumb to pressure from special interests and fail to enact laws or implement regulations that would make the economic playing field level for everyone. Taken together, the myriad laws and regulations—from antitrust to taxes, from regulatory oversight to bankruptcy, from foreign trade to pensions, from health care to investment practices—form a rule book that governs the way business operates, that determines your place in the overall economy.

Think of it as the United States government rule book.

It is a system of rewards and penalties that influences business behavior, which in turn has a wide-ranging impact on your daily life. From the price you pay for a gallon of gasoline or a quart of milk to the closing of a manufacturing plant and the elimination of your job. From the number of peanuts in your favorite brand of peanut butter to the amount of money you will collect in unemployment benefits if you are laid off. From whether the shirt or dress you are wearing is made in Fleetwood, Pennsylvania, or Seoul, Korea, to whether the company you work for expands its production facilities in the United States, thereby creating jobs, or opens a new plant in Puerto Rico or Mexico instead.

From whether the grapes you eat are grown in California or Chile, to the amount of money you will receive in your pension check when you retire—or whether you will even receive a pension check. From the amount of interest you earn on your passbook savings account to whether your weekly paycheck is cut when your employer sells out to a competitor.

It should be noted that conditions beyond the government rule book are also at work in the economy. They, too, play a part in determining one's fortunes. There is, for example, an entry-level work force that increasingly is unable to write a simple sentence or do elementary arithmetic. There is a preoccupation with resorting to litigation to settle most any type of conflict or slight, real or imagined. There is a systemic failure in schools to provide the basic technological education required for the business world of the twenty-first century.

Also, there is a declining work ethic that raises costs and contributes to the production of defective merchandise. There is a growing inability among workers to communicate adequately, or to read and understand the simplest instruction manuals. And there is an unthinking adherence to arcane work rules that breed inefficiency.

Nonetheless, if all these problems were erased overnight, the plight of the middle class would remain essentially unchanged. For it is the rule book that determines who, among the principal players in the economy, is most favored, who is simply ignored, and who is penalized. Those players include management, employees, customers, stockholders and the community where a business is located.

The players often have conflicting interests.

Arthur Liman, a prominent New York defense lawyer who represented convicted junk-bond creator Michael R. Milken, once put it this way: "I don't see how a board, elected by shareholders, can be expected to protect, for example, the interests of the community or the interests and diversity in the economy. That, perhaps, has to come from the rules of the game that are established by government, by democratic processes. I think boards have to represent the shareholders."

Indeed so. But those who establish the rules of the game long ago ceased to represent the middle-class players. As a result, the middle-class casualties of the government rule book already can be counted in the millions. By the dawn of the next century, they will be many times that number.

Here is a summary of what seems likely to come, barring a sweeping reversal in federal policy:

Workers will continue to be forced to move from jobs that once might have paid $8 to $20 an hour into jobs that will pay less. Some will be consigned to part-time employment. Some will lose all or part of fringe benefits they have long taken for granted.

Women and blacks will continue to move into the work force, but they will receive substandard wages, substandard pensions and substandard fringe benefits. For the first time, they will be joined by a new minority— white males in both manufacturing and service jobs.

Workers will be compelled to forgo wage increases to shoulder a growing percentage of the cost of their own health-care insurance. Some will find their coverage sharply limited. Some will lose their health-care coverage entirely.

The elimination of jobs that once paid middle-class wages will continue uninterrupted, due in part to an ongoing wave of corporate restructurings and bankruptcies, the continuing disappearance of some industries and the transfer of others to foreign countries.

More than a half-million men and women, including many with growing families, will be dumped into this sinking job market as the Defense Department begins to deal with budget cuts by prematurely discharging military personnel—most of whom had planned on a twenty-to-thirty-year career in the armed forces.

Local, state and federal taxes will continue to consume a disproportionate share of the incomes of ordinary workers. At the same time, the proportion of the incomes of wealthy Americans that goes untaxed will continue to grow.

Massive debt loads incurred by corporations and the federal government will require ever growing sums of money for interest payments, meaning less money for new plants and equipment, less money to create jobs, less money to rebuild a collapsing infrastructure—highways, bridges, water and sewer lines.

Men and women, banking on pensions they believe the federal government has insured, will discover at retirement that their pensions are not guaranteed. Some will receive only a fraction of the promised benefits. Some will receive nothing.

For the first time since the Great Depression, a growing number of workers will receive no pension at all. At the other extreme, about 20 percent of the work force will receive hefty pensions—in many cases they will collect more in retirement than they earned while at work.

None of this, it should be underscored, is related to a recession. Because these conditions are structural, built into the economy by the rule book's authors, they will be largely unaffected by any upturn in business.

Casualties of the New Economic Order

Larry Weikel and Belinda Schell know all about the future. For them, it arrived in 1990 when they paid the price for Wall Street's excesses—and Congress's failure to curb those excesses.

Weikel is forty-seven years old and lives with his wife in Boyertown, Pennsylvania. Their children are grown. Schell is thirty-three and lives with her husband and three children, two teenagers and a seven-year-old, in Royersford, Pennsylvania.

Both worked at the old Diamond Glass Company plant that had been a fixture in downtown Royersford for all of this century. Until, that is, the takeover craze of the 1980s led to its closing, to the elimination of their jobs and the jobs of 500 co-workers—and to profits of tens of millions of dollars for those behind it all.

Their stories are the stories of middle-class jobholders everywhere. In interviews across America, the authors heard a constant refrain. It was a litany sounded in city after city, from Hagerstown, Maryland, to South Bend, Indiana; from Hermann, Missouri, to Martell, California. Over and over, blue-collar and white-collar workers, midlevel managers—middle class all—talked of businesses that once were, but are no more. Sometimes the business was glass-making. Sometimes it was printing. Or timber. Or shoemaking. Or meat-packing. But always the words were the same.

They talked about owners and managers who had known the employees by name, who had known their families, who had known the equipment on the floor, who had walked through the plants and offices and stopped to chat. They talked about working with—and for—people who were members of an extended corporate family. And, finally, they talked—some with a sense of bewilderment, some with sadness, some with bitterness—of the takeovers, of the new owners and the new managers who replaced the old.

Sometimes those new managers knew the workers' names, but never the people behind the names. The new managers had only a nodding acquaintance with the equipment. And they were obsessed with meeting ever-rising production quotas.

Listen to Larry Weikel, who grew up in Spring City, Pennsylvania, went to Springford High School, joined the air force, spent four years in the service, returned home and, in 1966, went to work at the Diamond Glass Company, a family-owned business that dated from 1874: "Everybody knew everybody. Everybody was friendly. The supervisors were all nice. The owner would come in and talk to you. It was just a nice place to work. It was a nice family, you know . . . I loved to go to work."

Belinda Schell, born in Keyser, West Virginia, the daughter of a glassmaker, remembers how difficult it was to get a job at Diamond. Everyone, it seemed, wanted to work there. "It took me about two years to get into the plant," she said. That was 1984.

But already the plant was operating under the new economic rules. The company embarked on a course that thousands of other businesses had embarked on and would follow—because the rules by which the American economy operates actually encourage it.

That course went something like this: Take the company public, borrow a lot of money to expand by acquiring other glass companies, run up the price of the stock and sell it off at a nice profit.

At first, the process moved slowly. The company, which had changed its name to Diamond-Bathurst Inc., following a management buyout, picked up a second glassmaking plant in Vienna, West Virginia, from a bankrupt producer in 1981. Two years later, in 1983, it went public. Then, in April 1985, Diamond-Bathurst purchased Container General Corporation, a Chattanooga, Tennessee, glass manufacturer with twelve plants. And in July 1985, the company purchased most of the assets of Thatcher Glass Company of Greenwich, Connecticut, a manufacturer with six plants that was operating under the protection of a United States bankruptcy court.

Thatcher, like so many companies in the 1980s, had gone through a leveraged buyout in which managers and investors purchased the company with mostly borrowed money. So much borrowed money that the company eventually was forced into the bankruptcy court. That same month, Diamond-Bathurst moved from the drab second-floor offices above the aging Royersford plant into a modern office complex built into a hillside in the wooded and rolling countryside in Malvern, Pennsylvania. As Frank B. Foster 3d, the company's president and chief executive officer, put it at the time: "We became in three short months one of the largest glass-container manufacturers in the United States, with projected annualized sales of $550 million." To finance it all, Diamond-Bathurst borrowed big. Its debt rocketed 700 percent, going from $13 million in 1984 to $104 million in 1985.

Wall Street loved it. The stock shot up from a low of $6 a share to a high of $29. Later, it split. Sales climbed from $62 million to $408 million. Profits went from $2 million to $11 million.

The *Philadelphia Inquirer* in July 1985 quoted a First Boston Corporation securities analyst, Cornelius W. Thornton, as saying: "There's a whole lot of synergism in this deal. I don't think the question is can Diamond pull it off. I think they've done it." They hadn't. But Wall Street has a short attention span and many investors already had made a killing.

It soon became clear that Diamond-Bathurst would be unable to make the interest payments on its mountain of debt. The debt was made possible by a Congress that, at the time, was working on a tax bill that would eliminate the deductibility of most forms of consumer interest but retain the interest deduction for corporations.

Without that deduction, much of the corporate restructuring that took place in the 1980s, and the job loss that followed, might never have occurred, since the deals depended on the tax advantage. The use of debt to buy and dismantle companies—instead of to build them—was exploding. Congress, in hammering out the Tax Reform Act of 1986, chose to ignore that phenomenon.

In any event, Diamond-Bathurst posted a $6.2 million loss for 1986 rather than the profit that had been forecast by stockbrokers and company management. In June 1987, Moody's lowered the credit rating on Diamond-Bathurst's bonds. Company executives had already closed one manufacturing plant after another—in Indianapolis; Wharton, New Jersey; Mount Vernon, Ohio; Vienna, West Virginia, and Knox, Pennsylvania—abolishing the jobs of several thousands of workers.

It was not enough. In August 1987, a heavily indebted Diamond-Bathurst was acquired by a competitor, the new corporate headquarters in Malvern was closed and more than 250 salaried workers were dismissed. The buyer was Anchor Glass Container Corporation of Tampa, Florida, a descendant of a leveraged buyout.

When the new owners arrived in Royersford, Larry Weikel, by then a shift foreman; Belinda Schell, a clerk; and other workers noticed an immediate change. "It just became so competitive," Weikel said, "and things just started getting nasty and out of hand. It just seemed like they didn't care what you did to get the numbers. . . . They'd expect you to get on somebody about a problem that wasn't their fault to start with."

Schell said Anchor Glass sent in managers from its plants in other parts of the country, and they issued conflicting orders. Jobs were eliminated and the remaining employees were pressured to increase output. But there was no investment in more modern equipment or new technology. The final day of production came in August 1990. Weikel, Schell and the remaining 275 or so employees were out of work.

Once again, their stories were much like the stories the authors heard in scores of interviews across the country. With few exceptions, the former Anchor Glass workers have moved into jobs that pay lower wages and offer reduced health-care benefits. Weikel works part time at a marine-supply store run by his brother-in-law. His wife works in a sewing factory, earning about $6 an hour. When he lost his job, he refinanced the mortgage on the family home and has been draining their savings. Jobs that pay the $15 an hour he earned at Anchor Glass do not exist.

Said Weikel: "That's all I ever did in my life, work in a glass plant. I went to work there when I came out of the service and, you know, I really never learned anything because all I did was make bottles, and there's not much call for that. I could reeducate myself, I guess, but I don't want to get into another mess like that. I could get a job anywhere, I mean making $5, $6 an hour. But that's not worth my time. . . . I would do it if I was starving. But I'm not. My kids are grown and I'm not worrying about it that much anymore. I spent twenty-three years worrying about it. . . . All I really have to do is make enough money to feed my wife and myself."

Belinda Schell, with a growing family, had no choice but to go back to work. At Anchor Glass, she earned more than $10 an hour. At her new job, as a nursing home aide, she earns considerably less. It is an occupation that the federal government touts as a growth industry that will provide many jobs—mostly low-paying—as the aged population continues to grow.

Belinda Schell's husband, who like Weikel earned $15 an hour at Anchor Glass, found a job in another manufacturing plant in King of Prussia, Pennsylvania. He, too, earns less than he did.

Mrs. Schell said her brother-in-law encountered another obstacle when he sought a job at lower pay than he had made: "They would tell him he made too much money and he wouldn't be satisfied. He was making $16 at Anchor Glass and they said he wouldn't be satisfied making $8. But people like that don't know what it's like to go through a plant closing when you have a mortgage and children to feed. He has two children. He had just bought a new home the year before." She said her brother-in-law finally found other work, but at lower pay than he made at the glass plant. As for other co-workers, she said, "some of them that are working are only making $5 to $7 an hour, which doesn't compare with what we were making at Anchor. . . . I don't know anybody that is making what they made at Anchor Glass."

For Larry Weikel, the experience was disheartening: "You know what hurts me, that I was liked there at that plant at one time. And then for this to happen. . . . Twenty-three years in there, you know, and everything was great. And then an outfit comes in like this and destroys you.

"It seems like I prostituted my whole young life to that company and then they turn me out to pasture. . . . I spent Saturdays and Sundays down there. I didn't do anything with the kids. I didn't go to ball games. I didn't do that. I was always working. And then they turn around and do something like that to you."

Weikel, Schell and the other Diamond Glass employees were working under America's old economic rules that, for many, provided a job and good salary and health care and a pension for life in exchange for a commitment to the company.

The new rules were quite different, and the owners of the Anchor Glass company that bought Diamond Glass knew them intimately. In fact, you might even say that one of Anchor Glass's original owners helped to write those rules. He was former United States Treasury Secretary William E. Simon, who catapulted himself onto the *Forbes* magazine directory of the 400 richest Americans (his worth is estimated at $300 million) by taking advantage of the tax deduction for corporate debt.

Anchor Glass Container Corporation was itself the product of a leveraged buyout. It was formed in April 1983 by Wesray Corporation and executives of the glass-container division of the Anchor Hocking Corporation, one of the country's glass-making institutions. Wesray was an investment-banking firm founded by Simon along with Raymond G. Chambers, an accountant. It was one of the first of what would be many leveraged-buyout firms that acquired companies with mostly borrowed money.

After making cosmetic changes that often included job cutbacks and other short-term cost-reduction measures, the companies would be sold, in whole or in part, at a substantial profit—or taken public, another form of sale.

Newspapers and financial publications regaled readers with Simon successes during the 1980s—among them Anchor Glass. In an article published in October 1988, the *Los Angeles Times* reported that after Simon helped engineer the Anchor Glass buyout, "managers cut the work force, slashed expenses and made a successful acquisition." Simon, the *Times* said, "made more than 100 times his money."

When Anchor Glass purchased the old glass-container division of Anchor Hocking, the transaction was financed with the patented Simon debt formula: $76 million in borrowed money and $1 million investment by Wesray and others. You might think of that kind of arrangement this way:

Let's say you want to buy a house for $100,000. You visit your friendly neighborhood bank and offer to put about $1,500 down. That is not the kind of deal you can get.

But Simon and his associates got a much better one when they organized Anchor Glass. After Anchor Glass borrowed the $76 million, according to documents filed with the United States Securities and Exchange Commission (SEC), $48.5 million of that sum was reloaned to Simon and friends. They, in turn, used $24 million of that money to buy the land and buildings of the various glass plants. Then they leased the land and buildings back to their new company, Anchor Glass, for twenty years.

In other words, the new owner of the glass plants, Anchor Glass, would pay rent on the land and buildings to Simon and the other investors.

There was still more. Simon and his associates bought the furnaces and other glass-making equipment in the various plants in exchange for a note promising to pay $43.6 million. Then they leased the glass-making equipment back to Anchor Glass.

Several years later, Anchor Glass, in a report filed with the SEC, said the transactions were too generous to Simon and the other investors: "These arrangements were entered into when the company was privately owned, were not the result of arm's-length bargaining and on the whole were not as favorable to the company as could have been obtained from unrelated third parties."

There were other deals. Wesray picked up investment-banking fees for handling the purchase of the glass-container properties and the acquisition of Midland Glass Company. Anchor Glass purchased its casualty and liability insurance, and its employee health and benefit insurance, from two brokerage firms in which Simon and his colleagues also held an interest. That was worth more millions of dollars in fees. And finally, there was the Anchor Glass corporate headquarters in Tampa. It, too, was owned by Simon and associates, who leased the building to the company.

In March 1986, Anchor Glass, which had been a private company, offered stock for sale to the public. By February 1988, according to an SEC report, Simon had sold his holdings. His total profits from the deals are unknown. But they run into the tens of millions of dollars.

One more note: In October 1989, Anchor Glass was sold. The buyer was Vitro, S.A., a Mexican glass company that ships products into the United States, competing with American-owned companies. Vitro is part of the corporate empire of Mexico's Sada family, which is ranked by *Forbes* among the world's billionaire families. The Mexican company's first moves included a decision to close the glass plant in Royersford. And another plant in Vernon, California. And another plant in Gulfport, Mississippi. And another plant in San Leandro, California.

Downward Mobility

What happened to Weikel and Schell and other glass plant workers is not at all unusual. Nor is what happened to the company they worked for. Nor the money being made by investors and corporate executives. Their story is the story of millions of middle-class Americans who are being forced out of higher-paying jobs into lower-paying jobs, or who have lost a portion or all of their benefits, or both.

Vanishing Factory Workers. In a letter to Congress in January 1989, President Reagan spoke enthusiastically of the many jobs his administration had created since 1980: "Nearly nineteen million nonagricultural jobs have been created during this period. . . . The jobs created are good ones. Over 90 percent of the new jobs are full-time, and over 85 percent of these full-time jobs are in occupations in which average annual salaries exceed $20,000."

In fact, the job growth was centered in the retail trade and service sectors, which pay the lowest wages. Higher-paying jobs in manufacturing disappeared at a rate unmatched since the Great Depression. In the 1950s, businesses added 1.6 million manufacturing jobs. They added 1.5 million such jobs in the 1960s, and 1.5 million in the 1970s. But in the 1980s, corporations eliminated 300,000 manufacturing jobs. If the trend continues, 1 million or more will be erased in the 1990s.

While the number of manufacturing jobs fell 1.3 percent from the 1970s to the 1980s, dropping from an average of 19.6 million to 19.3 million, the number of retail-trade jobs climbed 32.5 percent, rising from 12.8 million to 17 million. The retail-trade workers, whose numbers are growing, earn on average $204 a week. The manufacturing workers, whose numbers are dwindling, earn $458 a week.

Those numbers understate the problem. For the percentage of the overall work force employed in manufacturing, people who make things with their hands—cars, radios, refrigerators, clothing—is plummeting. During the 1950s, 33 percent of all workers were employed in manufacturing. The figure edged down to 30 percent in the 1960s, and plunged to 20 percent in the 1980s. It is now 17 percent—and falling.

Orgy of Debt and Interest. One major reason for the declining fortunes of workers: American companies went on a borrowing binge through the 1980s, issuing corporate IOUs at the rate of $1 million every four minutes, twenty-four hours a day, year after year. By the decade's end, companies had piled up $1.3 trillion in new debt—much of it to buy and merge companies, leading to the closing of factories and elimination of jobs.

That debt required companies to divert massive sums of cash into interest payments, which in turn meant less money was available for new plants and equipment, less money for research and development. During the 1950s, when manufacturing jobs were created at a record pace, companies invested $3 billion in new manufacturing plants and equipment for

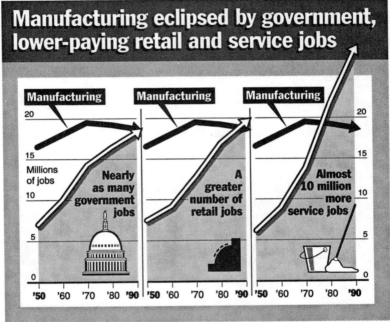

Manufacturing eclipsed by government, lower-paying retail and service jobs

SOURCE: Bureau of Labor Statistics

every $1 billion paid out in interest. By the 1980s, that pattern had been reversed: Corporations paid out $1.6 billion in interest for every $1 billion invested in manufacturing plants and equipment.

Similarly, during the 1950s, for every $1 billion that corporations paid out in interest on borrowed money, they allocated $710 million for research and development. By the 1980s, corporations spent only $220 million on research and development for every $1 billion in interest payments.

Through the 1980s, corporations paid out $2.2 trillion in interest, more than double their interest payments through the 1940s, 1950s, 1960s and 1970s—combined. It was enough money to create seven million manufacturing jobs, each paying $25,000 a year.

Bloated Pay for Executives. While companies are cutting jobs that pay middle-income wages and adding large numbers of lower-paying jobs, they are paying ever-larger salaries and bonuses to people at the top. Roberto C. Goizueta, chairman and chief executive officer of Coca-Cola Company, received salary and bonuses in 1990 totaling $2.96 million. Nearly four decades earlier, in 1953, a Goizueta predecessor, Hammond B. Nicholson, earned $134,600 in the top job at Coca-Cola.

To put the salary change in perspective, if the pay of manufacturing workers had gone up at the same pace, a factory worker today would earn $81,000 a year.

While the news media have written at length on corporate salaries, most publications have suggested that high-paid executives are the exception. They are not. An analysis of tax-return data shows that in 1953 executive compensation was the equivalent of 22 percent of corporate profits. By 1987, the latest year for which detailed figures were available, executive compensation was the equivalent of 61 percent of corporate profits.

Measured from a different perspective, in 1953 corporations paid their executives $8.8 billion in salaries, stock bonuses and other compensation. That year, those corporations paid $19.9 billion in federal income taxes. By contrast, in 1987 corporations paid their officers $200 billion in compensation, while they paid $83.9 billion in federal income taxes. That means businesses paid $2.3 billion in taxes for every $1 billion paid in executive salaries in 1953. By 1987, that pattern was reversed: Businesses paid $2.4 billion in executive salaries for every $1 billion in taxes.

The Downwardly Mobile. Measured in terms of buying power, the wages of manufacturing, retail-trade and other service-industry employees during the 1980s fell far short of their parents' and grandparents' earnings.

To understand why, let's go back in time, to 1952 and the opening of Levittown, Pennsylvania, the world's largest planned community, a symbol of a flourishing middle class. It took a factory worker one day to earn enough money to pay the closing costs on a new Levittown house, then selling for $10,000. More importantly, that was an era when the overwhelming majority of families buying homes relied on the income of one wage-earner. In 1991, it took a factory worker eighteen weeks to earn enough money to pay the closing costs on that same Levittown home, now selling for $100,000 or more.

Unfortunately, even if the average factory worker of the 1990s had the minimum down payment, his income would be insufficient for him to qualify for a mortgage in Levittown. That is because it now requires two incomes for most families to come up with a larger down payment and to meet higher monthly mortgage and tax payments. Workers in the retail and service industries are even worse off, which helps explain why so many Americans can't afford to own a house. This is especially true for young families, who in decades past were the traditional homebuyers.

On a more mundane level, a store clerk in 1952 had to work two hours to pay for 100 postage stamps. In 1991, a store clerk had to work six hours to buy 100 stamps.

All these things—shrinking paychecks, disappearing factory jobs, fat salaries for corporate executives, uncontrolled business debt, a deteriorating standard of living—are the visible consequences of the distorted government rule book.

Other consequences are harder to see. But look closely and you will find them. They range from mounting racial tensions between whites and blacks competing for a shrinking number of middle-class jobs to an increase in employee theft and shoplifting. From fraudulent worker-compensation claims approaching epidemic proportions to a growing refusal on the part of citizens to pay taxes that they owe. From a shifting of the responsibility for social-welfare programs from the federal government to the state governments to a shifting of similar burdens from the state governments to local governments. From an increase in domestic violence to a declining quality of care for residents of nursing homes.

What does the government rule book have to do with care in a nursing home?

Meet Mengabelle Quatre, a former resident of a California nursing home operated by Beverly Enterprises, Inc.

Actually, let's begin with Beverly Enterprises, the product of a new economic order—one envisioned by Michael Milken and his Wall Street associates and made possible by rules set down by Congress. Like so many other businesses of the 1980s, its rapid expansion was fueled by easy debt. The company grew by acquiring small, independent nursing homes and building new ones, financed with junk bonds, bank loans and, in part, tax-payer dollars through industrial revenue bonds.

The number of beds in its facilities increased from 51,300 in 1981 to 121,800 in 1986. Revenue rose from $486 million to $2 billion. Profits went from $16 million to $51 million. And its stock shot up from $2.50 a share to $22.50, generating millions of dollars in profits for investors.

Along the way, Beverly Enterprises emerged as the nation's largest nursing home operator. Its investment adviser, Drexel Burnham Lambert, Inc., which had managed a $100 million securities offering for the company in 1983, was bullish on the prospects of making ever more money on the elderly. In a 1985 report to its clients, Drexel Burnham recommended the purchase of Beverly Enterprises stock, saying there were many opportunities for expansion.

"There is still a formidable pool of small independents," the investment firm said, adding that "management's goal is a steady stream of small acquisitions."

In a report a year later, Drexel Burnham predicted the company's profits would reach $86 million in 1987 and said "there is no shortage of growth prospects for Beverly." And in May 1987, the *Wall Street Journal* reported that a Beverly executive had confirmed that estimates by securities analysts of profits for the year between $54 million and $71 million were "in the ball park."

It turned out to be a different ball park. For Beverly's earnings—like the earnings of so many businesses built on debt—evaporated. Instead of the $86 million profit forecast by Drexel Burnham, the company lost $33 million in 1987. It lost $24 million in 1988. And $104 million in 1989.

As the company sought to cut costs, it developed a reputation for paying low wages and having a high turnover rate among employees. Those two conditions often led to substandard care. The wages were so low and the staffing so minimal at some Beverly-operated nursing homes that regulatory authorities in one state after another cited the company time and again for patient neglect.

Beverly also lost a civil lawsuit in which damages were awarded to residents of its nursing homes in Mississippi who complained about a reduced quality of life that was due to general neglect and abuse. And the National Labor Relations Board joined the critics when an administrative law judge in November 1990 cited Beverly for unfair labor practices at thirty-three nursing homes in twelve states.

In an article published in December 1988 recounting Beverly's declining fortunes, the *New York Times* reported: "Perhaps the most damaging blow to Beverly's reputation occurred in California two years ago. The state alleged that poor care at a handful of Beverly's ninety homes caused nine deaths, and inspections turned up fifty life-threatening citations over a fifteen-month period."

All of which brings us to Mengabelle Quatre. Suffering from seizures and cancer of the bronchial tubes, unable to walk without assistance and otherwise confined to a wheelchair, she was admitted to a Beverly nursing facility on Oct. 13, 1989. Seven weeks later, on a quiet Saturday afternoon, Dec. 2, 1989, Mengabelle Quatre died at the age of sixty-nine at the Beverly Manor Convalescent Hospital in Burbank, California, not far from the make-believe world of Hollywood film studios.

A few lines from her death certificate sum up what happened:

"Death was caused by: Thermal injuries.

"Manner of death: Accident.

"Describe how injury occurred: Clothing caught on fire while smoking."

Confined to a wheelchair in a facility operated by Beverly Enterprises—the banner draped over the entrance proclaims "Love Is Ageless; Visit Us"—Mengabelle Quatre, a printer in a movie laboratory for thirty-five years, burned to death, in the middle of a hospital, while she was smoking a cigarette.

State investigators later described the incident: "[An employee] stated in an interview that at approximately 3:10 P.M. on Dec. 2, 1989, he heard someone screaming, ran to the patio adjacent to the TV room where he observed [the patient] on fire. He extinguished the fire and yelled for someone to call the paramedics." Mrs. Quatre was taken to an acute-care hospital where she died five hours later. According to the state investigation, "the county coroner reported that the resident had died of thermal burns . . . of yellow-brown to black discoloration over 50 percent of her body. The burns ranged between her front midthighs to the top of her head."

A California Department of Health Services investigation concluded that Beverly Enterprises "failed to ensure that [Quatre] smoked only in a designated area under supervision" and failed to implement a "plan which required the patient's smoking materials to be kept at the nurses station and the patient to smoke in a designated place supervised by the staff."

Life on the Expense Account

The government rule book that helped create the environment in which Mengabelle Quatre died also makes possible quite a different lifestyle.

Meet Thomas Spiegel. He is the former chairman and chief executive officer of Columbia Savings & Loan Association, a Beverly Hills–based thrift that the *New York Times* described in February 1989 as an institution that "has been extremely successful investing in junk bonds and other ventures." Spiegel is a major fund-raiser and financial supporter of political candidates, Democrats and Republicans alike. He and his family live in a six-bedroom Beverly Hills home—complete with swimming pool, tennis court and entertainment pavilion—that could be purchased for about $10 million.

Spiegel thrived at Columbia during the 1980s, a time when the executive branch of the federal government loosened regulatory oversight of the savings and loan industry. Working with his friend and business associate Michael Milken, whose Drexel Burnham Lambert, Inc. office was just down the street in Beverly Hills, Spiegel used depositors' federally insured savings to buy a portfolio of junk bonds, the high-risk debt instruments that promised to pay big dividends.

Columbia's profits soared. Earnings jumped from $44.1 million in 1984 to $122.3 million in 1985 and $193.5 million in 1986, before trailing off to $119.3 million in 1987 and $85 million in 1988.

Spiegel's compensation for those years averaged slightly under $100,000 a week. He spent $2,000 for a French wine-tasting course, $3,000 a night for hotel suites on the French Riviera, $19,775 for cashmere throws and comforters, $8,600 for towels and $91,000 for a collection of guns—Uzis, Magnums, Sakos, Berettas, Sig Sauers.

Not unusual outlays, you might think, for someone who collected a multimillion-dollar yearly salary. Only in this case, according to a much-belated federal audit, it was Columbia—the savings and loan—not Spiegel, that picked up the tab.

There is, to be sure, nothing new about lavish corporate expense accounts. The practice of converting personal living expenses to a deduction on a company or business tax return has been around as long as the income tax. It is a practice that Congress has been unable to curb. But in the 1980s, corporate tax write-offs for personal executive expenses as well as overall corporate excesses—from gold-plated plumbing fixtures in the private office to family wedding receptions in Paris and London—reached epidemic proportions.

The reasons varied. Among them:

■ The pace of corporate restructuring brought on by Wall Street created a climate in which once-unacceptable practices became acceptable, indeed, were even chronicled on radio and television, in newspapers and magazines.

■ In a monumental change in the rules, Congress deregulated the savings and loan industry, in effect opening the doors to the vaults of the nation's savings institutions, while at the same time discouraging meaningful audits or crackdowns when irregularities were detected.

■ The Internal Revenue Service lacks the staffing and time to conduct the intense audits of companies that would uncover such abuses. And even if the resources were available, an impenetrable tax code places too many other demands on the agency.

All this made possible a Tom Spiegel—and an army of other corporate executives who lived high on their expense accounts. Federal auditors eventually found that Spiegel used Columbia funds to pay for trips to Europe, to buy luxury condominiums in Columbia's name in the United States and to purchase expensive aircraft. From 1987 to 1989, for example, Spiegel made at least four trips to Europe at Columbia's expense, the auditors reported, staying at the best hotels and running up large bills.

They included, the report said: "$7,446 for a hotel and room service bill for three nights in the Berkeley Hotel in London . . . for Spiegel and his wife . . . in November 1988" and "$6,066 for a hotel and room service bill for three nights in the Hotel Plaza Athenee in Paris . . . in July 1989."

The Spiegels' most expensive stay was in July 1989 at the Hotel du Cap on the French Riviera, where the family ran up a $16,519 bill in five days. And when they weren't flying to Europe, the Spiegels spent time at luxury condominiums, acquired at a cost of $1.9 million, at Jackson Hole, Wyoming; Indian Wells, California; and Park City, Utah.

To make all this travel easier, Spiegel arranged for Columbia, a savings and loan that had no offices outside of California, to buy corporate aircraft, including a Gulfstream IV equipped with a kitchen and lounge. Federal auditors now say that Columbia paid $2.4 million "for use of corporate aircraft in commercial flights for the personal travel for Spiegel, his immediate family and other persons accompanying Spiegel." Columbia wrote off those expenses on its tax returns, thereby transferring the cost of the Spiegel lifestyle to you, the taxpayer.

The Federal Office of Thrift Supervision has filed a complaint against Spiegel, seeking to recover at least $19 million in Columbia funds that it claims he misspent. Spiegel's lawyer, Dennis Perluss, said Spiegel is contesting the charges.

"All of the uses that are at issue in terms of the planes and the condominiums were for legitimate business purposes," Perluss said.

But you are paying for more than Spiegel's lifestyle. You are also going to be picking up the tab for his management of Columbia. After heady earnings in the mid-1980s, Columbia lost twice as much money in 1989 and 1990—a total of $1.4 billion—as it had made in the previous twenty years added together. Federal regulators seized Columbia in January 1991. Taxpayers will pay for a bailout expected to cost more than $1.5 billion.

That final figure depends, in part, on how much the government collects for the sale of the corporate headquarters on Wilshire Boulevard in

Beverly Hills. When construction started, it was expected to cost $17 million. By the time work was finished, after Spiegel had made the last of his design changes—"the highest possible grade of limestone and marble, stainless steel floors and ceiling tiles, leather wall coverings"—the cost had soared to $55 million.

It could have been even higher, except that one of Spiegel's ambitious plans never was translated into bricks and mortar. According to federal auditors, he had wanted to include in the building "a large multilevel gymnasium and 'survival chamber' bathrooms with bulletproof glass and an independent air and food supply."

Just who Spiegel thought might attack the bathrooms of a Beverly Hills savings and loan is unclear.

An Indifferent Congress

Congress has done little to curb the abuses of the 1980s. Consider for a moment Congress's response to the leveraged-buyout and corporate-restructuring craze of the 1980s that led to the loss of millions of jobs. As mergers, acquisitions, hostile takeovers and buyouts swept corporate America in the 1980s, defenders of the restructuring process contended it was merely another stage of the free-market economy at work.

During an appearance before a congressional committee in April 1985, Joseph R. Wright, Jr., then deputy director of President Reagan's Office of Management and Budget, summed up the prevailing attitude: "There is substantial evidence that corporate takeovers, as well as mergers, acquisitions and divestitures are, in the aggregate, beneficial for stockholders and for the economy as a whole."

It is true that the restructuring of business is as old as business itself. So, too, the demise of corporations that are mismanaged or that manufacture products for which there is no longer any demand. Once, the Baldwin Locomotive Works sprawled over twenty acres in Philadelphia and more than 600 acres in Eddystone, Pennsylvania. At the company's peak, it employed 20,000 persons. When the market for steam locomotives disappeared, so, too, did Baldwin.

In those days, when factories and technologies died out—and workers lost their jobs—new factories, new technologies replaced the old. Always at higher wages. But what sets the current era apart from the past is this: There are no new manufacturing plants to replace today's Baldwins. And the remaining jobs pay less. While the government rule book encourages deal-making over creating jobs and rewards those who engineer new pieces of paper to be traded on Wall Street rather than those who engineer new products that can be manufactured and sold, Congress has displayed little interest in making changes.

From the mid-1980s on, lawmakers distributed news releases decrying corporate excesses. They made speeches deploring the loss of jobs. They conducted hearings exploring the possibility of enacting legislation to curb abuses. They issued reports reciting their findings.

At one point, the flurry of activity stirred concern on Wall Street. An article in a January 1989 issue of the *Wall Street Journal*, under the headline, "Wall Street Fears That Congress Will Put Brake on LBOs," began: "Fears are mounting on Wall Street that Congress may actually do something to slow down the gravy train of takeovers and leveraged buyouts."

The fears were misplaced. Lawmakers were content with giving the appearance of action: News releases. Speeches. Hearings. Reports. But nothing else. Especially no legislation.

As one congressional staff member put it when he explained why committee hearings trailed off: "There simply is no interest among lawmakers in this."

Indeed not. But Congress was merely following the lead of the White House and Presidents Reagan and Bush.

President Bush summed up his attitudes on corporate takeovers in a question-and-answer interview with *Business Week* magazine: "To the degree that there are egregious offenses in these short-term takeovers that result in increased debt, I think we ought to take a look. But I have no agenda on that. I'm always a little wary about the government trying to solve problems when, historically, the marketplace has been able to solve them."

Members of Congress, for their part, seemed satisfied with the arguments mounted by the experts who insisted that all was working well and that new laws were unnecessary. To Capitol Hill they came to testify, from the Harvard Business School, from Wall Street investment houses, from law firms specializing in mergers and acquisitions, from the offices of corporate raiders. People like Carl C. Icahn, who spoke on the virtues of corporate takeovers during an appearance before a House Energy and Commerce subcommittee in March 1984.

Icahn had already made hundreds of millions of dollars in raids on such companies as Texaco, Inc., Hammermill Paper Company, Uniroyal, Inc., and Marshall Field and Company.

It was the year before he would take over Trans World Airlines, Inc., a company from which he would personally extract millions of dollars, firing thousands of employees, and which he would pilot into bankruptcy court.

Downplaying concerns about layoffs that follow mergers and acquisitions, Icahn told lawmakers: "Generally, if the company is doing pretty well . . . there are not an awful lot of layoffs, and the layoffs that do occur are really getting rid of some of the fat that is not productive for society."

Similar views were expressed by Icahn's fellow raiders and others who profited from the restructuring of business—Wall Street investment advisers, bankers, lawyers, accountants, brokers, pension fund managers, arbitrageurs, speculators and a close circle of hangers-on. This army of dealmakers turned the government rule book to its own advantage, seizing on provisions that place a higher value on ever-larger profits today at the expense of long-term growth, more and better-paying middle-class jobs and larger profits in the future. In doing so, they made billions of dollars.

Popular wisdom has it that the worst has passed, that it was all an aberration called the 1980s. The age of takeovers and leveraged buyouts. The decade of greed. And greed has been officially declared dead by trend-trackers. A higher economic morality is supposedly in for the 1990s. Popular wisdom is wrong. The declining fortunes of the middle class that began with the restructuring craze will continue through this decade and beyond.

There are, an analysis suggests, two reasons: First, there is the global economy—the current buzz-phrase of politicians and corporate executives. As will be described in a later chapter, the global economy will be to the 1990s and beyond what corporate restructuring was to the 1980s.

Through the last decade, decisions that produced short-term profits at the expense of jobs and future profits were justified because they increased "shareholder value." In the 1990s, the same decisions are being made with the same consequences—only this time the justification is "global competition."

Second, the fallout from the 1980s will drag on for years, as more companies file for protection in bankruptcy court, more companies lay off workers to meet their debt obligations, more companies reorganize to correct the excesses of the past.

Wall Street's Greatest Accomplishments

Meet Edwin Bohl of Hermann, Missouri. He, like Larry Weikel and Belinda Schell, knows all about the future.

The place to begin Bohl's story is in 1988 with a company called Interco, Inc., a once-successful *Fortune* 500 conglomerate whose products included some of the best-known names in American retailing—Converse sneakers, London Fog raincoats, Ethan Allen furniture, Florsheim shoes. In that year the investment banking firm Wasserstein Perella & Co. set out to reorganize St. Louis–based Interco, a company with scores of plants operating in the United States and abroad.

Interco could trace its origins back more than 150 years. It was one of the country's largest industrial employers, with 54,000 workers. It had annual sales of $3.3 billion. It had paid dividends continuously since 1913.

In the summer of 1988, a pair of corporate raiders out of Washington, D.C., brothers Steven M. and Mitchell P. Rales, targeted Interco for take-over, offering to buy the company for $64 a share, or $2.4 billion. To fend off the Raleses, Interco's management turned to Wasserstein Perella, which came up with a plan valued at $76 a share. Interco obviously did not have that kind of cash lying around. So the plan called for the company to borrow $2.9 billion.

The financial plan was the sort that Wall Street embraced with great enthusiasm. Supporters of corporate restructurings insisted that debt was a positive force, imposing discipline on corporate managers and forcing them to keep a tight rein on costs. Said Michael C. Jensen, a professor at the Harvard Business School, who was one of the academic community's most vocal supporters of corporate restructurings, "The benefits of debt in motivating managers and their organizations to be efficient have largely been ignored."

As it turned out, Interco failed to be a textbook model for the wonders of corporate debt. Instead of encouraging efficiency, it compelled management to make short-term decisions that harmed the long-run interests of the corporation and its employees. Within two weeks of taking on the debt, Interco closed two Florsheim shoe plants—and sold the real estate. Interco announced that the shutdowns would save more than $2 million. That was just enough to pay the interest on the company's new mountain of debt for five days.

At the Florsheim plant in Paducah, Kentucky, 375 employees lost their jobs. At the Florsheim plant in Hermann, 265 employees were thrown out of work. None was offered a job at another plant.

Hermann is a picturesque town of 2,700 on the Missouri River, about seventy miles west of St. Louis. Settled by Germans from Philadelphia in the 1830s, it remains heavily German. The town's streets are named after noted Germans. The local telephone book reads more like a directory from a town on the Rhine than one on the Missouri. As might be expected from such a heritage, the deeply ingrained work ethic served the town's largest employer well. Beginning in 1902, that employer was known down through the years simply as "the shoe factory."

It was a model of stability for the town and one of the manufacturing jewels of the International Shoe Company, later Interco, its owner. Because of the factory's efficient work force, whenever Florsheim wanted to experiment with new technology or develop a new shoe, it did so at Hermann. The plant had a long history of good labor relations. And it operated at a profit. So why, then, did Interco choose to close the factory?

Listen to Perry D. Lovett, who was city administrator of Hermann when the plant shut down and who discussed the closing with Interco officials: "We talked to the senior vice president who was selling the property and he told me this was a profitable plant and they were pleased with it. The only thing was, this plant and the one in Kentucky they actually owned. The other plants they had, they had leased. The only place they could generate cash was from the plant in Hermann and the one in Kentucky.

"He said it was just a matter that this was one piece of property in which they could generate revenue to pay off the debt. And that was it. That brought it down."

In short, a profitable and efficient plant was closed because Interco actually owned—rather than leased—the building and real estate. And the company needed the cash from the sale of the property to help pay down the debt incurred in the restructuring that was supposed to make the company more efficient.

Hardest hit by the closing, Lovett said, were the older people: "Here were folks who had never worked anywhere else. . . . They had gotten out of high school and they went to work in the shoe factory."

So it was with Edwin Bohl.

Bohl began as a laborer in 1952. "I think I started for seventy cents an hour," he recalled. Except for two years out to serve in Korea, he worked at the plant, rising to a supervisory position, until its closing thirty-seven years later.

The announcement of the shutdown came without warning a few weeks before Christmas of 1988. There was a meeting that morning, Bohl remembered, in which there was talk about increased benefits and changes in the way shoes were made. "They had given me a bunch of new chemicals," he said, "that I was to use in the finishing department. They had told us that everything was looking good." A company executive was supposed to fly in from Chicago that same morning. No one said exactly why, but his plane was delayed.

"The minute we came back from lunch," Bohl said, "they called us supervisors together. . . . The man read us the papers and said there were no jobs held for anybody. . . . They told us they had to close the plant because of the restructuring. . . . They had to raise money. . . . They told [us] it was not because of the quality. We were rated the top in quality and cost. . . . We had no idea this would happen."

Unexpectedly, Edwin Bohl found himself on the unemployment rolls at the age of fifty-eight. He was given a choice: He could wait until he reached retirement age and collect his full pension. If he did so, he would have to pay for his own costly health insurance. Or he could take early retirement, with a sharply reduced pension, and the company would continue to pay his health insurance.

"I sacrificed 29 percent of my pension to get it [the health insurance]," he said, adding, "If I hadn't taken early retirement, my insurance would have been sky high. You really didn't have much choice." Later, Bohl, who was earning $19,000 a year at the shoe factory, found part-time work in the local Western Auto store. The job paid $4 an hour. By 1992, he was making $4.75 an hour.

Lamented Bohl's wife, Geraldine: "We thought this would be the best time of our life. Now he doesn't know when he's going to get a day off. You either take a poor retirement and have your insurance, or have your retirement and pay for high insurance."

As for Bruce Wasserstein and Joseph Perella, whose firm collected $9 million in fees for arranging the restructuring that left Interco with $2.9 billion in debt—which ultimately forced the company into United States

Bankruptcy Court—they have a somewhat different perspective of their efforts at reshaping corporate America. In February 1989, Perella modestly assessed his firm's contributions for the *Wall Street Journal:* "No group of people—not just me and Bruce—ever accomplished so much in such a short period of time in Wall Street's history."

CHAPTER TWO
LOSING OUT
TO MEXICO

WHAT WENT WRONG

American corporations are closing plants or slashing work forces in the U.S. and shifting the jobs to Mexico. Since 1965, more than 1,800 plants employing more than 500,000 workers have been built there, most by U.S. corporations.

2,800 (est.)

2,500

2,000

1,850

1,500

Hundreds of Mexican factories...

1,000

500

0

'65 '70 '75 '80 '85 **'90 '95**

800,000 (est.)

600,000

530,000

400,000

...with thousands of workers

200,000

0

'65 '70 '75 '80 '85 **'90 '95**

SOURCE: Secretariat of Programming and Budget, Secretariat of Commerce and Industrial Development, Mexico City

"What Are We Going to Do Now?"

Rosa Vasquez and Mollie James share a common interest. Vasquez works for the company that once employed Mollie James. That is where similarities end. James earned $7.91 an hour. Vasquez earns $1.45 an hour.

James lives in a six-room, two-story house on a paved street in a working-class neighborhood of Paterson, New Jersey. Vasquez lives in a one-room shack in a Mexican shantytown reachable only by foot along a dirt path. James's house has electricity and indoor plumbing. Vasquez's house has neither. When Mollie James wants to watch television, she turns on the set in her living room. When Rosa Vasquez wants to watch television, she connects a car battery to a thirteen-inch black-and-white set.

For thirty-three years, Mollie James worked for a company that manufactured electrical components for fluorescent lights in New Jersey. Now Rosa Vasquez works for the same company, making the same kinds of products at a new plant in Mexico.

Mollie James's story is that of many Americans in the 1980s. After decades of working for one employer, they suddenly found themselves out of work—unable to secure another job and deprived of benefits they had counted on for their later years.

Universal Manufacturing Company, the company that employed James, was founded in 1947 as a recent invention—fluorescent lights—grew in popularity. Universal manufactured a mechanism called a ballast that regulated the flow of electricity to the light.

Mollie James went to work at Universal's Paterson plant in 1955 for ninety-five cents an hour. She worked as a laminator, a tester, a machine operator and finally a press operator. "I could do any job in the plant," she said proudly. Although there was usually abundant overtime, James held a second full-time job for eighteen years to bring in more money to raise and educate her four children. Universal's original owners knew the workers and routinely walked through the plant talking to them, James recalled. "We were more or less like a family," she said. "The owner would come out and talk to us and would help us in any way that he could. He saw that many of us got homes through their help, by speaking to a bank or even making you a personal loan. They were concerned about the welfare of the workers." If something didn't work, James said, the owners wanted to know so they could make adjustments and produce a better product. "We were number one," she said.

In 1986, Universal was acquired by MagneTek, Inc. of Los Angeles. MagneTek had been formed in 1984 by a Los Angeles investment company, the Spectrum Group, headed by Andrew G. Galef, a business consultant who specialized in advising troubled businesses. The company was an early beneficiary of Michael Milken's junk bond machine. Drexel Burnham Lambert, Inc. served as MagneTek's investment adviser, underwriting millions of dollars in high-yield bonds that enabled the company to acquire Universal and other businesses.

Although Drexel is operating under United States Bankruptcy Court supervision and Milken is in prison for securities law violations, Drexel is still very much a part of MagneTek. Two limited partnerships made up of former Drexel employees and a Drexel subsidiary own 37 percent of the corporation's stock, according to reports filed with the United States Securities and Exchange Commission (SEC).

MagneTek went public in 1989 with investment analysts predicting a bright future. "We think this stock has above average intermediate term prospects," Merrill Lynch said in 1989, "[and] looks even more reasonably priced on prospects in the period beyond, which accounts for our buy, long term rating."

While it achieved record sales of $1.1 billion and record earnings of $34.6 million in 1991, MagneTek faces challenges in coming years to manage its huge debt. Starting in 1992, the corporation must make a series of steep principal payments. All told, $400 million will have to be repaid or refinanced by the year 2000. Galef, MagneTek's chairman, received $272,852 in bonuses from the company in the fiscal year ended June 30, 1991.

More important, the Spectrum Group—of which Galef is the sole stockholder—collects an annual fee to provide "management services" to MagneTek, according to SEC reports. In 1991, those fees totaled $678,000, and since 1986, MagneTek has paid Spectrum $3.6 million in such fees. Spectrum has similar arrangements with other companies that Galef reorganized, including the Warnaco Group, Inc., a textile manufacturer, and Exide Corporation, a maker of automotive and industrial batteries. Over all, Spectrum has collected millions of dollars in fees to advise these companies and assist in acquisitions.

Galef and his third wife live in the fashionable Bel Air section of Los Angeles, popular with entertainers and movie executives. Peter Bogdanovich, the film director, and Terry S. Semel, president of Warner Brothers, are among their neighbors. Their house on Copa de Oro (Cup of Gold) Road is valued at $3.9 million by the Los Angeles County assessor.

The flavor of Galef's lifestyle emerged in court papers filed in 1987 during a divorce action initiated by his second wife, Billie: "At Christmas we always had a large dinner party with at least 200 guests. . . . Travel was also extensive. Last July, we went to Australia, Hong Kong, China and Japan for approximately three weeks. We stayed, as we always do, in first-class hotels, ate at the best restaurants, and generally traveled by limousine.

"In September, we took the Concorde to Paris and London, where we spent a week, again staying at the best hotels and eating in the best restaurants."

While Galef and his wife were jetting about the world, his managers at the Paterson plant where Mollie James worked were assuring employees that nothing would change under MagneTek, the new owner. "They came through the plant and talked to each worker and told us we wouldn't have anything to worry about because they would always have operations in Paterson," James said. "They gave us the impression that we had great prospects here. They told us they were going to get us new equipment, new machinery."

All the promises notwithstanding, the new equipment failed to materialize. Instead, the existing equipment began to disappear. Mollie James and her co-workers would leave the factory one day, and a piece of equipment, such as a large stamping machine, would be in place, bolted to the floor. And then, she remembered: "You'd come in the next morning and it would be gone. There'd be a bare space on the floor."

Employees discovered later that the equipment had been shipped to other MagneTek plants. The company subsequently sent Paterson workers to those plants to train other persons to use the machines that had once provided work in Paterson. Incidents like that made employees wonder if the plant's days were numbered. Nonetheless, MagneTek continued to say it would never close Paterson. "They told us we were doing a great job," James remembered.

But one day a notice went up on the plant bulletin board. Effective June 30, 1989, Universal's thirty-eight-year-old Paterson plant would be shut. "It was very devastating," James said. "People asked, 'What are we going to do now?' We just always thought we would have a job." In July 1989, the plant that had once employed 500 people became a distribution center, receiving products made at other MagneTek facilities. James was offered a job in the shipping department. But at fifty-eight, she was unable to lift the heavy boxes. She was out of work.

Rush to the Border

As MagneTek stopped manufacturing in Paterson, the company reached full production at a 150,000-square-foot plant in Matamoros, Mexico, a burgeoning border town across the Rio Grande from Brownsville, Texas.

While Galef declined to discuss MagneTek's move to Mexico—"Mr. Galef usually doesn't do interviews," a secretary said—another company official explained the transfer. Robert W. Murray, vice president of communications and public relations, said that production operations at Paterson were transferred to a plant in Blytheville, Arkansas, and that part of the Blytheville operation was, in turn, moved to Matamoros.

Commenting on the shutdown of production in Paterson, Murray said, "On a local basis, it can be a tragedy. That, we regret. But to keep our 16,000 people employed, we need to stay in business. . . . But the market—the labor market that was once called the United States—is now North

America, and I include in that Central America. . . . Regions rather than countries are now competing on a world scale. We've got to cooperate with both our neighbors to the north, Canada, and with Mexico to the south to put together the kind of competitive package that can really compete on a world scale."

The MagneTek plant is part of Mexico's Maquiladora program, a venture started to persuade United States companies to establish assembly plants there. The government encourages such plants by setting a low tariff on finished goods shipped back to the United States. Originally, Maquiladoras assembled components shipped in from the United States by American corporations. Now many of these so-called assembly plants are full-scale manufacturing facilities performing the same type of work that was once done by American workers, but at much lower wages.

United States government agencies, notably the Commerce Department and State Department, have encouraged America's corporate flight to the border. In testimony before a Congressional subcommittee in December 1986, Alexander H. Good, director general of the United States and Foreign Commercial Service, summed up the government's position: "We are convinced the program has important economic benefits for both the U.S. and Mexican economies. . . . The Commerce Department supports participation in the Maquiladora program by U.S. industry because it helps U.S. companies to remain healthy in the face of intense international competition and it keeps U.S. employment as high as possible."

With this kind of backing from government rule makers, Maquiladora plants have blossomed along the border. The strip of land that runs for 1,500 miles from California to Texas has become a highway of *Fortune* 500 companies. All along the Mexican side of the border are names long associated with the other side—General Motors, Fisher-Price, Trico, Parker-Hannifin, Xerox, Ford, Kimberly-Clark, IBM, Samsonite, General Electric and Rockwell. All told, there are more than 1,800 plants employing more than 500,000 workers in Mexico—all since 1965.

With few exceptions, the new plants are replacing facilities that once provided jobs for United States workers. Like the Zenith Electronics Corporation plant in Reynosa, across the Rio Grande from McAllen, Texas. As recently as 1965, every color television set purchased in the United States was made by an American-owned company in a domestic plant. In that year, Americans purchased 2.6 million sets manufactured by companies such as Sylvania, Motorola, Admiral, Philco, Sunbeam, RCA, Quasar, Magnavox and Wizard.

Twenty-six years later, in 1991, sales of television sets to United States consumers soared to twenty-one million. But only one company was still making the sets in the United States—Zenith Corporation, at a lone domestic plant in Springfield, Missouri. By 1992, there were none. In October 1991 Zenith announced that it was ending production in Springfield in 1992 and shifting the jobs to a Zenith plant in Reynosa, Mexico.

For the American television industry, the end came with a swiftness that would have seemed inconceivable a generation ago, when more than two dozen American-owned plants were turning out all the television sets purchased in this country. That was before Japanese television manufacturers began dumping huge quantities of low-priced receivers on the American market.

When American manufacturers objected to what they called unfair trade practices, the Japanese claimed they were able to undersell American makers because their products resulted from greater cost efficiencies. But American television makers said there was no evidence to support that assertion. As proof, they pointed to the fact that the Japanese were selling television sets to Americans at much lower prices than they were selling them in Japan.

Zenith asserted in a 1977 report: "The fact that the Japanese manufacturers, whose lowest-priced nineteen-inch offerings in Japan are priced at about $500, are selling similar receivers to American private brand retailers at prices that permit resale in the United States at under $300, provides substantial support for the premise that those receivers are being dumped in the United States."

The United States Tariff Commission had agreed, saying in a 1971 ruling that the television "industry in the United States is being injured by reason of the importation of television receivers from Japan, which are being sold at less than fair value." Fines and duties totaling several hundred million dollars were later assessed against the Japanese television makers. But years of legal wrangling and diplomatic maneuvering followed, with the Japanese companies ultimately paying only nominal amounts.

Zenith also filed a lawsuit against the major Japanese manufacturers, charging them with violating United States antitrust and antidumping laws. The case found its way to the United States Supreme Court, which ruled in favor of the Japanese. By the time litigation and the regulatory proceedings were over, the American television industry was history.

Every American-owned company had either shut down its television production line or been sold to the Japanese. Except Zenith. The company known for innovation and quality—"The quality goes in before the name goes on"—continued to maintain one production plant. Zenith's sprawling Springfield plant—it covers an area the size of twenty-nine football fields—was the town's largest private employer and a steady source of earnings for 1,750 local residents.

Until 1992. Having lost $500 million in revenue over the previous five years, the company announced that it had to cut costs. When labor contracts expired in 1992, a total of 1,350 employees would be let go and the work shifted to Mexico. In a statement that has become all too familiar to middle-class Americans, Jerry K. Pearlman, Zenith's chairman and president, explained that the Springfield shutdown, while "painful," was necessary for Zenith to remain competitive: "This further consolidation of our operations is a necessary component of Zenith's programs to reduce costs and improve profitability."

The chief reason, Zenith officials emphasized, was Mexico's low wage rate. Wages ranged from $5 to $11 an hour at Springfield; in Mexico they were $1.60 an hour. Actually, the average wage rate at Springfield was $7 an hour. That translated into an annual income of under $15,000, meaning that, by national standards, that the work force in Springfield was, on average, at the low end of the pay scale for the American middle class.

Robert W. Mingus, president of Local 1453 of the International Brotherhood of Electrical Workers, which represents the Zenith workers, does not blame the company for the shutdown. He blames the last four presidents, the Commerce Department and members of Congress, both for not doing more to counter Japanese moves, and for making it possible for United States industry to relocate to Mexico. "We're encouraging our industrial base right out of this country," he said.

In Matamoros, where Mollie James's company relocated, Maquiladora operations are similar to those found in Tijuana, Mexicali, Juarez, Nuevo Laredo and other border towns. Plants make everything from cosmetic brushes to auto flashers. Rosa Vasquez, twenty-six, one of 1,500 employees—mostly female—at the MagneTek facility in Matamoros, began working the 4:30 P.M.-to-1:30 A.M. shift in July 1988, the year the plant opened. She earns 179,000 pesos, or about $59, a week.

In 1989, MagneTek, in a report filed with the Securities and Exchange Commission, cited the benefits of this low-wage haven: "The company has consolidated manufacturing and relocated product lines to facilities having lower per-unit labor and overhead costs. For example, the company has established a full-scale manufacturing facility in Mexico, where it benefits from lower wage rates."

Mollie James doesn't understand. "The company said we were hurt by foreign trade," she said. "But this company has plants in Mexico. Why isn't that foreign trade?" Rosa Vasquez does understand. She needs the money from the plant—even if it is only enough to buy essentials. Asked how she spends her earnings, she answered, "The children, food, clothing for the children, clothing for us."

To get to and from work, most MagneTek workers must ride crowded, stuffy yellow vans called Maxi-Taxis that were designed for twelve passengers, but that carry twice that many in cramped, often sweltering conditions for journeys that take up to an hour. In this sense Vasquez is fortunate. She walks to work.

Her home is one of about 200 primitive dwellings in a colony of poor people called "Vista Hermosa" bordering the MagneTek plant. Vista Hermosa (which means "beautiful view" in Spanish) is a collection of ramshackle dwellings, made of wood or cement blocks, in varying stages of disrepair. Wooden outhouses serve as toilets. People light their houses with kerosene lamps. Chickens and pigs wander about.

Vasquez and her husband live behind the plant, where the roar of MagneTek's air-conditioning system can be heard twenty-four hours a day. She describes her home as a "small wooden house." It is actually one room, twelve feet long and ten feet wide, with a tin, peaked roof. It contains a double bed, two small dressers, a table, a cupboard, clothes hamper, two chairs and a propane stove.

Vasquez and her husband, Alberto, a carpenter, live at the house during the week while their two children stay nearby with her parents. Although she works until 1:30 A.M., she rises early to take her small boys to preschool each morning, riding thirty minutes by bus each way. She and her husband believe in education. The only object on the walls of their modest home is a poster showing a child bent intently over a desk with the slogan above, *"Total Principio es Dificil."* An ode to hard work, the expression translates roughly as, "Starting all over is difficult."

For entertainment, the family watches television at the house of Rosa Vasquez's parents, using a car battery to power the set. Every two weeks a brother puts the battery in an old car and drives around to charge it up.

President Bush and other promoters of free trade with Mexico are fond of pointing to Mexico's large population as a potential market for American-made products under a hemispheric free trade agreement. They see finished products moving back and forth across the border. Items once made in the United States would be manufactured instead in Mexico and shipped north for sale to American consumers. Other products would continue to be manufactured in the United States and shipped south for sale to Mexican consumers.

American workers, they say, have nothing to fear from such an arrangement because it would open the door for United States products in Mexico's vast domestic market. The president cited the benefits of an unrestricted trade policy during a speech in Houston in April 1991: "I don't have to tell anyone in this room about Mexico's market potential: eighty-five million consumers who want to buy our goods. Nor do I have to tell you that as Mexico grows and prospers, it will need even more of the goods we're best at producing: computers, manufacturing equipment, high-tech and high-value products."

That is the theory. Reality is quite different.

There is no doubt that under a free trade agreement more United States companies would rush to establish plants in Mexico to take advantage of low wage rates. But there is little likelihood that the Mexican masses would be able to buy many goods made in the United States in return.

That is because their wages—even those earned by the Rosa Vasquezes, which are at the high end of the Mexican wage scale—do not translate into a standard of living comparable to that enjoyed by Rosa's counterpart, Mollie James. As a result, the material goods that are common features of middle-class American households are beyond the reach of the Vasquezes.

Like refrigerators. Even if Vista Hermosa had electric power, and even if the Vasquezes could afford electricity, they still couldn't afford a refrigerator. In Matamoros, refrigerators sell for $450, or about two months' wages. Even so, Rosa Vasquez feels fortunate. She has a job, which is more than Mollie James can say.

After the Paterson plant closed in 1989, Mollie James collected unemployment benefits for six months and then went back to school. She learned how to repair computers but has yet to find anyone who will hire her. "When you are . . . going on fifty-nine, it is very hard to get a job," she said. "Any time you put your age down, they say nicely, 'We will contact you.'" For eighteen months she paid for her own health benefits, but it became too expensive at $114 a month. "I hope for the best," she said.

Mollie James liked her job and took pride in her work. In the 1970s, she had to overcome management's reluctance to allow a woman to operate a large metal stamping machine. But she passed the thirty-day tryout and ran the machine until the plant closed. "I've seen men lose fingers," she recalled, "but thank God I never lost anything."

Except, in the end, her job.

CHAPTER THREE
SHIFTING TAXES—
FROM THEM
TO YOU

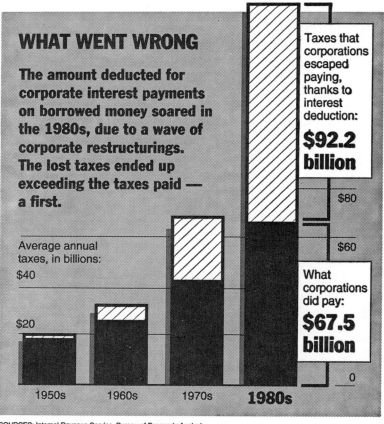

WHAT WENT WRONG

The amount deducted for corporate interest payments on borrowed money soared in the 1980s, due to a wave of corporate restructurings. The lost taxes ended up exceeding the taxes paid — a first.

Average annual taxes, in billions:

$40

$20

1950s   1960s   1970s   **1980s**

Taxes that corporations escaped paying, thanks to interest deduction:

$92.2 billion

$80

$60

What corporations did pay:

$67.5 billion

0

SOURCES: Internal Revenue Service, Bureau of Economic Analysis

The Magic Wand

Once upon a time, in a faraway land called Texas, two men owned a bank. They called it Guaranty Federal Savings & Loan. The two men paid themselves lots of money and loaned other people lots of money. But they wanted to make even more money, so they met with people from a distant kingdom with very tall buildings, called Wall Street.

They liked the Wall Street people very much and decided to buy pieces of paper from them called bonds. They bought and sold the pieces of paper over and over again. When they made money doing this, they kept it for themselves. When they wanted even more money to build castles of sand in yet another kingdom, they just took it out of the bank.

This worked okay. Until one day when the bank ran out of money. Then some government people came to Dallas to look into the way they ran the bank. These people called the two men crooks and put them in a building with bars on the windows.

The government people took the bank away from the two men and sold it to a big Texas company. Then the government people gave the big Texas company lots of money so the bank wouldn't run out again. Best of all, the government people also gave the company a very special magic wand that came with the bank.

The wand is called NOL, and it is wondrous. It makes taxes disappear. The government actually invented the wand. By waving the wand, the big Texas company that now owns the bank can make taxes vanish for years and years and years. The money it used to pay in taxes it can now keep for itself. Isn't this a nice deal for the big Texas company?

Nicer than you think.

First of all, the wand invented by the government people is available to only a select few. You, for example, can't have one. What's more, you pay for the wands that do get passed around.

NOL stands for net operating loss deduction, a tax break that allows corporations to reduce this year's taxes—and next year's taxes, and so on—because of money lost last year. Through the 1980s, the NOL enabled corporations to escape payment of more than $100 billion in income taxes.

But it is not the largest of the many generous write-offs available to businesses. The deduction that corporations can take for interest paid on borrowed money costs the government nearly $100 billion in a single year, dwarfing the amount that NOLs diverted from the United States Treasury. The deduction for interest on corporate debt has long been part of the United States tax code. But in the 1980s' frenzy of unchecked corporate restructuring, as businesses raced to see which could borrow the most money, it ballooned out of control.

A catalogue of other deductions—ranging from the write-off for so-called intangibles to special deals that exempt select businesses and investors from payment of taxes—runs to many more billions in lost tax revenue. All these are reasons that individual taxpayers are picking up an ever-larger share of the national tax burden while corporations pay a steadily decreasing share.

Corporations such as Temple-Inland, Inc., the big Texas company that got the magic wand when it acquired Guaranty Federal Savings & Loan Association of Dallas. That is the savings and loan run by the two men from Dallas, Paul Sau-Ki Cheng and Simon Edward Heath. The Wall Street people were from Drexel Burnham Lambert, Inc. and E.F. Hutton and Company, Inc. By the time Cheng and Heath had finished working their financial wizardry, Guaranty Federal was insolvent. Federal regulators seized it in 1988 and turned it over to Temple-Inland.

As a result of what the government has charged was "fraudulent bond-trading" transactions along with illegal dealings that led to the conviction of Cheng and Heath, the savings and loan ended up with a net operating loss of more than $300 million. Now, and for many years to come, Temple-Inland can use those old losses incurred by the savings and loan's former owners to reduce its taxable income and avoid paying taxes.

What makes the Guaranty Federal story so remarkable is this: First, taxpayers are paying, and will continue to pay, to bail out the failed savings and loan—that is, to restore depositors' money. Then, taxpayers will pay yet again, to make up for the taxes Temple-Inland won't be paying because its profits can be offset by the savings and loan losses incurred years earlier by two men now in jail.

Direct cost of the bailout: An estimated $3.9 billion, which will go straight from you and other taxpayers to Guaranty Federal and its new owner, Temple-Inland. Indirect cost: An estimated $590 million in lost tax revenue. That missing revenue will be made up by you and other taxpayers—or be added to the federal debt, in which case you'll pay the interest charges on it.

The tax beneficiary, Temple-Inland, is a diversified corporation based in Diboll, Texas. The company's interests, which include forest products, building materials, mortgage banking, and insurance, generate more than $2 billion in annual revenue. Its largest stockholder is Oppenheimer Group, Inc., parent of Oppenheimer & Company, Inc., the Wall Street investment banking and securities firm.

In 1990, the first full year that Temple-Inland took advantage of the Guaranty Federal tax breaks, its federal income tax payments plummeted 66 percent. According to a report filed with the United States Securities and Exchange Commission, the company's profits rose from $207 million in 1989 to $232.5 million in 1990. But its taxes fell from $84 million to $29 million. If you were in the $30,000-to-$40,000 income group and received a similar tax break, you'd have an extra $48 every week in your paycheck.

Guaranty is only one of hundreds of savings and loans that taxpayers are rescuing, Temple-Inland only one of scores of companies profiting from the bailout. The ultimate cost to taxpayers: A half-trillion dollars. If you make $20,000 to $30,000 a year, you might think of that sum this way: Every dollar that you and all others in your income group pay in federal income taxes for the next decade will, in effect, go to the savings and loan industry.

For this, you can thank the people in Washington—a succession of Congresses and presidents, administrators and regulators, Democrats and Republicans, who write the government rule book, the accumulation of laws and regulations that provide the framework for the country's economy.

As might be expected, some people profit handsomely from the rule book. Like Ted Arison of Miami Beach, Florida, and Tel Aviv. You may not recognize the name. But you've probably seen the TV commercials for his company. The ones starring Kathie Lee Gifford (cohost of the syndicated television show "Live With Regis and Kathie Lee"), who, in assorted costumes, dances across the decks of the "fun ships" of Carnival Cruise Lines, Inc. singing "Ain't We Got Fun."

From 1985 to 1988, Carnival Cruise Lines, which promises evenings of "dazzling entertainment, romantic dancing and fast-paced casino action" aboard a fleet of ships with names such as *Fantasy* and *Ecstasy,* produced total profits of $502.5 million.

The corporate income tax rate during those years ranged from 46 percent in 1985 to 34 percent in 1988, meaning that Carnival paid about $200 million in federal taxes. Right?

Wrong. Carnival paid not a cent in United States corporate income taxes on that half-billion dollars in profits. Its corporate tax rate was zero. That is because Carnival benefits from a government rule book that exempts shipping companies incorporated in foreign countries from having to pay United States income taxes.

It is a special-interest provision, like so many others, that friendly members of Congress have preserved through repeated revisions in the Internal Revenue Code—revisions that they often call "tax reform." Although Carnival's offices are in Miami, and its Caribbean-bound ships leave from Miami, the company is incorporated in Panama. Its subsidiaries are organized in Liberia, the Bahamas, the British Virgin Islands and the Netherlands Antilles.

Carnival's situation is not unique. Hundreds of corporations have eliminated or drastically reduced their federal tax bills through similar special-interest tax laws. But the immunity from federal corporate income taxes helps explain why Ted Arison, sixty-seven, the Israeli-born founder of the company, was designated by *Forbes* magazine in 1991 as one of the fifteen richest people in the United States, with wealth estimated at $2.3 billion.

How is it possible for any corporation to escape paying taxes after passage of the 1986 Tax Reform Act, the legislation that members of Congress hailed as restoring fairness to the American tax system? The legislation that Senator Bob Packwood, the Oregon Republican who was one of the two chief architects of the tax law, said was so tough that "there will not be a profit-making corporation in the country that can escape taxation." The legislation that Senator John F. Kerry, Democrat from Massachusetts, said "will make that kind of unfairness a thing of the past" and permit "the American people to move once again to trust their federal government."

They said it. The tax act did not do it. For the five years preceding passage of the tax act, Carnival recorded profits of $279 million, and paid no federal income taxes. In the two years following passage, it recorded profits of $349 million—on which it paid no federal income taxes.

In June 1987, several months after the sweeping tax-overhaul legislation was signed into law, Carnival Cruise Lines issued a stock-offering document confidently predicting that its tax-free status would continue. The registration statement, filed with the SEC, states: "The company is not subject to United States corporate tax on its income from the operation of ships, and the company does not expect such income to be subject to such tax in the future."

The 1986 act did make one change that affected Arison personally. It required large shareholders like him to report a portion of their company's earnings on their individual income tax return. But the company had a solution for Arison's personal tax bill, as it disclosed in a report filed with the SEC in March 1990. As Carnival explained it, if the company's taxable income amounted to, say, $200 million, a stockholder who owned 80 percent of the company's stock (as Arison, in fact, did at the time) would be required to report $160 million in income on his personal tax return. At an effective tax rate of 30 percent, he would owe taxes of $48 million.

Not to worry. Carnival would declare a dividend equal to the $48 million and give it to the stockholder (that is, to Arison) to pay his taxes. As Carnival put it in the SEC report: "The company anticipates that it will pay quarterly dividends aggregating with respect to each year an amount at least equal to the principal shareholder's tax rate."

If there were a comparable deal for you, it might function something like this: Let's say you earn $30,000 to $35,000 a year working for the Kellogg Company, the Battle Creek, Michigan, company that manufactures and markets Corn Flakes, Raisin Bran, Frosted Mini-Wheats, and other ready-to-eat cereals and convenience foods. At the end of the year, your federal tax bill is $3,710. So Kellogg declares a special dividend and gives you a check for $3,710.

Sure. In the real tax world, you must pay your own income taxes, and the Kellogg Company must—and does—pay corporate income taxes. For Carnival and companies like it, the rules are different.

Today, Arison's company still pays no federal income taxes on its cruise operations, which accounted for 78 percent of its overall revenue in 1990. But when Carnival acquired Holland America Line in January 1989, it was obliged to begin paying some income taxes. The reason: Holland America operates tours and hotels within the United States that do not enjoy the same tax immunity granted to the cruise business.

Thus, in 1989 and 1990, Carnival paid $11 million in federal income taxes on profits of $411 million. That is a tax rate of 2.7 percent, about half the rate paid by individuals and families with incomes of $7,000 to $9,000.

Carnival's tax-free status for its cruise operations has been one of its big selling points with Wall Street, driving up the stock price and helping make Arison a billionaire. Time and again, securities analysts have singled out Carnival's tax advantage and assured investors that there was little reason to fear that Congress would end the preferential treatment.

In October 1987, the securities firm Bear Stearns and Company issued an investment report advising its clients: "We are not aware of any initiatives now being considered by Congress to amend the 1986 tax changes in ways that will be detrimental for Carnival. In fact, when sponsors of the bills were working out final provisions last year, several interested parties were aiming to include language that would have further solidified exemptions." Translation: Friendly members of Congress were prepared to write an amendment to the Internal Revenue Code guaranteeing the tax exemption of Carnival and similar companies.

One year later, in a November 1988 investment report, Provident National Bank of Philadelphia reaffirmed the Bear Stearns view: "We believe that future taxation is not likely, and would point out that the company has taken a number of safeguards aimed at preserving its tax-free status for the foreseeable future." And in December 1989, the Robinson-Humphrey Company, Inc., another securities firm, recommended that its clients buy Carnival stock in part because the company "does not pay U.S. federal income taxes."

This exemption is but one of the thousands of provisions that make up the government rule book, for which you pick up the tab.

Middle-Class Tax Squeeze

To understand why you pay the taxes you do, think of your paycheck as part of two government pies. The first pie is made up of total income taxes collected from all individuals and all corporations. The amount that you, as an individual, pay is determined, in part, by the amount Congress says companies should pay. If Congress collects more from businesses, you pay less. If Congress says some businesses may pay reduced taxes, you pay more.

The second pie is made up of combined income taxes and Social Security taxes collected from individuals. The amount that you pay if you earn, say, $25,000 to $35,000 is determined, in part, by the amount that Congress says people who earn more than $100,000 should pay. If Congress collects more from people at the top, you pay less. If Congress says people at the top should pay less, you pay more.

Now consider a few statistics drawn from an analysis of a half-century of government tax and economic data. They will explain why you are accounting for an ever-larger slice of the two government pies.

ITEM: During the 1950s, when more Americans than ever attained middle-class status, the federal government collected $478 billion in combined individual and corporate income taxes in the decade. Of that, corporations paid 39 percent, individuals 61 percent.

During the 1980s, individual and corporate income tax collections soared to $4 trillion. Of that $4 trillion, the corporate share dwindled to 17 percent, the individual share swelled to 83 percent.

ITEM: Corporations have succeeded in reducing their share of the tax burden, in part, through a provision in the government rule book that permits a virtually unlimited deduction for interest on debt. During middle-class America's golden years, the 1950s, corporations paid $44 billion in interest on borrowed money and more than four times that amount, $185 billion, in federal income taxes.

By the 1980s, an era of frenetic corporate borrowing and unabashed congressional support of special interests, that pattern was reversed. During that decade, corporations paid out $2.2 trillion in interest on borrowed money and $675 billion in income taxes.

Thus, in the 1950s, companies paid $4 billion in taxes for every $1 billion they paid in interest. In the 1980s, they paid $3 billion in interest for every $1 billion paid in taxes. That means if your income was less than $30,000 a year during the 1980s, every penny that you—and the other seventy million people who were in that income bracket—paid in federal income tax the entire decade went just to offset the taxes lost through the deduction for interest on corporate debt.

ITEM: Congress has written the government rule book so that Social Security taxes consume an ever-larger share of the weekly paychecks of low- and middle-income Americans, while the affluent are exempted from similar increases. As a consequence, the average family or individual has less money to spend for housing, food, clothing and education.

Look at the plight of median-income families, those who fall in the middle of the American economy, with half of all workers earning more, half less. During the 1950s, median-income families each paid a total of $744 in Social Security taxes for the entire decade—or 1.7 percent of their income. In the 1980s, they paid $19,114 in Social Security taxes—or 7 percent of their income.

For more affluent families—say, those with incomes of ten times the median—the Social Security burden increased, but was comparatively much lighter. During the 1950s, affluent families also paid $744 in Social Secu-

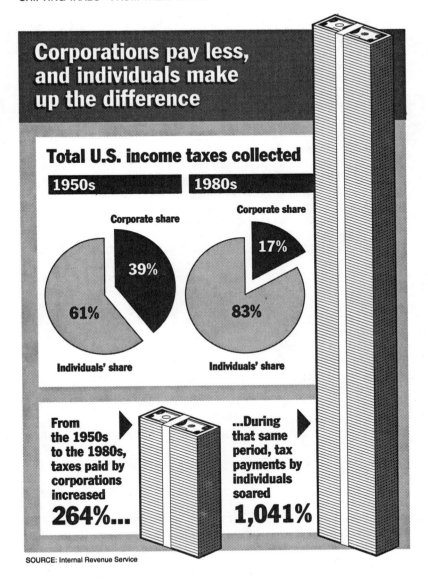

Corporations pay less, and individuals make up the difference

Total U.S. income taxes collected

1950s

Corporate share

39%

61%

Individuals' share

1980s

Corporate share

17%

83%

Individuals' share

From the 1950s to the 1980s, taxes paid by corporations increased

264%...

...During that same period, tax payments by individuals soared

1,041%

SOURCE: Internal Revenue Service

rity taxes. That amounted to two-tenths of 1 percent of their income. In the decade of the 1980s, the more affluent families paid $26,683 in Social Security taxes—still less than 1 percent of their income. Viewed another way, after payment of Social Security taxes, affluent families retained 99 percent of their salaries. Median-income families kept less than 93 percent.

ITEM: The Social Security tax and federal income tax combined are weighted against middle- and lower-income workers, making it more difficult for both groups to maintain their standard of living or to improve their lot.

In 1970, persons with incomes between $25,000 and $30,000 were solidly upper-middle class, earning about three times the median family income of $9,867. They paid, on average, $5,092 in combined income and Social Security taxes. By 1988, another generation in the same $25,000 to $30,000 income category had fallen several rungs down the economic ladder. Their earnings actually dropped below the median income of $32,191. To make matters worse, they paid $4,794 in combined income and Social Security taxes, or only $298 less than their more prosperous counterparts of 1970.

ITEM: While maintaining or increasing the tax burden on middle- and low-income workers, Congress has cut taxes for many of the nation's wealthiest people by one-third or more. In 1970, individuals and families with incomes between $500,000 and $1 million paid, on average, $304,408 in combined federal income and Social Security taxes. By 1989, individuals and families in that income group paid $168,714—or $135,694 less than nineteen years earlier. That amounted to a tax cut of 45 percent.

By way of comparison, during the same period, the combined income and Social Security taxes of people in the $25,000-to-$30,000 income group fell from $5,092 to $4,645—a decline of 9 percent. If the 7.6 million individuals and families in that middle-class group had benefited from the same tax-rate cut as the more affluent taxpayers, they each would have received a tax reduction of $2,291—instead of the $447 they got.

As you might expect, the people who write the tax laws have painted a different picture.

Dan Rostenkowski, the Democratic representative from Illinois who is chairman of the House Ways and Means Committee and one of the two principal authors of the 1986 Tax Reform Act, portrayed himself as the defender of the middle class during debate on the legislation. At one point, Rostenkowski posed these rhetorical questions for his colleagues: "Today's vote is very straightforward. Do we want to give this country tax reform—or don't we? Do we want to give back to middle-income taxpayers the fairness they do not believe will ever come? Or do we want to stand for the status quo which goes hard on the poor—and easy on the rich?"

The answer—documented in tax data—is that Congress has stood for the rich. In 1985, the year before the tax overhaul bill was passed, those with incomes between $30,000 and $40,000 paid combined federal income and Social Security taxes of $6,663. That was 19 percent of their income. In 1989, three years after "tax reform," they paid $6,177, or 17.6 percent. That amounted to a 7 percent cut in tax rates.

By comparison, during that same period, those with incomes between $500,000 and $1 million saw their combined taxes fall from $243,506 to $168,714. That amounted to a 31 percent cut in tax rates—nearly five times the rate-cut for middle-class taxpayers.

If Rostenkowski and his colleagues were adamant about the good deeds they were doing for the middle class in 1986, they were equally insistent that the pending bill would transfer the tax burden from individuals to corporations. Rostenkowski said: "The bill will shift more than $120 billion in tax liability from individuals to corporations—restoring a balance that existed at the start of this decade." Senator Jay Rockefeller, the West Virginia Democrat, said that "what the bill really does is broaden the tax base and shift the tax burden from individuals to corporations."

Not really. In February 1986, months before passage of the 1986 tax act, Congress estimated that corporate tax collections under existing law would amount to $410 billion from 1987 through 1990. The new tax law, which Congress sold as transferring taxes from individuals to corporations, resulted in actual corporate collections of $375 billion during the four years. Instead of generating $120 billion in new corporate tax revenue, the law produced $35 billion less than had been projected under the old law.

As for Rostenkowski's claim that the act would restore the balance between corporate and individual tax payments that had existed in the early 1980s, consider this: In 1980, corporations accounted for 21 percent of total income taxes collected from individuals and corporations. In 1990, corporations accounted for 17 percent. That was down 4 percentage points. Not up.

It is such creative math that has led to an exploding federal deficit, which is a major factor in your falling standard of living.

Legalized Loan-sharking

Despite three laws passed by Congress mandating a phased elimination of the federal deficit by 1991—and then by 1993, and then by 1995—the red ink this year is expected to top $350 billion, a record. If so, it will exceed the deficits of the 1930s, the 1940s, the 1950s, the 1960s and part of the 1970s—all combined.

To better appreciate the consequences of congressional arithmetic, you might consider that in 1960, $9 of every $100 that individuals paid in federal income taxes went not for education or health or social services, but for interest on the debt. In 1991, it was $30 of every $100. The interest payments represent the largest transfer of wealth in this century—with the money going from middle-class job holders to the investors who own the debt.

To put what is happening in more personal terms, think about the federal debt this way. Some years ago, your parents borrowed money from your rich uncle and now you must pay back the loan. Let's suppose that, as in most families today, both you and your spouse work, and your combined paychecks total $600 a week, which makes you a certified member of the middle class. Now, give your rich uncle $180—or 30 percent of your income. Give him another $180 next week. And every week, for the rest of your life.

And presume that when you die, your children will keep paying it. Except they will make the payments to the rich uncle's children.

It is the ultimate loan-sharking operation, one that organized crime leaders could only dream about. For all that money will go for interest on the debt. The debt itself will never be paid.

Oh, that uncle? He may be American. But chances are increasing that he is Japanese, Swiss, German or Arab, since foreign nationals own a growing share of the United States debt. As recently as 1969, foreign investors held just $10 billion of the United States debt, or less than 5 percent of the total federal debt held by the public. By 1990, the $10 billion had ballooned to $405 billion, or 17 percent of the debt in public hands.

Based on projections for the rest of this century, it is a sure bet that a growing portion of the taxes withheld from your paycheck each week will be going to pay interest on the debt. That is because Congress and the president are on a roll. Make that twelve Congresses and five presidents.

At midnight on Monday, Sept. 30, 1992, the United States Government will close the books on its twenty-third consecutive year of deficit spending. That is the longest-running streak of red ink in the nation's history. The previous record—sixteen consecutive years—ran from 1931 to 1946, the hard years of the Great Depression and World War II.

Today, an entire generation has come of age never knowing a federal government that spent less than it took in. The last time that Congress and the president chose to operate within the country's means, actually posting a surplus, albeit a modest one of $3.2 billion, was 1969. That will go into the economic record books as the last balanced budget of the twentieth century.

Lest you think the annual federal deficits have little relevance to your daily life, mull over these numbers: During the 1980s, the government paid out $1.13 trillion in interest on its debt, which consists of all the yearly deficits added together. That is $1.13 trillion in taxpayer dollars.

To put the number in perspective, consider what the federal government will spend in 1992 to reduce the infant mortality rate in the United States. Keep in mind that infant death rates in some United States cities rival the rates of developing nations. That $1.13 trillion would be enough money to double current spending on programs to reduce infant deaths— and to continue spending at that level, year after year, until the second half of the twenty-first century. Or you might want to think about that $1.13 trillion this way: If your weekly paycheck was $700 or less during the

1980s, every penny you paid in federal income taxes went to the people who own that debt.

In many cases, they are people and corporations and institutions that don't pay federal income taxes as you do. Or they pay taxes at a rate below what you pay. Which means a chunk of your weekly paycheck was transferred to wealthy investors. And that chunk will grow substantially. During the 1980s, interest payments averaged $113 billion a year. So far in the 1990s, interest payments are averaging $195 billion a year.

How have a succession of Congresses and presidents fashioned a policy that has produced the civilized world's first permanent deficit? In part, by engaging in practices for which other people are sent to prison. In part, by playing a Washington game called Creative Math.

During his inauguration address in January 1981, President Reagan railed against the deficits that the federal government had been accumulating. "For decades," he said, "we have piled deficit upon deficit, mortgaging our future and our children's future. . . . To continue this long trend is to guarantee tremendous social, cultural, political and economic upheavals." The deficit that year, attributable to Congress and the administration of President Jimmy Carter, was $74 billion. The following year, the first under President Reagan, the deficit jumped to $120 billion—history's first $100 billion–plus deficit.

One year after that, in 1983—the year by which Reagan promised he would produce a balanced budget—the deficit spiraled to $208 billion. It had taken the federal government more than two centuries to pile up a $100 billion deficit in a single year. Reagan doubled that mark in one year.

Members of Congress, Democrats and Republicans alike, caught on to the Creative Math quickly. In 1985, Congress, with great fanfare, enacted the Balanced Budget and Emergency Deficit Control Act. More popularly known by the name of its authors, Gramm-Rudman-Hollings, it imposed automatic spending cuts if the government failed to meet fixed deficit-reduction goals. It provided for the deficit to be reduced to $172 billion in 1986, $144 billion in 1987, $108 billion in 1988, $72 billion in 1980, $36 billion in 1990 and zero in 1991.

Senator Ernest F. Hollings, Democrat from South Carolina, told his colleagues the law assured that "we are going to have truth in budgeting." He said, "The lack of truth in budgeting is why we have gotten by with the charade of what a magnificent job we have done each year on the budget, how we have cut the budget and brought the deficit down—only to learn later that, on average, the deficit has increased about $20 billion each year."

Reagan was equally enthusiastic when he signed the legislation, foreseeing the end of government deficits in five years: "For years we've been warning that the growing deficit reflects a dangerous increase in the size of government. . . . Now Gramm-Rudman-Hollings locks in a long-term commitment to lowering and eventually eliminating deficits."

As it turned out, the first year, 1986, set the tone for the future. In

The federal debt

Interest payments on U.S. government debt are nearly equal to all our spending on education...

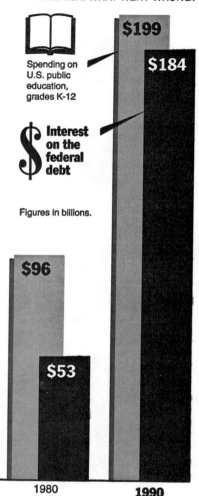

Spending on U.S. public education, grades K-12

Interest on the federal debt

Figures in billions.

$199

$184

$96

$53

$41

$14

$16

$7

1960   1970   1980   **1990**

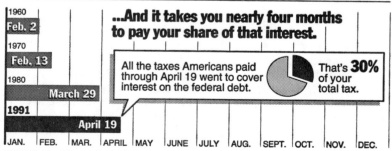

...And it takes you nearly four months to pay your share of that interest.

1960
Feb. 2
1970
Feb. 13
1980
March 29
1991
April 19

All the taxes Americans paid through April 19 went to cover interest on the federal debt.

That's **30%** of your total tax.

JAN. | FEB. | MAR. | APRIL | MAY | JUNE | JULY | AUG. | SEPT. | OCT. | NOV. | DEC.

SOURCES: Internal Revenue Service, Federal Reserve Board

1981, President Carter had forecast a budget surplus of $138 billion for 1986. In 1984, President Reagan forecast a $177 million deficit for 1986. And in 1985, Gramm-Rudman-Hollings set the maximum deficit at $172 million for 1986. The deficit eventually hit $238 billion.

That was off $66 billion from the Gramm-Rudman-Hollings mandated maximum of $172 billion. Off $61 billion from President Reagan's predicted deficit of $177 billion. Off $376 billion from President Carter's predicted surplus of $138 billion. So much for the way lawmakers and presidents count.

Truth to tell, the numbers were worse. The real deficit was $283 billion. But Social Security and other trust funds had surpluses. So Congress and the president took the $45 billion surplus in the trust funds—money that in part was to have been set aside for future Social Security payments—and spent it instead for other government programs, thereby masking the true size of the deficit. That is a practice for which other people go to prison.

By law, money in a trust fund may be spent only for the specific purpose for which the trust fund was created. Unless you happen to be Congress or the president. In which case you may remove $138 billion from Social Security and other trust funds—which Congress and two presidents did through the 1980s—and divert the money elsewhere.

In any event, the deficit numbers were going the wrong way. To deal with the errant figures, Congress passed another version of the Gramm-Rudman-Hollings law in 1987, setting revised deficit goals. The new deficit figures: $136 billion in 1989, $100 billion in 1990, $64 billion in 1991, $28 billion in 1992 and zero in 1993. Once again, though, the numbers did not seem to add up quite right. The 1989 deficit ended up at $153 billion, instead of the promised $136 billion.

Not to worry. Congress did what only Congress can. It came up with a supplemental deficit-control law called the Omnibus Budget Reconciliation Act of 1990. Lawmakers promised that it would soak up nearly $500 billion in red ink over the next five years.

The *New York Times*, in an article recounting passage of the measure in October 1990, called it "the most important legislation ever written to reduce the budget deficit." The *Wall Street Journal* labeled it the "most serious deficit-cutting package in modern times." And the *Philadelphia Inquirer* described it as "the largest deficit-reduction package in history" and "a first step toward reversing the fiscal legacy of the freewheeling '80s."

It was unprecedented. Senator Warren B. Rudman, the New Hampshire Republican who was coauthor of the ongoing Gramm-Rudman laws, said so: "For the first time since I've been here, we've made a real effort at deficit reduction." In February 1991 President Bush, speaking, appropriately, before the Economic Club of New York, declared, "Thanks to the budget reforms that began last fall, the deficit will be virtually eliminated by 1995."

In truth, it was ever more Creative Math. Label it voodoo budgeting. The deficit for 1991—which Gramm-Rudman No. 1 of 1985 said absolutely would be zero, and Gramm-Rudman No. 2 of 1987 said absolutely, positively would be no more than $64 billion, and the Omnibus Budget Reconciliation Act of 1990 said would be certainly no more than $245 billion—set an all-time record: a whopping $269 billion.

That is the make-believe deficit. The one that is pared down because Congress and the president divert the surplus Social Security taxes that you pay to other purposes. Remember, the Social Security taxes withheld from your paycheck are not being set aside for your retirement. That money is paid out immediately to currently retired people. That means that, when the government collects more Social Security taxes than it needs to pay today's retirees, the left over sum is considered surplus.

Actually, when Congress raised the Social Security rates some years ago, lawmakers and the president promised that any surplus would be set aside for your retirement. The reason: The retired ranks are swelling faster than the work force. As a result, there will not be enough workers to support Social Security payments to those who retire early in the next century. But that's another matter.

When the 1991 Social Security surplus was subtracted from the government spending books, the real deficit totaled $321 billion. That is more money than the federal government spent for all its programs and services in 1979. The outlook for 1992, when everyone, Congress and presidents, Democrats and Republicans, once projected the beginning of budget surpluses: a real deficit of $400 billion. Or more.

The number may be more meaningful if you compare the federal government's spending practices with the way you manage your own or your family's budget. Suppose that two decades ago, in 1972, you earned $11,000. That was the income of the average family that year. Suppose, also, that each year since then your income grew to keep pace with the average family, so that in 1991 you earned $36,000. Suppose, further, that the relationship between your income and the amount of money you spent each year was proportional to the income and spending of the United States government.

If you spent at that pace, the outstanding charges on your VISA or Master Card charge account in 1992 would total about $184,000. Every month you would write a check for $2,800 to cover the interest costs alone.

After paying Social Security and federal income taxes, you would have no money left. No money for food. No money for housing. No money for clothing. In fact, you would have to borrow money for all those purposes. In a few more years, as the deficits continue to pile up, you would not have enough money to pay your income and Social Security taxes. And a few years after that, you would have to borrow money just to pay the interest.

That is the way Congress and presidents manage the national family budget.

Is it possible, you might ask, that Congress one day will do what it has promised to do for years—eliminate the deficit and thereby reduce the amount of money collected from weekly paychecks to cover the interest payments on its trillions of dollars in borrowed money?

Not if experience is any guide.

Nearly two decades ago, Congress, amid much fanfare and self-praise, enacted the Congressional Budget and Impoundment Control Act of 1974. It was intended to give Congress greater control over federal spending. The measure created budget committees in the House and Senate and established a Congressional Budget Office to provide lawmakers with the expert advice they said they needed to manage the government's fiscal policy.

Alan Cranston, the Democratic senator from California, called the budget act "probably the most important bill that has been passed or considered by Congress during the time I have been in the Senate." Representative Bill Frenzel, Minnesota Republican, said the act "will set up procedures that will tend to force us to establish our own spending priorities, to control our overspending more sensibly and to strike a better balance between our income and our expenses."

And Representative Al Ullman, an Oregon Democrat, said the act "will make Congress a more respected institution and a more effective partner in our federal government. I believe it will be recognized as the major fiscal reform of the twentieth century, and a fundamental new element in the framework of our democratic structure."

In the eighteen years since passage of the legislation crafted to give Congress the sophisticated advice and legislative machinery to regulate government spending, lawmakers have compiled eighteen consecutive annual deficits—ten of them record-breakers. That is far short of what Representative Frank Annunzio, Democrat from Illinois, had promised on June 18, 1974, when the House passed the Congressional Budget and Impoundment Control Act: "This landmark legislation will enable the Congress to be responsible for devising the budget and for meeting our obligations, with no deficit spending, and in the event that we collect more money than we spend, this money will be used to pay off our national debt."

Runaway Write-offs

Long ago, businesses borrowed money to build plants, to buy equipment and to make new products, thereby creating jobs. In those times, there was a certain logic to allowing companies to write off the full interest expense on their tax returns. But in the 1980s, the interest deduction became an instrument to dismantle America—not to build it.

Businesses borrowed money to raid other businesses and sell off their assets. That led to the closing of factories, the elimination of middle-income jobs, and the paying of astronomical sums to owners, investors and corporate executives who brought it all about. All this was subsidized by tax-payers—through the deduction for interest payments.

Like the takeover of RJR Nabisco, Inc., the company that makes such diverse products as Winston cigarettes, Oreo cookies, Shredded Wheat, Camel cigarettes, Ritz crackers and Grey Poupon mustard. Kohlberg Kravis Roberts and Company, the Wall Street investment-banking and buyout firm, acquired RJR Nabisco in April 1989 after winning a bitter bidding war with a company management team headed by president F. Ross Johnson. To pull off the deal, Kohlberg Kravis saddled RJR Nabisco with more than $20 billion in long-term debt, including $5 billion in junk bonds sold by Drexel Burnham Lambert.

The *New York Times,* quoting Wall Street investment bankers, de-scribed Drexel Burnham's sale of securities variously as "awe-inspiring" and as evidence that "the [Drexel] machine functions very well." In truth, the Drexel "machine" was headed for bankruptcy court, but in the interim the RJR deal produced awe-inspiring fees of hundreds of millions of dollars for its partners, Kohlberg Kravis, assorted lawyers and other professionals.

Taxpayers, on the other hand, lost billions. During the last nine months of 1989 and all of 1990, RJR Nabisco wrote off more than $3 billion in cash interest payments, according to documents filed with the SEC. That al-lowed the new owners to avoid payment of $1 billion or more in corporate income taxes.

You might think of that $1 billion–plus this way. If you are a middle-class individual or family living in Fort Wayne, Indiana, or Sioux City, Iowa, every dollar you paid in federal income taxes in 1989 and 1990 went to offset the lost tax revenue from the RJR Nabisco buyout. Actually, every dollar you pay in income taxes for the rest of this century will go for that purpose.

While middle-class taxpayers everywhere must make up the lost cor-porate tax revenue, the executives who arrange the deals are profiting handsomely from them. At the same time, they personally are paying United States income taxes at the lowest rate in decades. In 1992 the maximum rate for individuals will be 31 percent. In 1990 and prior years it was 28 percent. Back in 1960, it was 91 percent.

Take Steven J. Ross, chairman of the board and co–chief executive officer of Time Warner, Inc., the world's largest media and entertainment company. Time Warner was created in July 1989 when the former Time, Inc., publisher of *Time* magazine, acquired a majority of the stock of Warner Communications, Inc., the motion picture, television and entertainment company.

As was the case with RJR Nabisco, the acquisition left the new com-pany heavily in debt. In 1989 and 1990, according to reports filed with the SEC, Time Warner deducted $2.1 billion in interest payments. The write-off allowed the company to avoid payment of $700 million in federal income taxes. In fact, the SEC reports show that Time Warner, with total revenue of more than $19 billion over the two years, did not pay any federal income taxes.

For his services in 1990, Ross received regular cash compensation amounting to $3.3 million. Then there was a special $74.9 million bonus, bringing his total Time Warner income for the year to $78.2 million.

While RJR Nabisco and Time Warner may be exceptions in terms of the dollars involved, similar stories on a smaller scale are recurring across corporate America. Consider the interest and tax payments of three other companies, as compiled from reports filed with the SEC.

Supermarkets General Holdings Corporation. The company, based in Woodbridge, New Jersey, is one of the country's ten largest supermarket retailers. It operates more than two hundred supermarkets, including Path-mark and Purity Supreme, and about forty Rickel Home Center outlets in the Northeast, mid-Atlantic and New England states.

For the two fiscal years ending in February 1989 and 1990, Super-markets General reported operating income—that is, income before pay-ment of interest expenses and taxes—of $343 million. Interest expenses totaled $498 million, wiping out the operating income and producing losses for both years. Federal income taxes paid: zero.

To be accurate, Supermarkets General paid $13 million in income taxes for the two years. But thanks to the net operating loss provision, the company received refunds of taxes paid in previous years amounting to $36 million. That left the company $23 million ahead in the tax game.

USG Corporation. The company, based in Chicago, was founded in 1901 and is better known by its former name, United States Gypsum Com-pany. USG manufactures and markets building products and is the coun-try's largest producer of gypsum wallboard.

During 1989 and 1990, USG reported total operating income of $487 million. Interest expenses amounted to $589 million, wiping out all of the operating income. Federal income taxes paid: zero.

Burlington Holdings, Inc. The company, based in Greensboro, North Carolina, is better known by its old name, Burlington Industries, Inc. It makes an array of textiles, including fabrics for clothing, carpets, uphol-stery and draperies.

During 1989 and 1990, Burlington reported operating income of $389 million. Interest expenses amounted to $504 million, wiping out all of the operating income. Federal income taxes paid: zero.

Now add up the numbers for the three companies. Operating income came to $1.2 billion. Interest expenses totaled $1.6 billion, thereby elim-inating operating income. Total federal income taxes paid: zero.

How does that compare with your personal tax bill? Let's say, when you filled out your tax return for 1991, your total income from all sources came to $35,000. If you paid $1—that's one dollar—in federal income taxes, you were taxed at a higher rate than were the three companies.

Remember that the tax records of Supermarkets General, USG and

Burlington Holdings are representative of many corporations. Remember, also, that this was after passage of the 1986 Tax Reform Act, which was so widely hailed as restoring equity to the tax system and assuring that corporate America would pay its fair share.

Beyond corporations that do not pay their fair share of taxes because of a preferential government rule book, there is yet a darker side to the story, one with bleaker implications for the American middle class. The expenditure of those hundreds of millions of dollars borrowed, and the hundreds of millions of dollars that were—and will be—paid in interest by the three companies did not create a single new job.

In fact, to meet their interest payments, Supermarkets General, USG and Burlington Holdings, whose debt grew out of the corporate restructuring mania fueled by the government rule book, did what so much of the rest of corporate America has done in the same situation: They slashed their work forces. And they received a tax break for doing it.

What's more, the very deduction that wipes out current tax bills—the interest write-off—creates yet another tax-avoidance mechanism to shelter future profits: the net operating loss deduction—the magic wand that makes taxes disappear.

As with so many sections of the tax law, Congress originally agreed to the net operating loss deduction as an "emergency" measure to promote fairness. It was enacted in 1919 specifically to help ease business recovery from World War I.

Representative Claude Kitchin, a North Carolina Democrat who was chairman of the House Ways and Means Committee, explained what he called the "net loss relief provision" during debate on a pending tax measure in February 1919. Kitchin said that the tax writers "agreed that it was wiser and safer" to limit the deduction to one year, "for the transition period from war conditions to peace conditions." The provision, he said, would be "just for this year, 1919."

Time passed.

Seventy-three years, to be precise, and Kitchin's "loss relief" amendment is embedded in the Internal Revenue Code. For most of those years, the net operating loss deduction was not widely used by businesses and thus did not represent a significant loss of tax revenue. That changed in the 1980s, when investors, speculators and takeover artists saw an opportunity to turn the tax code into instant profits for themselves.

One company charted the course. In 1970, the Penn Central Transportation Company, which had been formed two years earlier with the merger of the old Pennsylvania Railroad and New York Central, collapsed into bankruptcy. When it finally emerged from bankruptcy proceedings in 1978, the reorganized company, now called Penn Central Corporation, bore scant resemblance to the railroad of old. Gone were the rail cars, freight yards and train stations. In their place were diversified holdings in housing, recreation and energy.

But the new Penn Central kept one "asset" from its dying days as a railroad: two billion dollars in net operating losses—thanks to that temporary 1919 "emergency" provision. To make full use of it, Penn Central acquired profitable companies and began using the old Penn Central's losses to reduce taxes owed by the newly acquired companies. While the operating income mounted, adding up to $1.8 billion from 1978 to 1984, the company paid no federal income taxes.

"Our income stream is not subject to current federal income tax as a result of our loss carryforwards," the company said in its 1983 annual report.

Since coming out of bankruptcy in 1978, Penn Central has written off more than $1 billion of the net operating losses, avoiding payment of hundreds of millions of dollars in federal income taxes. By 1990, Penn Central still had about $1 billion in net operating losses left over. Making use of them remains one of the company's primary objectives. As its officers told stockholders in 1989: "We must invest Penn Central's substantial cash resources and make use of its debt capacity . . . and, at the same time, fully utilize the value of the company's remaining $1 billion in net operating loss carryforwards."

Then there is the Chicago-based Itel Corporation. The company generates annual revenue of $2 billion from its interests in rail-car and marine-container leasing, dredging, and the distribution of wiring and cable systems. It also generates hefty tax-free profits, courtesy of the net operating loss deduction. Those profits have helped secure a spot in the *Forbes* directory of the 400 richest Americans for Samuel Zell, the Chicago investor who controls the business.

From 1984 to 1989, according to SEC reports, Itel recorded $563 million in operating income, that is income before interest payments and taxes. Its federal income tax payments: zero.

"Federal income tax is not accruable or payable by Itel," the company's 1988 annual report said, "because income that would otherwise be taxable is offset by the utilization of its substantial . . . tax loss carryforwards."

So what is the bottom line for the net operating loss deduction, which proponents defend as necessary to help start-up companies through their early money-losing years and to even out the tax bills of companies whose income fluctuates from one year to the next? At best, it has evolved into a device to transfer payment for a corporation's ill fortune from its stockholders and managers to individual taxpayers. In many cases, it has also become a lucrative tax-avoidance scheme enabling shrewd investors to use others' losses to cut their own corporate tax bills.

Actually, with the net operating loss deduction, a company can do more than avoid payment of future taxes. It can also go back in time and collect a refund of taxes paid. Losses incurred in 1991, for example, can be subtracted from taxable income for three previous years, enabling a com-

Corporations discover the NOL, a tax write-off bonanza worth billions

By 1988, U.S. corporations were getting $51.4 billion in tax write-offs from the NOL deduction.

$50 billion

$40 billion

Cost of NOL deductions

Companies escaped paying the 34% corporate income tax on $51.4 billion in write-offs in 1988, costing the U.S. Treasury $17.5 billion.

Use of the net operating loss deduction began to skyrocket in the early '80s.

$30 billion

$20 billion

A little-used rule: Only $1.6 billion in net operating loss tax write-offs in 1950.

$10 billion

Figures in 1988 dollars.

0

| 1950 | 1960 | 1970 | 1980 | '88 |

SOURCE: Internal Revenue Service

pany to obtain a refund check from the United States Treasury for taxes paid in those years.

By now, you may be wondering how you can do the same. Thumb through the pages of the Internal Revenue Code and see if you can find a similar provision for workers whose income is derived from a daily job. A provision saying that, if you paid $3,000 in income taxes last year but lost your job this year and are living off your savings and unemployment benefits that are about to expire, you can obtain a refund of the $3,000 you paid last year. What? You can't find anything like that? Of course not.

But your loss is someone else's gain. In 1969, corporations wrote off $2.5 billion in net operating losses, or 3 percent of their taxable income. By 1988, those deductions had soared to $51.4 billion, or 13 percent of their taxable income. Thus, net operating loss deductions increased 1,956 percent during those years.

This is just the beginning. Absent a change in the rule book, the deduction will grow larger in years to come because more corporations are winding up in United States Bankruptcy Court, creating yet more net operating loss deductions for future use. This means that middle-class individuals and families will continue to subsidize the failed business practices of the 1980s—practices that produced massive profits for corporate managers and investors, and bankruptcy, unemployment and reduced wages for workers.

Even unlawful business dealings that produced net operating losses are now being converted to tax savings for the favored few. The new owners of Guaranty Federal, the failed Texas savings and loan, for example, are benefiting from the fraudulent losses of their predecessors, who went to jail.

Tax Breaks for Fraud

The story begins with Guaranty's former owners, Paul Sau-Ki Cheng and Simon Edward Heath, Dallas real estate promoters. One-time classmates at Southern Methodist University in Dallas, Cheng and Heath had gone into the real estate business after graduation from college in 1977.

They began by building single-family homes in the Dallas area. In 1984, their real estate company, Pacific Realty Corporation, acquired Guaranty Federal Savings and Loan, a savings bank in Galveston that dated from 1938. After moving the thrift's headquarters to Dallas, Cheng and Heath began doing business with Drexel Burnham Lambert's Beverly Hills office, presided over by the junk-bond king, Michael Milken.

Early in 1986, Cheng and Heath were "advised and encouraged by personnel" at Milken's office to launch a takeover, according to a federal complaint later filed against them. The target was the U.S. Home Corporation, a Houston-based builder of single-family, modular and mobile homes. The advice seemed invaluable, since Drexel Burnham was the homebuilder's investment banker and had underwritten a $50 million junk bond issue for the company the year before. Now Drexel Burnham was advising another party to make a run at one of its own clients—a client crippled by debt that Drexel Burnham had arranged.

With Drexel Burnham's encouragement, Cheng and Heath, through their real estate company, began acquiring U.S. Home's stock. The cash came mostly through loans from other Texas savings and loans. After picking up 9 percent of U.S. Home's shares, they offered in July 1986 to buy the remaining stock for $367 million. U.S. Home's board of directors rejected the deal and the takeover bid collapsed. That was good news for U.S. Home.

It was bad news for Cheng and Heath. They had paid nearly $30 million, mostly borrowed money, to acquire shares of U.S. Home that were worth only $23 million when the deal fell through. They were $7 million in the hole. As the value of their stock holdings declined, they were confronted with hefty interest payments on the money borrowed to buy the shares.

A solution soon appeared. According to a Federal Deposit Insurance Corporation (FDIC) lawsuit, it was a "fraudulent bond-trading" scheme involving speculation in Treasury bonds that worked like this: The two businesses that Cheng and Heath controlled—Guaranty Federal, their government-insured thrift, and Pacific Realty, their real estate company— opened brokerage accounts with Drexel Burnham and E.F. Hutton to handle buy-and-sell orders for Treasury bonds.

The crux of the scheme was to manipulate Treasury-bond trading between the two accounts at each brokerage house—assigning losses to the federally insured savings and loan association and profits to Cheng and Heath's private real estate subsidiary. Drexel and Hutton installed special phone lines in Cheng's Dallas office and in his home connecting him directly to their trading desks. From September 1986 to April 1987, Cheng made nearly 1,500 transactions, buying and selling more than $21 billion in Treasury bonds for Guaranty Federal and an additional $16.8 billion for Pacific Realty.

"From the very beginning of the trading scheme period," the FDIC contended, "the excessive trading resulted in significant and constant losses to Guaranty Federal, the insured institution, while Pacific Realty consistently realized significant gains." Guaranty Federal lost money every month and Pacific Realty made money every month through what the FDIC described as "unsafe and unsound speculation."

The strategy worked nicely for Cheng and Heath. According to the FDIC complaint, they earned $11.1 million for Pacific Realty and two family trusts. Drexel Burnham and E.F. Hutton also prospered, earning about $49.6 million in commissions and markups from the nearly 1,500 trades. Individual brokers collected between $7.5 million and $15 million for their services.

The big loser was Guaranty Federal. The savings and loan lost $28.5 million on the trades and an additional $40 million later when it sold bonds at depressed prices, bringing the overall loss to $68.5 million. In a civil lawsuit still pending at the end of 1991, the FDIC is seeking judgments against Cheng, Heath and the brokerage firms for $130 million in actual damages and $390 million more in punitive damages. Drexel Burnham and Hutton have contested the FDIC allegations.

The federal agency, if it proves its case against Cheng and Heath, may have difficulty collecting. On Aug. 6, 1990, both men filed for protection from creditors under the U.S. Bankruptcy Code.

Cheng, who listed his occupation as "real estate investment adviser" on the bankruptcy petition, said his income the previous year was $1.8 million. Nonetheless, he reported he had only $55,000 in cash and bank deposits and that he owed an estimated $150,000 in federal income taxes. Heath was in even more dire straits, it seemed. He said his income the previous year was $1.5 million but that he had only $2,200 in cash and bank deposits.

In any event, nine days later, on Aug. 15, 1990, a United States District Court jury in Dallas convicted Cheng and Heath of defrauding Guaranty Federal in transactions unrelated to the bond-trading scheme. They were found guilty of bank fraud, wire fraud, misapplying Guaranty Federal money and making false entries in the thrift's books in connection with a $10 million loan on a Florida property. Cheng subsequently was sentenced to thirty years in prison, Heath to twenty years.

All these transactions helped to undermine Guaranty Federal, adding it to the growing list of savings and loans that have collapsed and now are being bailed out by the federal government at a projected cost to taxpayers of a half-trillion dollars.

On Sept. 30, 1988, the Federal Home Loan Bank Board declared the thrift insolvent. That same day, the federal agency merged Guaranty Federal with two smaller failed Texas thrifts. The surviving entity was renamed Guaranty Federal Savings Bank and sold to Temple-Inland, Inc.

As part of the federal rescue plan, Temple-Inland agreed to put in $75 million in cash and to buy $50 million worth of Guaranty Federal preferred stock in 1990 and 1991. The Federal Savings and Loan Insurance Corporation (FSLIC), in turn, agreed to cover any losses on Guaranty Federal assets, which had a book value of just under $1.7 billion. That meant if Guaranty Federal owned an office building that was worth, according to its books, $10 million, but could be sold for only $5 million, the FSLIC would kick in the $5 million difference.

Better still, to make the sale of the failed thrift more attractive, the government gave a note to Guaranty Federal's buyers promising to pay $700 million—and to pay interest on that note. Even better, the interest income is tax-free.

To summarize: Temple-Inland put up $125 million. The FSLIC—courtesy of the taxpayers—put up $700 million, plus a promise to make up any losses suffered on assets valued at $1.7 billion. And Temple-Inland collects interest on a $700 million promissory note—but is excused from paying taxes on that interest.

You can't do that. If you could, it would be like collecting the interest on $10,000 in your savings account—and then not having to report the money as taxable income. So: You pay taxes on the interest you receive on your passbook savings account. Some of your tax money is given to Guaranty Federal as interest on the government's promissory notes, but that interest is tax-free to the owners of Guaranty Federal.

And then there is, of course, the magic wand, as explained in the report to the Resolution Trust Corporation: "The Internal Revenue Code also permits the consolidated entity to use accumulated net operating loss carryovers and other loss carryovers of the failed institutions to offset taxable income of the acquiring association following the acquisition." Translation: The losses suffered by Guaranty Federal, due, at least in part, to the criminal conduct and the bond-trading activities of its former owners, may be used to reduce the taxes owed by its new owners.

From the beginning, Wall Street liked the deal. Prudential Bache Securities, in a report issued in October 1988, offered this observation on the advantages of Temple-Inland's new savings and loan business: "Temple-Inland should derive nearly $15 million to $20 million of tax benefits, according to management, from this investment in the current quarter. Next year, the benefit could be anywhere from $20 million to $50 million, followed by approximately $13 million to $15 million per year."

Donaldson, Lufkin & Jenrette, another Wall Street brokerage firm, in a report issued in May 1989, commented on why Temple-Inland's stock was selling below what the investment house believed the price should be: "We attribute the market's hesitancy in valuing the transaction to date to management's reluctance to advertise just how lucrative the deal is. . . . Temple-Inland will not have to pay taxes on S&L earnings until after 2000. The three units are currently carrying over $550 million in operating loss carryforwards."

So how much is this going to cost you? The meter is still running, but an August 1990 report to Resolution Trust placed the estimated total cost of the Guaranty Federal bailout—cash and tax breaks—at $4.5 billion. That means that the equivalent of every penny paid in federal income taxes by all the residents of Portland, Oregon, for the next several years will go to rescue Guaranty Federal and to reimburse its new owners for losses.

Lest you believe that the people responsible for the government rule book—and who make all this possible—are troubled by the consequences of their handiwork, ponder the words of Ronald A. Pearlman, one of those rule writers. Pearlman was assistant secretary for tax policy in the Treasury Department for the Reagan administration. That is the executive-branch office that recommends the tax contents of the government rule book. Later, Pearlman became chief of staff of Congress's Joint Committee on Taxation. That is the committee with overall responsibility for the rule book's tax contents. Now, he is a member of Covington and Burling, a Washington law firm that often succeeds in influencing the rewriting of the government rule book for the benefit of its clients.

During a 1991 interview with *Tax Notes*, a Washington publication, Pearlman was questioned about the net operating loss deduction. Echoing the views of many members of Congress, Pearlman said:

"Others may say the tax system is too generous in the way it deals with loss carryovers. That's not a concern I share."

CHAPTER FOUR

THE LUCRATIVE BUSINESS OF BANKRUPTCY

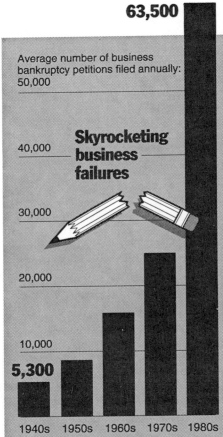

63,500

Average number of business bankruptcy petitions filed annually:

50,000

40,000

Skyrocketing business failures

30,000

20,000

10,000

5,300

1940s 1950s 1960s 1970s 1980s

WHAT WENT WRONG

Congress streamlined the Bankruptcy Code in 1978, making it easier for shaky companies to keep operating. Then came the heavy corporate borrowing and leveraged buyouts of the 1980s.

Result of that combination: Bankruptcy petitions filed in the 1980s soared — four times as many as in the 1960s.

SOURCE: Administrative office of U.S. Courts

$500-an-Hour Jobs

It was May 22, 1990, Rosalind Webb's last day of work after more than thirty years at the Bonwit Teller store in downtown Philadelphia. The store was one of fourteen Bonwit branches that were closing after Bonwit's parent company filed for bankruptcy protection.

That morning, Rosalind Webb did what she customarily did—she boarded the No. 48 bus near her home in North Philadelphia and rode twenty-five minutes to her job in the shipping department of the store.

Somewhere aloft, Wilhelm Mallory, Steven Hochberg and Peter Dealy did what they customarily did, too. Mallory flew from San Diego to New York, and billed a client $250 an hour for his travel. His associate, Dealy, flew from Los Angeles to Las Vegas, and billed $300 an hour. Hochberg flew from New York to Atlanta and charged $150 an hour for his time in the air.

What kind of work warrants such fees for sitting in an airplane? The same kind that charges $225 an hour for Richard Schmid to pack and unpack boxes.

Mallory, Dealy, Hochberg, Schmid—they are all in a business that reorganizes companies and puts people like Rosalind Webb out of work. The bankruptcy business. It pays well.

Mallory billed $1,250 that day for his five-hour flight. That money—more than Rosalind Webb earned in three weeks—came out of the dwindling cash reserves of a floundering business that was eliminating Webb's job to save money.

With the surge in bankruptcies growing out of the excessive debt load that crushed many companies in the 1980s, there are more jobs than ever like those of Mallory, Dealy, Hochberg and Schmid. But there are many millions more people like Rosalind Webb, who have been thrown out of work. They are, overwhelmingly, middle-income employees who are being forced into lower-paying jobs, part-time employment, premature retirement or unemployment. In the process, they are losing all or part of their pensions and having to settle for reduced benefits, or no benefits at all.

So it is with Webb, who is unemployed and must pay $181 a month for medical insurance. "All those years I had health insurance and didn't need it," she said. "Now I need it and don't have it."

Rosalind Webb, like millions of Americans, is snared in an economic shift in the United States in which the middle class is being squeezed and the ranks of the working poor are growing, while new jobs paying up to $500 an hour are being created for a select group of professionals—lawyers, accountants, bankers, investment advisers, brokers and management specialists.

For all this, you can thank a series of Congresses, presidents and the heads of regulatory and administrative agencies who, during the 1970s and 1980s, rewrote the rules governing the federal tax and bankruptcy systems. These changes, along with Congress's failure to enact measures correcting growing inequities in the economy, benefited special interests at the expense of everyone else.

Consider Congress's handling of two issues—corporate debt and bankruptcy. While making sweeping revisions of the Internal Revenue Code throughout the 1980s, lawmakers agreed to leave intact a provision that allows corporations a virtually unlimited tax write-off of interest paid on borrowed money. This, even though corporate debt was ballooning to its highest level this century and was being used increasingly to buy and then dismantle companies, not to build them.

That decision followed an overhaul of the United States Bankruptcy Code in 1978—the first revision in forty years—that made bankruptcy easier for troubled businesses. Companies were given more flexibility to stay in business while they attempted to resolve their financial problems. The result: a bankruptcy code that encouraged an explosion in corporate bankruptcies brought on, in part, by an explosion in corporate debt that Congress failed to discourage through tax law revisions.

All this is incorporated in the government rule book, that agglomeration of laws and regulations that, through incentives and disincentives, sanctions and prohibitions, determines the course of the United States economy.

In the case of bankruptcy, a few numbers compiled from an analysis of a half-century of bankruptcy data tell the story. During the 1980s, businesses filed, on average, 63,500 bankruptcy petitions a year nationwide. That was up 155 percent over the 24,900 petitions a year filed in the 1970s, and up 302 percent over the 15,800 filed in the 1960s. The 1980s, in fact, produced the largest growth in bankruptcy cases since the Great Depression of the 1930s.

Not only is the number of bankruptcies spiraling; so, too, is the size of the companies flocking into bankruptcy court. When the Penn Central Transportation Company, parent company of the old Pennsylvania Railroad and New York Central Railroad, sought protection from its creditors in 1970, it was the largest bankruptcy in United States history—the first ever to exceed a billion dollars. For years, it was the bankruptcy against which all others were measured.

No more. Since 1985, more than fifty companies with assets of more than $1 billion each have filed bankruptcy petitions—including nearly a dozen with assets that exceeded Penn Central's $6.9 billion. The combined assets of large companies seeking bankruptcy court protection swelled to more than $70 billion in 1990.

Big-business bankruptcy has become so brisk that a new trend has emerged: the repeat bankruptcy customer. Braniff, Inc., the airline, first sought protection in bankruptcy court in May 1982. It emerged two years later, in March 1984, but made a return appearance in September 1989. It emerged again in July 1991, and returned for a third time the following month. Continental Airlines went into bankruptcy court in 1983. And again in 1990.

All this has been a bonanza for the burgeoning bankruptcy industry—the lawyers, accountants and other specialists who charge up to $500 an hour for their time.

They get paid to fly about the country, from courthouse to courthouse, from business to business. They get paid to talk for a few minutes on the telephone. They get paid to pack files. They get paid to unpack files. They get paid to pick up their mail. They get paid to sort their mail. They get paid to schedule conferences. They get paid to attend conferences. They get paid to keep a list of the conferences. They get paid to keep track of the way they spend their time. They get paid to fill out expense reports. And they get paid to eliminate the jobs of people who work for two weeks to earn what they charge for one hour.

Meet Ming the Merciless. He is otherwise known as Sanford C. Sigoloff, sixty-one, a Los Angeles businessman who describes himself as "internationally renowned for his work in corporate turnarounds and restructurings." Indeed, newspaper, magazine and television reports have praised his work as a doctor of ailing companies. The *New York Times* called him one of the "masters of the corporate turnaround." The *Los Angeles Times* described him as a "corporate savior."

But employees of companies that Sigoloff has managed remember him better as "Ming the Merciless." Ming, the evil ruler of the planet Mongo in the Flash Gordon serial, is one of the more unsavory characters in science fiction. It is a nickname that Sigoloff relishes. In fact, he gave it to himself to signify his single-minded dedication to cost-cutting.

Sigoloff and a small group of longtime allies direct Sigoloff and Associates, a "crisis management" firm in Santa Monica, California, whose clients have fallen on hard times. Its biggest client to date: L.J. Hooker Corporation the United States subsidiary of an Australian real estate company that once had annual revenue of more than $1 billion.

Beginning in 1987, the Australian Hooker went on an American buying spree, snapping up such well-known department store chains as Bonwit Teller and B. Altman and Company. These and other acquisitions were made, naturally, with borrowed money. So much borrowed money that Hooker quickly collapsed under the weight of its debt and entered bankruptcy court on Aug. 9, 1989.

That same day, Sigoloff, who had been retained to guide the company and its subsidiaries through bankruptcy reorganization, distributed a news release: "Daily operations will continue as usual, stores will remain open

The 30 biggest bankruptcies in U.S. history

Assets, in billions of dollars, the year before bankruptcy filing.

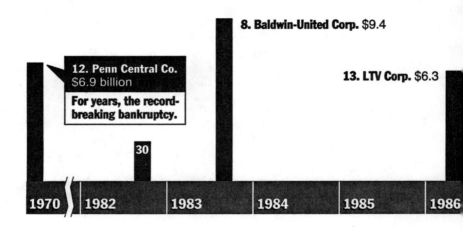

8. Baldwin-United Corp. $9.4

12. Penn Central Co.
$6.9 billion

For years, the record-breaking bankruptcy.

13. LTV Corp. $6.3

30

| 1970 | 1982 | 1983 | 1984 | 1985 | 1986 |

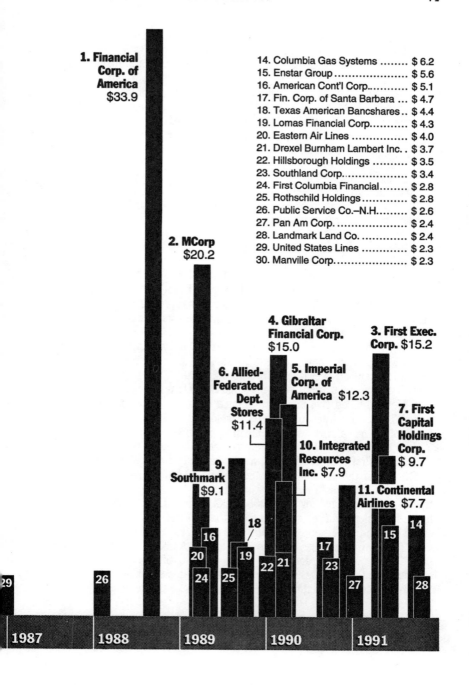

1. Financial Corp. of America $33.9

2. MCorp $20.2

14. Columbia Gas Systems .... $ 6.2
15. Enstar Group .... $ 5.6
16. American Cont'l Corp........... $ 5.1
17. Fin. Corp. of Santa Barbara ... $ 4.7
18. Texas American Bancshares.. $ 4.4
19. Lomas Financial Corp........... $ 4.3
20. Eastern Air Lines .... $ 4.0
21. Drexel Burnham Lambert Inc. . $ 3.7
22. Hillsborough Holdings .... $ 3.5
23. Southland Corp................... $ 3.4
24. First Columbia Financial........ $ 2.8
25. Rothschild Holdings............. $ 2.8
26. Public Service Co.–N.H......... $ 2.6
27. Pan Am Corp. .... $ 2.4
28. Landmark Land Co. .... $ 2.4
29. United States Lines .... $ 2.3
30. Manville Corp..................... $ 2.3

4. Gibraltar Financial Corp. $15.0

3. First Exec. Corp. $15.2

6. Allied-Federated Dept. Stores $11.4

5. Imperial Corp. of America $12.3

7. First Capital Holdings Corp. $ 9.7

10. Integrated Resources Inc. $7.9

9. Southmark $9.1

11. Continental Airlines $7.7

18

16

20

19

22 21

17

15

14

29

26

24

25

23

27

28

1987   1988   1989   1990   1991

and transactions . . . will go on just as before the filing. Paychecks will be issued at the same time as if no proceeding had been filed."

Four months later, the paychecks began to stop. First, Sigoloff closed B. Altman, the 124-year-old New York–based department store chain with seven stores in New York, New Jersey and Pennsylvania. About 1,700 jobs were lost. Next, he liquidated all but two of Bonwit Teller's sixteen stores, eliminating about 2,500 jobs in a department store empire that dated back ninety-four years. He closed all six stores of Sakowitz, the upscale Houston-based retailer that had been in business for eighty-eight years, eliminating 450 jobs. He sold off most of Hooker's real estate holdings, throwing more employees out of work.

Hooker employed about 12,000 full- and part-time people in August 1989 when Sigoloff took over. When a Hooker spokesman was asked in late 1991—two years later—about the number then employed, he answered: "Today the number is sixty-two."

Author: "6,200?"

Hooker spokesman: "No, sixty-two."

Author: "Sixty-two people?"

Hooker spokesman: "People. Exactly."

While the 1980s corporate restructuring boom resulted in the loss of 12,000 Hooker jobs, for Sigoloff and Associates it produced $6.5 million in fees in the first year alone. And the fees continue—such as the ones charged for riding in airplanes.

Sigoloff and his colleagues flew often from Los Angeles, near their Santa Monica home base, to New York, Atlanta and other eastern cities where Hooker had operations. On Feb. 12, 1990, Sigoloff flew first class from Los Angeles to New York and billed $500 an hour for the five-hour trip. He also billed two hours' time for a conference that day on Bonwit Teller. Three days later, on Feb. 15, Sigoloff billed $500 an hour for three hours of phone calls, a one-hour meeting and five hours for "Travel: New York to Los Angeles." For the round trip, he collected $5,000.

In the first year that Hooker was in bankruptcy, Sigoloff logged about 175 hours in the air, charging more than $90,000 in fees for riding on airplanes. First class. Peter Dealy, a senior associate, logged 200 hours in the air. Fees collected for travel: $55,000. James M. Van Tatenhove: 250 hours in planes, collecting fees of more than $75,000. Seymour Strasberg spent 212 hours aloft and billed $60,000.

The charges are fees billed by Sigoloff and Associates, not necessarily paid directly to those doing the work. Overall, Sigoloff and Associates earned more than $500,000 for time the associates spent in planes during the first twelve months that Hooker operated under the bankruptcy court's protection.

The Sigoloff firm is by no means unique. It is part of a growing frater-nity that manages ailing companies and charges such fees. In fact, so many management consultants have entered the field that they have formed their own group. It is called, appropriately, the Turnaround Management Association. The association, composed of more than 400 managers, consultants, bankers, lawyers and accountants, holds an annual conference and bestows awards on companies deemed the most successful turnarounds of the year. Its 1990 conference had as its theme, "Corporate Reconstruction: Managing the Aftermath of the 1980s."

James A. Schuping, the association's executive vice-president, foresees a bright future: "The misfortune of the economy and a great many of the companies that are suffering right now are to the advantage of our people because that's their specialty. We look for this business failure phenomena to continue well throughout the decade."

A look at the billing practices of Sigoloff and Associates offers a glimpse at that future. Packing and unpacking files, for example. That chore led to several thousand dollars in billings by Sigoloff associate Richard F. Schmid, who managed Hooker's real estate operations in Washington, D.C. Schmid accumulated the file-packing fees as he prepared to move Hooker's offices in May 1990 from one suburban Washington location to another.

A sampling from his billing logs:

May 14, 1990—"Worked on packing files for office move." Schmid billed four hours at $225 an hour, collecting $900.

May 15, 1990—"Monitored removal of certain items of furniture, files and equipment. . . ." Four hours, $900.

May 17, 1990—"Continued selective packing of files for . . . move." Two hours, $450.

May 22, 1990—"Pack desk files for Chantilly move. Empty credenza and bookcases—sort files for storage." Three and one-half hours, $787.50.

May 23, 1990—"Packing for Chantilly move." Four hours, $900.

Finally, on May 24, the move took place, with the Hooker office relocating from Vienna, Virginia, to nearby Chantilly.

After the move, Schmid began a new series of entries on his expense reports:

May 24, 1990—"Unpack boxes and set up at Chantilly." Four hours, $900.

May 29, 1990—"Unpack files for use at new office." Two hours, $450.

May 31, 1990—"Continue unpacking boxes and set up office space." Three and one-half hours, $787.50.

A Sigoloff spokesman, Michael Sitrick, said the firm's fees are reviewed and approved by bankruptcy court. As for flying time: "Sandy said they work while they're on airplanes. His comment was: 'They don't sit and watch movies.'"

When Sigoloff initially applied for fees for travel time in 1989, the United States trustee, who monitors fees in bankruptcy court, expressed concern about the "substantial time" spent traveling, according to papers filed in United States Bankruptcy Court in New York. But the objection was later dropped after consultations with Hooker's lawyers. Hooker's counsel,

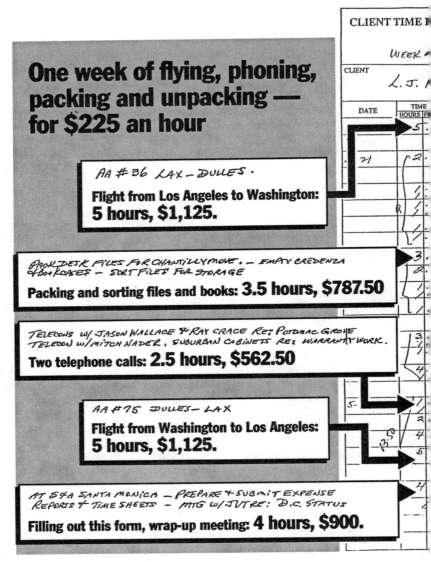

One week of flying, phoning, packing and unpacking — for $225 an hour

CLIENT TIME

WEEK

CLIENT
L. J.

DATE | TIME HOURS

AA #36 LAX — DULLES.

Flight from Los Angeles to Washington: 5 hours, $1,125.

PACK DESK FILES FOR CHANTILLY MOVE. — EMPTY CREDENZA + BOOKCASES — SORT FILES FOR STORAGE

Packing and sorting files and books: 3.5 hours, $787.50

TELECONS W/ JASON WALLACE + RAY CRACE RE: POTOMAC GROVE TELECON W/ MITCH NADER, SUBURBAN CABINETS RE: WARRANTY WORK.

Two telephone calls: 2.5 hours, $562.50

AA #75 DULLES — LAX

Flight from Washington to Los Angeles: 5 hours, $1,125.

AT S&A SANTA MONICA — PREPARE + SUBMIT EXPENSE REPORTS + TIME SHEETS — MTG W/ JUTRE: D.C. STATUS

Filling out this form, wrap-up meeting: 4 hours, $900.

SOURCE: U.S. Bankruptcy Court

A time sheet showing fees charged by one staff member at a consulting firm, Sigoloff & Associates.

ORD CONTROL FORM

SIGOLOFF & ASSOCIATES, INC.

3340 Ocean Park Boulevard, Suite 3045
Santa Monica, California 90405
(213) 452-2218 Fax: (213) 452-9547

SUN. FRI·
MAY 20 THRU MAY 25

NER

CLIENT NUMBER	CONSULTANT
071	R. O. Solmon
	R. F. Schmid

DESCRIPTION OF WORK PERFORMED

AA #36 LAX - DULLES .

DISCUSSIONS W/ EDNA KING RE: OFFERS ON OFFICE
FURNITURE TO BE SOLD AT 8330 BOONE BLVD. — PRICED ITEMS
BASED ON BOOK VALUES — EXPECT TO GET BETWEEN 25 + 40%
OF BOOK VALUE — IT MAKES NO ECONOMIC SENSE TO STORE THE STUFF.
TELECON + FAX EXCHANGE W/ DONOVAN RE: POT. GROVE MODEL SALE
2 TELECONS W/ JASON WALLACE RE: GRACE AGREEMENT .
TELECON W/GRACE RE: TAKEDOWN SCHEDULE ON LOTS.
TELECON W/ MATT BECK OF MT. VERNON REALTY — EXPECTS OFFER
ON POT. PLANT TOWNS BY 5/31
MEETING W/ RICK CENTRA. RE: SALES STATUS
GEN'L ADMIN.

PROD. DESK FILES FOR CHANTILLY MOVE . — EMPTY CREDENZA
+ BOOKCASES — SORT FILES FOR STORAGE
REVIEWED SEVERAL OFFERS FOR FURNITURE — AGREED TO
SELL 4 LOTS "AT AVERAGE OF 43.5% OF BOOK VALUE .
MTG W/ HENSON RE: STATUS OF PAVING AT FRANKLIN MANOR
MTG W/ HANNER RE: WARRANTY STATUS AND SCHEDULE FOR
FURTHER FIELD PERSONNEL REDUCTIONS
GEN'L ADMINISTRATION

COMPLETE HAULING FOR CHANTILLY MOVE
TELECON W/ MUSCHEL RE: LEASE TERMINATIONS
TELECON + FAX , JOHN DONOVAN RE: WALKTHRU SCHEDULE
AND REVISED CLOSING SCHEDULE ON GREENE CLOSING .
PACKING FOR CHANTILLY MOVE .
GEN'L ADMINISTRATION

TELECONS W/ JASON WALLACE + RAY CRACE RE: POTOMAC GROVE
TELECON W/ MITCH NADER , SUBURBAN CABINETS RE: WARRANTY WORK .
MEETING W/ MT. VERNON REALTY RE: STATUS OF SALES
EFFORTS ON BEHALF OF 6 PROPERTIES
UNPACK BOXES + SET UP AT CHANTILLY
AA #75 DULLES - LAX

AT S+A SANTA MONICA — PREPARE + SUBMIT EXPENSE
REPORTS + TIME SHEETS — MTG W/ JVT RE: D.C. STATUS

The running tab

SUNDAY
$ 1,125

MONDAY
$ 3,150

TUESDAY
$ 5,287.50

WEDNESDAY
$ 7,537.50

THURSDAY
$10,575

FRIDAY
$11,475
total for week

Alan B. Hyman of the New York law firm of Proskauer Rose Goetz and Mendelsohn, told the court the travel time fees were necessary because Hooker's operations were "all over the country."

"We've been advised by Sigoloff," Hyman said, "that the way they keep the time records, and charge, they charge travel time for the exact time of the flight." Sigoloff later wrote that the travel fees were justified because "we are working on Hooker business . . . we bill only for the scheduled time of the flight, not the actual time, which is often significantly longer on a cross-country flight."

As for entries such as "packing" and "unpacking" boxes, Sitrick, the Sigoloff spokesman, said that Richard Schmid might have been searching for financial records. "Dick is a terrific financial guy but maybe not a real good time-slip keeper," Sitrick said. "I know Dick Schmid. Dick is a very senior guy. He would have one of his subordinates packing and unpacking boxes. He wouldn't be packing and unpacking." Schmid later wrote that his decision to move Hooker's Washington operations and to lay off most of its staff saved creditors a substantial amount of money.

"This move saved the creditors $13,000 per month in rent, over $80,000 in payroll and benefits for the twenty employees who were terminated, and at least another $10,000 per month on telephone, supplies and other costs," Schmid wrote. "And, yes, the five key employees and myself who remained did indeed sort, evaluate and pack the files with critical documentation pertaining to ongoing lawsuits, as well as proprietary L.J. Hooker business records which were essential to an orderly liquidation."

Sigoloff himself later confirmed the need for Schmid to personally handle the packing and unpacking of the boxes: "In this particular circumstance, the files involved were highly sensitive payroll, termination and other management information requiring strict confidentiality."

Schmid's billing practices were in keeping with those of his co-workers, who collected fees for performing seemingly routine tasks. Richard A. Stemm, who was handling creditors' claims against Hooker, billed $90 an hour to "return car to airport" and "to make travel arrangements" and to "rearrange flight, hotel checkout, car return and standby" for a flight.

And then there was the "master calendar." That's the schedule of meetings, court appearances and other dates affecting the business of L.J. Hooker. Sigoloff and Associates collected thousands of dollars in fees to revise, update and delete information from this schedule.

Excerpts from bankruptcy court records: On June 14, 1990, a long-time Sigoloff associate, Wilhelm Mallory, who was overseeing Hooker's retail properties, billed 6.75 hours, or $1,688, for "master calendar task review." Sigoloff, the highest-paid member of the firm, billed $500 an hour every time he worked on the calendar.

On Jan. 5, 1990, he spent an hour on "master calendar assignments." The next day, he billed three hours for work on the "professional master calendar." The day after that he collected $3,000 in fees for the "review of corporate master calendar/professional master calendar." On Jan. 9, it was two hours of fees for "review of master calendar draft II." Then on Jan. 31, after all the work on the master calendar that month, it was time for what Sigoloff described as "master calendar cleansing."

Sigoloff collected fees for working on the master calendar wherever he happened to be. On July 30, 1990, while on the French Riviera, Sigoloff phoned his office to "review Hooker master calendar." For the call, he billed his usual hourly rate—$500.

As is so often the case in bankruptcy proceedings, some of the most detailed work is keeping track of fees. And there are fees for keeping track of fees. Sigoloff and Associates staff billed thousands of dollars in fees to record expenses, to fill out time sheets, to prepare an application to bankruptcy court for fees, to appear in court to answer questions the judge might have about the fee requests. Every three months, Sigoloff and Associates petitioned bankruptcy court in New York for payment of its fees.

The compiling, writing, revising and drafting of the final fee application generated yet another round of fees. On Nov. 17, 1989, Arthur Cayley billed three hours at $175 an hour for work on the "fee application." Three days later he billed five more hours for work on the fee application. The day after that he billed four more hours for work on the application. On Dec. 14, Cayley billed three hours and fifty minutes for giving "support for fee application."

After the application was completed, Sigoloff filed it with bankruptcy court in New York, seeking $1.8 million in fees and expenses for August through October 1989.

Bankrupted by Debt

Not everyone does so well off the bankruptcy boom. Ask Joyce Buckner, who lost her job as a $6.05-an-hour meat slicer at the Toppers Meat Company in Sedalia, Missouri. The plant was closed in 1990 after Doskocil Companies, a midwestern meat processor that owned Toppers, entered bankruptcy.

"I went to school for a while but financially that wasn't working," she said. "I did try to find work but some of the jobs were at night, and when you have children, it's just not possible. It took about seven or eight months before I found a job."

Buckner eventually found work packaging bullets in a plant that manufactures ammunition. "I'm just there," she said, "because I need the money. The hourly wage isn't that great. It's $5 an hour. Less than what I was making but a little bit above minimum wage."

Doskocil was an American success story until, like so many other businesses, it got caught up in the takeover and debt revolution of the 1980s. The Hutchinson, Kansas, company had carved out a niche in the highly competitive world of meat packing by making pizza toppings for some of the largest fast-food chains. Doskocil grew by adding plants, employees and products until 1987, when it decided it wanted to really grow. Not slowly by selling more products and building more plants, but by acquiring a competitor.

With the help of Drexel Burnham Lambert, Inc., the investment banking firm that is in bankruptcy court, Doskocil sold $50 million in high-risk, high-yield junk bonds to finance an acquisition. The next year it launched a hostile takeover of Wilson Foods, an Oklahoma City meat packer that was six times as large as Doskocil. Doskocil had sales of $215 million, compared with Wilson's $1.3 billion. Doskocil had 900 employees, compared with Wilson's 5,000. Doskocil had five plants, compared with Wilson's twelve.

Wilson had a corporate history dating to 1853, when it was one of the first of the great national meat packers. Doskocil dated from 1963, when founder Larry Doskocil slaughtered a hog in a former chicken coop on the outskirts of Hutchinson and sold the parts. Nevertheless, the times were such that a small company with access to the easy money of Wall Street could take on larger prey.

Although Wilson initially rejected the bid, the Doskocil company eventually won out after a bitter three-month battle. The takeover fight generated millions of dollars in fees for lawyers, investment bankers and accountants. For Wilson, the price was steep, creating a loss in the last quarter of 1988 for "costs and expenses" to fight the Doskocil raid.

"These charges of approximately $11.8 million," Wilson reported to the SEC, "consisted primarily of financial, legal and bank commitment fees which were incurred by Wilson in its defense of the unsolicited tender offer."

The Doskocil company formally took control of Wilson in January 1989, firing the president, chief executive officer and more than 100 salaried employees at Wilson's corporate headquarters in Oklahoma City. Just fifteen months later, the deal that took millions of dollars in fees to put together came apart. Unable to sell off parts of Wilson as planned, Doskocil could not pay the interest on the huge debt it took on to buy Wilson. Citing a "liquidity crisis," Doskocil filed for bankruptcy protection on Mar. 5, 1990. Squeezed for cash, Doskocil sought to lower costs by closing plants or imposing layoffs or wage cuts at other plants.

Carol Jean Smith was one of the casualties. For more than six years, she had made meatballs for pizza toppings at the Doskocil-owned Toppers plant in Sedalia, seventy miles east of Kansas City. She earned $6.25 an hour. Then in May 1990, two months after Doskocil filed for bankruptcy, she lost her job. The Sedalia plant closed. Permanently.

To Carol Jean Smith and her co-workers, the shutdown came as a shock. "We thought the plant was doing okay," she said. "Everyone was always telling us what a good plant it was. Then they began laying off people and we began to wonder if they were going to close the plant. But they said no. They had no plans to do that.

"But then before it happened, we knew something was up. They began calling people in for a meeting. Even those who were on vacation got a call and were told to come to the plant. The meeting was in the cafeteria. The manager read a letter saying they were going to close the plant in two weeks. We were all shocked. We couldn't believe it."

After that, Carol Jean Smith looked for a job, but did not find steady work. Meanwhile, she cleaned houses—at $5 an hour.

If the Doskocil bankruptcy has been a financial hardship for Carol Jean Smith, Joyce Buckner and others who lost jobs that paid $6 an hour, it has been a windfall for another group of workers. Lawyers, accountants and consultants from across the country have swarmed to United States Bankruptcy Court in Topeka, Kansas, to grab a share of the fees for representing a variety of interests.

Nightingale and Associates, Inc., of New Canaan, Connecticut, bills at a rate of $250 an hour as management consultant for the Official Committee of Unsecured Creditors of Doskocil. Andrews and Kurth, a Houston law firm, bills $250 an hour as counsel for the Official Committee of Unsecured Creditors of Doskocil. Stutman, Treister and Glatt, a Los Angeles law firm, collects up to $400 an hour as Doskocil's lead bankruptcy counsel.

Paul, Weiss, Rifkind, Wharton and Garrison, a New York law firm, bills $435 an hour as special counsel for the Official Unsecured Creditors' Committee of Wilson Foods. Price Waterhouse, the national accounting firm, collects up to $300 an hour as accountants for the Official Unsecured Creditors' Committee of Wilson Foods. Pepper, Hamilton and Scheetz, a Philadelphia law firm, bills $260 an hour as attorney for the Official Unsecured Creditors' Committee of Wilson Foods. Kensington and Ressler, a New York law firm, bills $220 an hour as counsel for Doskocil.

Not so long ago, such cross-country travel in the pursuit of bankruptcy business was rare. That is because such fees were rare. Until Congress rewrote the bankruptcy section of the government rule book in 1978, bankruptcy cases were processed in United States district courts, along with other civil cases. But most of the daily work in bankruptcy was presided over at a lower level by so-called referees, who were appointed by district court judges. Fees were comparatively modest. So was the number of bankruptcy lawyers.

When Congress revised the code, it created a separate bankruptcy court to deal solely with bankruptcy cases. Fees closer to the going corporate rate could then be charged. The result was predictable: Cases, fees and the number of lawyers specializing in bankruptcy soared. So much so that *Working Woman* magazine singled out bankruptcy practice as one of the twenty-five best career choices for women.

"Just a few years ago," the magazine said in July 1990, "corporate bankruptcy law, like real estate law before it, was the poor sister of the bar . . . but the Bankruptcy Reform Act of 1978 allowed judges to award fees in line with regular corporate rates. Bankruptcy law suddenly became more lucrative, and large law firms that previously had farmed out bankruptcy work to smaller firms began to develop in-house departments."

Today, in many jurisdictions, bankruptcy court judges routinely approve the fees. Sometimes they explain their reasons. Like the charges for "word processing expenses" billed in 1990 by the New York law firm of Debevoise and Plimpton, which represents L.J. Hooker Corporation's creditors. These were not stenographic fees, but fees for the use of the firm's computers. The law firm billed $25 an hour for its own staff to use its own computers during regular working hours to prepare letters and legal documents, and $50 an hour outside of the normal workday.

Arthur H. Amron, a member of the firm, explained the procedure to the court: "There's a usage charge, that is an hourly fee for the use of the system. There's an overtime usage by the word-processing department outside of the normal hours. That is a charge added on to the usual charge for overtime use."

Replied Judge Tina L. Brozman: "I think that billing practices citywide have changed. I am not sure that I necessarily agree with them, but if it's standard, I think my mandate is to compensate firms as they are compensated in other matters and not to be niggardly."

During that particular hearing, at which Judge Brozman approved the awarding of millions of dollars in fees, she did reject one expense item—a $16 tip on an $88 taxi bill turned in by an Australian bank.

"Take out the tip," said Judge Brozman. "We will deal with it at—" Attorney Alan Hyman interrupted with a little bankruptcy court levity: "It's expensive to take a cab to Australia."

As might be expected, the generous fees have prompted strong reactions from creditors, who get only what's left. Consider those with a stake in the reorganization of American Continental Corporation in Phoenix. American Continental was the parent company of Lincoln Savings and Loan Association, the California thrift controlled by Charles H. Keating, Jr., that was seized by federal regulators in April 1989.

The American Continental bankruptcy case and related litigation have been a perpetual money machine for scores of lawyers, accountants and other professionals. One law firm alone, Wyman, Bautzer, Kuchel and Silbert of Los Angeles, estimated in February 1991 that it had "devoted approximately 40,000 hours, the equivalent of twenty lawyer years, of professional services" to the American Continental case. When another law firm filed petitions in bankruptcy court in Phoenix, seeking payment of more than $1.5 million in interim fees in the case, a man and woman from Riverside, California, wrote the court complaining that the lawyers were "asking for money faster than the U.S. Mint can make money."

They were among the thousands of investors, many of them retirees, who had purchased American Continental bonds and who stood to lose most of their money. They argued that if American Continental had "this kind of money in the bank to pay attorneys, then the investors should be paid off first and the attorneys afterwards." A Westminster, California, investor, adding up the fee requests from several law firms, told the court: "All the available monies will be discharged to counsels and the creditors will be left holding the bag; again."

To be sure, not all bankruptcy court judges are so liberal in dispensing fees. Judge Joseph L. Cosetti, who presides over bankruptcy proceedings in Pittsburgh, has rejected fees for some expenses that New York judges have approved. Among them: The charges for word-processing, or computer use, during the bankruptcy reorganization of Allegheny International, Inc., a Pittsburgh-based conglomerate, whose interests ranged from steel to Sunbeam appliances.

In an opinion dealing with fees, Judge Cosetti took special note of the billings for computer time: "Secretarial time, both regular and overtime, as well as charges for word-processing, are clearly overhead. . . . Therefore, those entries are disallowed." He also disallowed charges for meals and local cab fares. He cut the hourly fees charged by lawyers, saying they were too high. And he complained that lawyers from the same firm were billing for too much time in office meetings, and that multiple lawyers from the same firm appeared in court.

Nonetheless, the fee petitions were so voluminous—as they are in many cases—that Judge Cosetti conceded it was impossible to go over every claim. He wrote: "Unfortunately, the court lacks the resources because of its other cases to review, line-by-line, every fee petition filed in this case. The fee petitions which are the subject of this opinion, when stacked together, are over two feet high."

Law firms spend many hours preparing fee applications that even the most conscientious judges lack the time to sift through. How many hours?

Well, in one month, a couple of lawyers and legal assistants in the Atlanta law firm of Trotter, Smith and Jacobs billed 150 hours—at rates up to $215 an hour—to prepare one fee application in the bankruptcy reorganization of Southmark Corporation, a Dallas real estate and financial services firm.

Herewith a sampling from Trotter, Smith reports for April 1990:

"Review . . . of court's Dec. 18, 1989, order to determine date next fee application by Trotter Smith & Jacobs must be filed." "Drafting . . . of memorandum . . . regarding filing date for next fee application by Trotter Smith & Jacobs." "Preparation . . . of file containing prior fee application information."

"Conference . . . regarding need to assign legal assistant to begin collecting documents and information for third application by Trotter Smith & Jacobs for interim award of attorneys' fees and reimbursement of expenses."

"Conference . . . regarding assignments to individual attorneys for writing narrative summaries to include in application by Trotter Smith & Jacobs for interim award of attorneys' fees."

"Preparation, assembly and review . . . of distribution packets to thirteen billing attorneys . . . regarding the preparation of summaries to be used in connection with the preparation . . . of the third fee application . . . for interim awards and reimbursement expenses."

Paper Jobs

Not too surprisingly, the nation's bankruptcy courts are choking on paper. Keeping track of hearings attended, hearings rescheduled, letters sent, letters not received, expense reports compiled and expense reports filed, obviously requires a massive amount of record-keeping. When the paperwork goes astray, as it is wont to do when lawyers and judges and courts process tens of millions of pieces of paper, one result is ever more fees as everyone debates the legal subtleties of errant legal documents.

Consider the events of a single day in a single bankruptcy court proceeding and keep in mind that similar debates are taking place in courtrooms across America. Again, at $100 to $500 an hour.

The city is Pittsburgh. The company is Allegheny International, a once high-flying conglomerate. The date is Aug. 11, 1988. The place is a sixteenth floor courtroom in the federal building in downtown Pittsburgh.

A dozen lawyers are engaged in an animated discussion with bankruptcy court Judge Joseph Cosetti. The issue: Whether one of thousands of notices Allegheny mailed to potential creditors was properly sent. The creditor, Equibank, Pittsburgh's third-largest bank, argues that the notice was incorrectly addressed.

The notice was mailed from Allegheny's corporate headquarters, in the Equibank building in Pittsburgh, to Equibank's corporate headquarters, which are in the same building. The bank's lawyer contends that the notice was sent to Equibank's "mail room department and a gentleman or person by the name of D. Miller," rather than to the bank's corporate trust department.

Equibank's lawyer: "I have witnesses here today who will be testifying that there is no current D. Miller as an employee of Equibank, nor has there ever been a D. Miller in the employ of the corporate trust department for the last fifteen years." Because of Allegheny's error, he says, Equibank missed the deadline to file its claim.

"It's our position," he continues, "that we did not receive the notice, that this constitutes excusable neglect under Rule 9006 (B) (1) [and] that we should be permitted to file the late proof of claim."

The judge: "Now, this is being opposed, as you know, by all the other committees and every party who can get their hands on a typewriter."

Equibank's lawyer: "Yes, your honor."

Creditors' lawyer: "It was addressed to a Mr. Miller, but in our response we also cite case law which indicates that as long as it's sent to the right firm and the right place and, in fact, it was sent to two places." He leafs through his papers and notes that in addition to the notice to D. Miller in Equibank's mail room, another was sent to the attention of William Barnum, also at Equibank's corporate offices.

The judge: "So there were two notices?"

Creditors' lawyer: "Yes."

Equibank's lawyer: "Well, your honor, if I may interpose here. . . . Mr. Barnum is, in fact, the chief at Equibank's dining room. And how he could be expected to provide notice to the corporate trust department is quite frankly beyond me." Laughter fills the courtroom.

Creditors' lawyer: "This request does clearly come after the expiration of the May 31st time period. So I don't even think we need to get to the question of excusable neglect because the request was made late."

The judge is familiar with the legal doctrine of "excusable neglect." But he notes he is not certain it can be invoked in the Equibank situation. "My view is that the . . . cases don't give much excusable neglect merit to slightly wrong addresses," he says.

In any event, the judge will think it over. If he agrees to allow the claim, he will inform the parties. Then they will have another hearing. The reason: to decide the value of the claim.

Cases like Allegheny International are so complex and so voluminous that they have forced bankruptcy courts to take special steps to handle the flow. Around the country, bankruptcy courts have limited their hours, rented additional space, hired more clerks, contracted with private firms to take over tasks once performed by court employees, restricted access to records, installed telephone answering machines to route the flow of requests and invoked other emergency measures to try to manage what one bankruptcy court official described as a "tidal wave" of paper.

In St. Louis, ten additional clerks have been hired to deal with the largest bankruptcy in the city's history, Interco, Inc., whose holdings include such familiar names as Florsheim shoes and Broyhill furniture. In Phoenix, the bankruptcy case of American Continental is so gargantuan that the clerk's office retained a legal-services management firm, which rented an entire warehouse to store documents that fill nearly 10,000 boxes. That is for just one case. In Los Angeles, the influx of documents is so great that the clerk's office is beginning to resemble a supermarket, with specialized lanes to handle specific requests.

Inside the main door are these signs above the public counter: "Advanced Request Here," "Return Files Here," "Request Files Here," "Photo Copying" and "Cashier." Unlike most supermarkets, however, there are no express lanes in bankruptcy court.

In Manhattan, the bankruptcy court clerk's office has created a special division to try to manage the volume of paper produced by a series of massive bankruptcies stemming from the era of easy debt. Until four years ago, all bankruptcies—however large or small—were filed in Room 525 on the fifth floor of the historic old United States Custom House at the foot of

Manhattan. Today most still are—except L.J. Hooker, Eastern Airlines, Ames Department Stores, Drexel Burnham Lambert, Integrated Resources, Pan American Airways, Best Products and other mega-bankruptcies. They are in a new office down the hall.

Until the summer of 1989, Room 510 was a dark, unused storage area, piled high with old furniture from the days when the building was New York's principal custom house. Today it looks much like a typical clerk's office found in bankruptcy courts across America. Except that it is handling fewer than three dozen cases. They are so enormous they require a section all their own.

"The purpose of that room was because we simply could not deal with the public otherwise," said Cecilia Lewis, the bankruptcy court clerk. After the large cases began to be filed, she said, the court discovered "there were not enough telephone lines, not enough people, not enough copies of the petition available to give to people."

The bankruptcy court operation in Manhattan moved to its present location only five years ago from cramped quarters in the United States Courthouse at Foley Square.

"We have only been in this building since 1987 and we are totally out of space," said Lewis. "At the time we moved in, this was a large expansion."

What accounts for the runaway growth of paperwork? In four words: the government rule book.

When Congress rewrote the rule book in 1978 to revise the bankruptcy law, it opened the floodgates to a specialized proceeding called Chapter 11. Under the old law, companies in trouble tended to file petitions under a section of the code called Chapter 7. That section provides for the liquidation of the company. Its assets are sold and the proceeds distributed to creditors. The business ceases to exist. Chapter 11 is different. It allows a company to continue operations and existing management to stay in control. The company reorganizes under court supervision, protected from its creditors. Chapter 11 had existed previously, but the new law made it a more appealing option.

The change came at a time of shifting values in the world of business, when bankruptcy began to lose the stigma once attached to it. Those same shifting values permitted corporate managers to engage in practices they once would have avoided—such as unrestrained borrowing—out of fear of bankruptcy. And they permitted executives whose faulty judgments resulted in the failure of their businesses to seek sanctuary in bankruptcy court and, perhaps more important, retain their jobs.

So it was that corporate debt surged to record levels in the 1980s as a result of the new attitude toward borrowing. In the past, corporate managers saw debt as a necessary tool for corporate growth, but one to be used cautiously. But in the 1980s, fueled by the virtually unlimited tax deduction for interest paid on corporate borrowings, debt was seen as a positive force, a way to impose discipline on a company's operations.

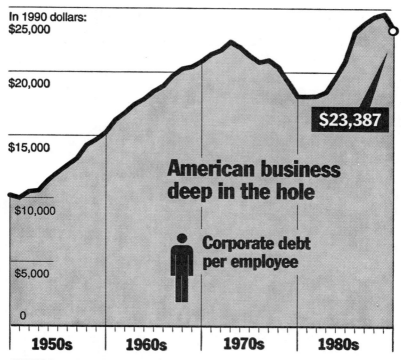

In 1990 dollars:
$25,000

$20,000

$23,387

$15,000

**American business
deep in the hole**

$10,000

● **Corporate debt
per employee**

$5,000

0

1950s | 1960s | 1970s | 1980s

SOURCES: Bureau of Labor Statistics, Federal Reserve Board

Steven N. Kaplan, an assistant professor of finance at the University of Chicago, summed up this attitude in testimony before a Congressional committee in 1989: "The large debt service payments force managers to find ways to generate cash and prevent managers from spending money unproductively." The results of that trend have become painfully evident. The very factor that was supposed to impose discipline—the high debt service payments—instead became a liability that drove many into bankruptcy court.

An analysis of a half-century of bankruptcy caseloads shows what happened: From 1976 to 1979, businesses filed, on average, 3,700 bankruptcy petitions each year under Chapter 11. During the 1980s, with the new law in effect, businesses filed, on average, 15,200 petitions each year under Chapter 11. That was an increase of 311 percent. By contrast, Chapter 7 petitions rose just 43 percent, from an average of 28,200 to 40,300.

Viewed from a different perspective, in the late 1970s only one of every nine businesses that went into bankruptcy court sought to reorganize. In the 1980s, it was one of every three.

The dramatic growth in Chapter 11 proceedings—in which a business conducts its affairs under the supervision of the courts and an army of lawyers, accountants and management consultants—brought on the avalanche of paperwork.

As with so many legislative actions involving the government rule book, lawmakers failed to understand the consequences of their bankruptcy code revisions in 1978. Malcolm Wallop, a Republican senator from Wyoming, promised that "no longer will needless litigation in several courts be required to determine all the matters involved in a bankruptcy case." Don Edwards, a Democratic congressman from California, hailed the Bankruptcy Reform Act, saying that it "encourages business reorganizations by a streamlined new commercial reorganization chapter."

No more needless litigation? Streamlined?

As for the end of litigation, take a look at the bankruptcy proceedings of Integrated Resources, Inc., the New York financial services company that collapsed in February 1990. There has been litigation involving unpaid merchandise, breach of contract, unpaid rent, default on promissory notes, fraud and misrepresentation in the sale of partnership interests, securities law violations, fraud and negligence in the sale of investment programs, conspiracy and fraud in the marketing of partnerships, nonpayment of notes, and a class-action lawsuit by stockholders.

There is so much litigation overall that in 1990 Andrews Publications of Westtown, Pennsylvania, began publishing a twice-monthly newsletter, the *Failed LBO Litigation Reporter*, just to report on bankruptcy cases in state and federal courts. Frank Reynolds of Andrews Publications said that the *Failed LBO Litigation Reporter* follows major bankruptcy cases with an eye on "who might be liable for the mess and who is going to sue who and what is the proportion of the liability among various parties."

As for "streamlined," take a look at the number of law firms representing some of the interests in the Hooker bankruptcy case. There are Attorneys for the Creditors Committee, General Counsel to the Debtor, Special Counsel for Debtor, Attorneys for Debtor, Cocounsel to Debtor, Special Labor Counsel, Attorneys for the Official Committee of Unsecured Creditors, Special Local Counsel, Attorneys for Plaintiff, Special Corporate Counsel, Special Counsel for the Debtors Trade Creditors, Consultants for Debtors and Accountants to the Official Creditors' Committee. All those committees beget a prodigious volume of paperwork, which, in turn, begets prodigious fees.

When L.J. Hooker, the United States division of the Australian real estate company, filed for bankruptcy in New York in August 1989, it submitted one petition for Hooker Corporation—and fourteen separate petitions for fourteen Hooker subsidiaries. Consequently, each time Hooker filed an accounting, it submitted fifteen separate statements covering operations and liabilities. One such statement, Document No. 47, was 1,510 pages long, seven inches thick, weighed ten pounds, and contained the names of 15,000 potential creditors of one Hooker subsidiary—Bonwit Teller.

At the bankruptcy court in Dallas, there was the Southmark Corporation, the real estate combine. Instead of fifteen subsidiaries, Southmark had 550 subsidiaries and 350 public and private real estate partnerships. The collapse of hundreds of those entities in turn spawned about 850 lawsuits. In Phoenix, the bankruptcy cases grew so large that the bankruptcy court was compelled to retain a private firm, Ameriscribe Management Services, Inc., to handle the flood of legal documents.

So it is with the reorganization of Circle K Corporation, a convenience store chain based in Phoenix that in 1990 had annual sales approaching $4 billion. By late 1991 Circle K had produced nearly 5,000 legal documents—some of which were thousands of pages long—that have been submitted to the court and Ameriscribe.

It is "generating huge, huge amounts of paper," said Mark A. Scipione, an Ameriscribe official. When the company filed its list of assets and liabilities, Scipione said, they were "twenty-five volumes long. There were 40,000 pages of creditors.

"We had some people call and say, 'I want that list of assets and liabilities.' And I said, 'Sure, do you want to pick them up with a truck or should I send them air freight?' "

CHAPTER FIVE
THE FOREIGN CONNECTION

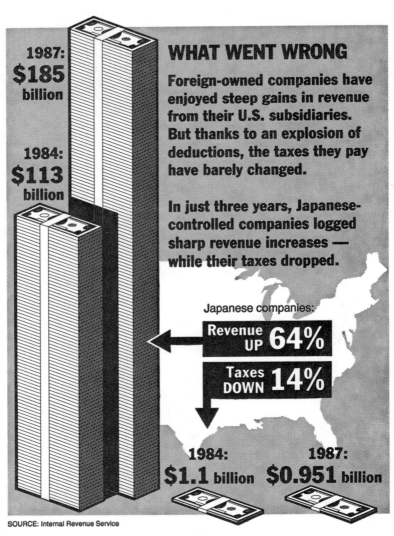

1987:
$185
billion

1984:
$113
billion

WHAT WENT WRONG

Foreign-owned companies have enjoyed steep gains in revenue from their U.S. subsidiaries. But thanks to an explosion of deductions, the taxes they pay have barely changed.

In just three years, Japanese-controlled companies logged sharp revenue increases — while their taxes dropped.

Japanese companies:

Revenue **UP 64%**

Taxes **DOWN 14%**

1984:
$1.1 billion

1987:
$0.951 billion

SOURCE: Internal Revenue Service

Global Economy

Want to take advantage of the stew of rules, regulations and laws that govern the United States economy and the conduct of business in America? And maybe make a few million dollars and cut your taxes along the way? Here are a few tips:

■ Become a fugitive from justice and set up operations in a foreign country to conduct business, even to deal with government agencies back home.

■ Become a citizen of a foreign country in order to play American stock and bond markets or even to buy and sell American businesses, at lower tax rates than you would get staying at home in the United States.

■ Form an American subsidiary of a foreign-owned company so you can pay lower taxes than your United States–owned competitors.

■ Start an American company, and then move your factory, jobs and investment dollars overseas.

Any one of those setups is now to your advantage because of the way the rules that govern business in this country have been written and rewritten over the last twenty years.

Why would the United States government rig the game that way? In part because of the influence exercised by special interests in Congress and in federal agencies. In part because of good intentions gone awry.

One of the consequences: American companies and companies worldwide are now conducting a replay on a global scale of a business practice that became common in the 1960s. That was the decade when United States companies began playing off one region of the United States against another, one state against another, one city against another. The objective was to locate a new plant or relocate an existing one in whatever area would offer the greatest tax incentives—so the company would have to pay the smallest amount of local and state taxes—and where employee wages and fringe benefits could be held down the most.

Now that practice has gone global, as corporations and financiers play off one country against another, one national tax system against another, one country against its possessions. President Bush put a glowing light on it in February 1991 in his annual report on the state of the economy that he delivered to Congress: "The benefits of global economic integration and expanded international trade have been enormous, at home and abroad. United States firms gain from access to global markets; United States workers benefit from foreign investment in America. . . . Competition and innovation have been stimulated, and businesses have increased their efficiency by locating operations around the globe."

The aptly named Marc Rich quite likely feels the same way. You may not recognize his name. But you quite likely have used one of his products. Rich, a member of *Forbes* magazine's directory of the 400 richest Americans, operates a highly secretive and successful commodities business around the world. Through a maze of closely controlled companies, he buys and sells billions of dollars worth of oil, copper, nickel, wheat, alumina and other commodities.

What makes this remarkable is the fact that Marc Rich is a fugitive from the United States government. Back in 1983, Rich, two associates and one of his companies, Clarendon, Ltd., were accused by the federal government of failing to pay taxes on profits from rigging the price of crude oil during the 1979–1980 energy shortage, then hustling the money out of the country. To continue doing business, Clarendon pleaded guilty to the charges and paid $172 million in taxes and penalties.

Rich fled the country, apparently unwilling to risk the possibility of a trial, conviction and a sentence that could add up to more than 300 years in prison. Ever since the indictment, Rich has been operating from Zug, Switzerland, where he lives in a multimillion-dollar mansion. Except, of course, when he is relaxing at his multimillion-dollar estate at Marbella on the coast of Spain. That is the estate, according to published accounts, with the swimming pool carved into a cliff overlooking the Mediterranean.

Whether in Switzerland or Spain, Rich directs the buying and selling of assorted commodities—he virtually controls the aluminum market—in the United States and around the world.

He also has had an impact on the jobs of American aluminum workers. People like Joseph Gladden of Ravenswood, West Virginia, who, along with 1,700 other employees, has been locked out of the aluminum smelting plant that is owned by a company called Ravenswood Aluminum Corporation. Gladden, forty-one, began working at the plant in 1971, when it was owned by Kaiser Aluminum and Chemical Corporation. Those were the days when American business operated in a way that came to seem hopelessly antiquated and naive to the wheeler-dealers who moved in during the 1980s, with the federal government paving every step of the way. The days when a company actually built a plant and ran it for the long term.

For Gladden, those days ended in 1986. That is when the first of a dizzying series of changes ensued. Joseph Gladden was about to meet the global economy. It began that year when the British takeover artist Alan E. Clore seized control of the company. Clore lasted until the stock market crash of October 1987, when he defaulted on bank loans. The next buyer was an American takeover artist, Charles E. Hurwitz of Houston. To pay down the debt incurred when he bought Kaiser Aluminum, Hurwitz sold off pieces of the old company, including the Ravenswood plant.

Enter the third set of new owners in three years—bankrolled by a mysterious company with multiple ties to Marc Rich.

How is it possible for a fugitive to conduct business as usual in the United States?

The answer, once again, is the government rule book, the handiwork of a succession of lawmakers and presidents, regulators and administrators, who have chosen to write the rules to favor special interests—from wealthy individuals such as Marc Rich to influential businesses—rather than create a level economic playing field for everyone. Nowhere is the imbalance more evident than in the rules—or, more accurately, the absence of rules—relating to foreign investment in the United States, foreign trade, the conduct of United States businesses abroad, unrestrained imports, and the global economy.

The transformation of once-American-owned businesses such as the Ravenswood plant into outposts controlled from abroad is part of a larger picture that is unfolding across America.

The blockbuster movie you went to see or rented at the neighborhood video store, *Home Alone*, was distributed by Twentieth Century–Fox, which is owned by Australia's News Corporation, the global media conglomerate of Rupert Murdoch. The television game show you watch faithfully every evening, "Jeopardy," is produced by Columbia Pictures Entertainment, which is owned by Japan's Sony Corporation, the global electronic and media company.

The bestseller that you read, Stephen King's *The Stand: The Complete and Uncut Edition*, was published by Doubleday and Company, which is owned by Germany's Bertelsmann, AG, a global communications company. Even your favorite fast-food hamburger place, Burger King, is owned by Britain's Grand Metropolitan PLC. The deep-heating ointment used to ease your aches and pains is made by the Mentholatum Company, Inc., which is owned by Japan's Rohto Pharmaceutical Company. The Arrow shirts you buy are made by Cluett Peabody, which is owned by France's Biderman Group.

The Tropicana orange juice on your breakfast table is made by the Tropicana Company, which is owned by Canada's Seagram Company, Ltd. The Stroehmann bread you like so much is made by Stroehmann Bakeries, which is owned by Canada's George Weston, Ltd.

The locks on your doors are made by Yale, which is owned by Britain's Valor PLC.

And your favorite vacation golf course, the Pebble Beach (California) Golf Course, is owned by a Japanese investor, Minoru Isutani.

Once, all were American-owned.

To be sure, foreign-controlled corporations in America are still a comparatively small slice—7 percent—of total United States business receipts. But from 1979 to 1987, the revenue of foreign-controlled corporations rose from $242 billion to $685 billion—an increase of 183 percent. The revenue of U.S.-owned companies went up only 52 percent.

While the 1987 statistics are the latest available, it is believed, given the large number of foreign acquisitions of United States businesses since then, that their annual revenue has reached $1 trillion.

The growing presence of foreign goods and foreign-owned properties in the United Sates has been accompanied by generous tax breaks that the people in Washington have extended to foreign corporations and foreign investors. Internal Revenue Service data show that companies owned by the Japanese, Germans, British and other foreign interests are claiming far larger deductions on their United States tax returns than American companies do.

The oversized write-offs mean that foreign-owned companies are more likely than American companies to file tax returns showing little or no profit. This allows them to pay little or no United States income tax. In 1987, only 41 percent of foreign-owned companies reported a profit on their U.S. tax returns. By comparison, 55 percent of U.S. companies showed a profit.

That means fifty-nine of every one hundred foreign-owned companies doing business in the United States reported—for federal income tax purposes—that they lost money. In the case of United States businesses, forty-five of every one hundred said they lost money. A House Ways and Means subcommittee investigation of thirty-six foreign-owned businesses, including electronics and automobile companies, showed that more than half "paid little or no federal income tax."

One tax break that has proved popular is the net operating loss deduction, which, you may recall, began to grow dramatically in the 1980s. The Ways and Means subcommittee reported that in one case an electronics company reported total sales of $4 billion over seven years—but only $15 million in tax liabilities. It turned out that "the company always had net operating losses available to zero out any tax. In ten years, the company ultimately paid no federal income tax," according to Patrick G. Heck, assistant counsel for the committee.

Revenues of foreign-controlled companies in the United States rose 50 percent from 1984 to 1987. Their taxes went up 2 percent. Japanese-controlled companies in this country have done well, both in boosting their sales and avoiding United States income taxes. Their revenue rose 64 percent from 1984 to 1987, going from $113 billion to $185 billion. Yet the federal income taxes paid by these Japanese-controlled companies went down, rather than up—falling 14 percent, from $1.1 billion in 1984 to $951 million in 1987.

If you enjoyed the same increase in income that the Japanese companies achieved, your annual salary would have gone from, say, $30,000 to $49,200 in those three years. Simultaneously, the federal income taxes you paid would have dropped from $2,729 to $2,347.

Residents of foreign countries who buy and sell stocks, bonds and government securities in this country do even better. In 1988, residents of Japan collected $8.4 billion from their investments in this country, mostly in interest and dividends. They paid $510.6 million in United States income taxes on that money. That is a tax rate of 6.1 percent. By contrast, American workers with incomes between $40,000 and $50,000 paid taxes at an 11.6 percent rate.

Residents of the United Arab Emirates fared even better. They collected $312.9 million from their American investments. They paid $443,000 in U.S. income taxes. Their tax rate: One-tenth of 1 percent.

American workers struggling to achieve a middle-class lifestyle, on the other hand, were taxed at fifty-three times that rate. Individuals and families with incomes between $13,000 and $15,000 paid taxes at a 7.4 percent rate.

But take a closer look at the deal the United States government has arranged with the United Arab Emirates and other countries. In theory, foreigners are taxed lightly on their income in the United States because it is assumed they pay income taxes in their home countries. That's the theory. Reality is quite different.

The United Arab Emirates, for example, imposes no income taxes on its citizens. It does levy a religious tax. But, as one United States government tax official explained: "They have no enforcement mechanism. No reporting. You're just supposed to pay it because [of] your conscience. My understanding is it's a rather modest tax in terms of collection."

Let us review: If you have $1,000 in your passbook savings account, you must pay income tax on the interest you receive. If a resident of the United Arab Emirates has $1 million in the same bank, that person pays no United States income tax on the interest.

Overall, wealthy residents and corporations in foreign countries collected $31.8 billion, mostly in interest and dividends, from their United States investments in 1988. They paid $1.7 billion in United States income taxes. That is a tax rate of 5.3 percent—less than the 5.8 percent rate paid by Americans who earn $7,000 to $9,000 a year.

Viewed another way: American workers who earned between $30,000 and $40,000 in 1987 paid, on average, $3,710 in income tax. If they had been taxed at the same rate that Congress granted residents of the United Arab Emirates, their average tax bill would have totaled $49.

How is all this possible? There are a number of interwoven reasons, all related to the government rule book:

Enactment of laws and regulations to encourage an uncontrolled global economy. Outdated tax-treaty concepts. The State Department's long practice of catering to special foreign interests. The IRS's inability to commit sufficient resources to audit corporate tax returns in general, and foreign-owned corporations in particular. And the complexity of the Internal Revenue Code.

For some measure of that complexity, consider one aspect of a business that operates globally—the pricing and sale of products among affiliated companies. Let's say the Global Widget Company manufactures a part used in making widgets at a factory in a country with a low corporate tax rate, say 10 percent. It costs Global Widget $5 to make the part, which it

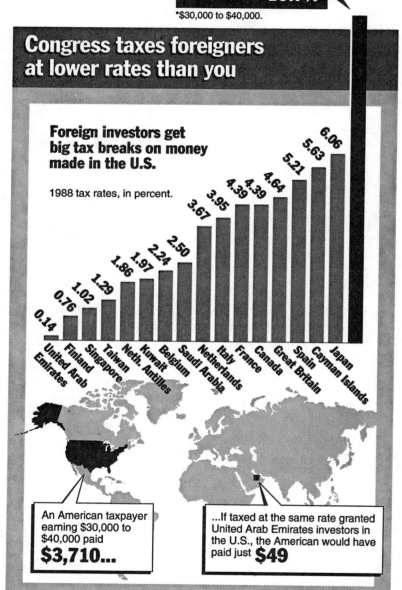

Rate for middle-income* U.S. taxpayers: **10.7%**

*$30,000 to $40,000.

Congress taxes foreigners at lower rates than you

Foreign investors get big tax breaks on money made in the U.S.

1988 tax rates, in percent.

0.14 — United Arab Emirates
0.76 — Finland
1.02 — Singapore
1.29 — Taiwan
1.86 — Neth. Antilles
1.97 — Kuwait
2.24 — Belgium
2.50 — Saudi Arabia
3.67 — Netherlands
3.95 — Italy
4.39 — France
4.39 — Canada
4.64 — Great Britain
5.21 — Spain
5.63 — Cayman Islands
6.06 — Japan

An American taxpayer earning $30,000 to $40,000 paid **$3,710...**

...If taxed at the same rate granted United Arab Emirates investors in the U.S., the American would have paid just **$49**

SOURCE: Internal Revenue Service

sells to its United States subsidiary for $50. The United States subsidiary, in turn, sells the part to the American public for $55.

The United States subsidiary books a profit of $5 on the widget part and pays taxes, after deduction of expenses, at a 34 percent rate. Global Widget's plant reports a profit of $45 in the low-tax country, where the part is produced, and pays taxes, after deduction of expenses, at a 10 percent rate.

So it is that corporations constantly shift their costs to countries with high tax rates, in order to maximize their deductions, while they shift their profits to low-tax havens to keep tax payments down.

Exporting Jobs

Diverting operations and tax write-offs to the best possible locale is hardly peculiar to foreign-owned companies. In fact, it was invented by United States companies, with the assistance of members of Congress who rewrote the government rule book in 1976 to encourage the practice. They did so when they amended the Internal Revenue Code to provide tax credits for American companies that established subsidiaries in United States possessions, notably Puerto Rico, where the islanders are United States citizens.

In essence, the provision allows subsidiaries to transfer profits from Puerto Rico to their parent companies in the United States—without paying taxes on those profits. Thus the United States government will provide a tax break to a company if it terminates the jobs, say, of 800 workers in Elkhart, Indiana, who earn an average of $13 an hour. That is, the company will get the tax break if, at least in part, it replaces the $13-an-hour workers in Elkhart with $6-an-hour workers at a plant it builds in Puerto Rico.

Meet George Skelton. Until April 1991, he was one of 800 production workers at the Whitehall Laboratories plant in Elkhart. That was the month his job was eliminated. On Nov. 1, 1991, Whitehall Laboratories, a division of American Home Products Corporation, closed the Elkhart plant permanently; the last of the 800 still on the job were thrown out of work.

Some of the products once manufactured there are now being turned out at a new facility in Guayama, Puerto Rico.

As for American Home Products, the Puerto Rican subsidiary has already allowed the company to escape payment of millions of dollars in United States income taxes, not to mention saving millions of dollars in salaries.

Said the fifty-two-year-old Skelton: "All the companies that have moved down there, so far as I know, are good, healthy, rich companies. It's like giving welfare to the rich, the way I'm looking at it. Robbing from the poor and giving it to the rich."

For that, thank members of Congress and the 1976 Tax Reform Act that amended the tax code. While provisions in the Internal Revenue Code encouraging investment in Puerto Rico date to 1921, the 1976 law added a twist that led to a corporate stampede to the island.

Under the old law, the subsidiary of a United States company operating in Puerto Rico had to pay federal income taxes on its profits earned there when it transferred the profits back to this country. In other words, a company could accumulate its profits, year after year, on the island, and pay no United States income tax. But taxes had to be paid when the subsidiary paid dividends to its parent company. The new law exempted the dividends—or profits in Puerto Rico—from the United States income tax, and allowed the profits to be shipped back to the United States tax-free.

There is no comparable tax provision for individual taxpayers. If there were, it would go something like this: If you had two jobs, one in Chicago and the other in Gary, Indiana, you would pay federal income taxes only on the money you earned in Gary. The money you earned in Chicago would be tax-free.

Since passage of the 1976 tax act, corporations have terminated the jobs of tens of thousands of factory workers in the United States, replaced them with lower-paid workers in the possessions, mostly Puerto Rico, and escaped payment of billions of dollars in federal income and other taxes. Pharmaceutical companies, in particular, have embraced this provision. So much so that Puerto Rico boasts the world's largest concentration of drug companies.

The effect on United States mainland workers may be measured in announcements by pharmaceutical companies over the last few years.

In October 1987 the duPont Company announced that it planned to transfer production of prescription drugs from a plant in Garden City, New York, to a plant in Puerto Rico—and terminate the jobs of 168 Garden City workers.

In October 1988 the then–SmithKline Beckman Corporation announced that it would transfer production of prescription drugs from Philadelphia to Puerto Rico—and terminate the jobs of 800 Philadelphia production workers.

In April 1990 the Bristol-Myers Squibb Company announced that it would transfer production of a cardiovascular drug from a plant in New Brunswick, New Jersey, to Puerto Rico—and terminate the jobs of 500 New Brunswick workers.

Let's look at one company, American Home Products, a New York–based health-care conglomerate that had sales of nearly $7 billion in 1990. Its Whitehall Laboratories division manufactures nonprescription products with such familiar names as Advil and Anacin-3, Preparation H and Dristan.

In February 1989 American Home Products told stockholders that "completion of a new facility in Puerto Rico in the fourth quarter of 1988 . . . will enable Whitehall to achieve significant cost efficiencies while maintaining the highest manufacturing standards." In October 1990 American

Home Products announced that within one year it intended to close the Whitehall plant in Elkhart and transfer some of the work to its new plant in Puerto Rico. Among the products to be manufactured in Puerto Rico: Anacin, Dristan, Denorex and Advil.

The move exacted a heavy toll on the Elkhart work force, whose average length of service was fifteen years. More than half of the production workers were women. A survey showed that after one year, of 100 employees laid off, only about half had found other work. In many cases they were forced to accept part-time employment. Their average pay was $6 an hour. Before, it had been $13.40. When they worked at Whitehall, they had good benefits, including company-paid health insurance. By one estimate, 70 percent of the Elkhart workers lost their medical insurance when the plant closed in November 1991.

George Skelton, who lost his job in April 1991, is among those who can attest to the plummeting wages. It took five months before he found another manufacturing job, operating an injection-molding machine in a rubber company. At Whitehall Laboratories, he earned $13.40 an hour. In his new job, he earned $7 an hour. And how many former co-workers does he know who were able to find new jobs that matched their Whitehall salaries?

"Basically," he says, "everybody that's found a job I know of is [making] half or less than what they were making [at Whitehall]."

Mary Soellinger, fifty-seven, who worked at Whitehall eight years, did not even do that well. Laid off early in 1991, by year's end she still had not been able to find work.

"I suppose I could probably get in at McDonald's," she said, "but I really don't feel that it is fair to push people into minimum-wage jobs, because you can't live on minimum wages."

But Mary Soellinger and George Skelton's loss—and the loss of the other Elkhart workers—is American Home Products' gain. Listen to the words of Smith Barney, Harris Upham and Company, a Wall Street investment firm that reported in April 1990 on the tax good-fortunes of American Home Products: "In 1985, American Home Products initiated tax-sheltered manufacturing in Puerto Rico. . . . As a result, American Home Products' tax rate declined 13.9 percentage points from 1983 to 1988."

For a personal comparison, if a family with an income between $30,000 and $40,000 in 1988 had benefited from a comparable reduction, the taxes they paid would have fallen from $3,708 to $2,558—a saving of $1,150.

Companies have long called investors' attention to the reduced tax rates they enjoy on their Puerto Rican operations. In January 1990, the Rorer Group, Inc., now known as Rhone-Poulenc, S.A., a pharmaceutical manufacturer headquartered in Fort Washington, Pennsylvania, whose products include Maalox, reported that its profits were up and its tax rate was down: "Rorer's results were positively affected by a lower effective tax rate, which was 31 percent for 1989, compared with 35 percent in 1988.

This reduction in rate was achieved primarily as a result of further tax benefits from manufacturing in Puerto Rico."

In July 1991 the Upjohn Company, a pharmaceutical and health-care company headquartered in Kalamazoo, Michigan, announced record second-quarter sales of $859 million, a profit before taxes of $175 million and a lower tax rate. Commenting on its tax outlook for the rest of the year, Upjohn reported: "The estimated annual effective tax rate for 1991 is 27 percent, compared to 32 percent a year ago. The lower rate resulted primarily from a greater proportion of total earnings from low-tax Puerto Rican operations and a lesser proportion of foreign income taxed at relatively higher rates."

George Skelton, whose annual income has been sliced almost in half, has difficulty understanding the Washington wisdom underlying the tax break: "Everybody says, 'Well, they're [Puerto Rico] just like a state.' Well, they're not just like a state. 'Cause they don't pay taxes. And our states sure in hell don't get those kinds of tax breaks.

"In my opinion, either you're in the game or you're out of the game. To me, they ought to be able to become a state, or else, if they're not a state, they ought to be treated like a foreign country. They ought to have tariffs put on them and they should have to pay taxes on their profits and everything.

"We're headed toward a $5 trillion national debt. And $350-billion-a-year deficits. And yet we're giving tax breaks to corporations like that to take jobs that would be paying toward that debt. It looks like a hell of a situation for our children and our grandchildren."

How much is the Puerto Rican tax rule costing you?

According to Treasury Department data, companies claiming the possessions tax credit escaped payment of $14 billion in income taxes during the 1980s. For the United States government to make up that lost revenue required every penny in tax paid by all middle-class taxpayers in Santa Rosa, California; Lakeland, Florida; and Portland, Maine, through the 1980s. And then some.

But what about all the new jobs created in Puerto Rico with that tax money?

Well, in the pharmaceutical industry alone the lost tax revenue to the United States government adds up to $60,000 for every $6-an-hour job created. Thus, it would be cheaper for the United States government—and all American taxpayers—to send annual subsistence checks to those island residents who work for American drug companies, and keep the jobs here. In other words, Congress is spending $60,000 of taxpayers' money to eliminate one job in the United States that pays $28,000 a year and to create one job in Puerto Rico that pays $12,000.

While United States companies are exporting ever more jobs, the growing foreign influence in this country is showing up in other, more subtle ways. Take patents, for example.

For American business, the year 1986 represented a first: For the first time a foreign-owned company, Hitachi, Ltd., secured more United States patents than any American-owned company. It has been downhill ever since.

As recently as 1977, according to statistics compiled by the United States Patent and Trademark Office, the ten corporations that received the largest number of patents broke down this way: Seven were American-owned. Three were foreign-owned. By 1989 those statistics were reversed. Seven of the top ten corporate patent-holders were foreign-owned. Only three were American-owned.

In 1977 the top four companies were all American. The General Electric Company ranked No. 1 with 822 patents for the year. GE was followed by IBM, Westinghouse Electric Corporation and Xerox Corporation.

In 1989 the four American companies were replaced at the top of the list by four foreign companies—all Japanese. Hitachi headed the list with 1,053 patents, followed by Toshiba Corporation, Canon, Inc., and Fuji Photo Film Company, Ltd. GE had fallen to the No. 5 slot, and IBM had dropped to No. 9. Between 1977 and 1989, four American companies disappeared from the ranks of the top ten: Westinghouse, Xerox, AT&T and the duPont Company.

The makeup of the foreign companies on the list also had changed significantly. In 1977 two companies were German, one was Dutch. There were no Japanese companies. By 1989 there were five Japanese companies among the top ten, one German, one Dutch.

In 1977 American companies received two of every three patents granted to corporations. By 1989 it was one of every two.

While the Japanese and other foreign interests are churning out patents for new technologies and products, the United States, courtesy of the government rule book, is churning out something else: master of business administration degrees (MBAs).

All through the 1970s and 1980s, American colleges and universities turned out ever larger numbers of MBAs, a process that coincided with the steady erosion of the country's once-dominant manufacturing base. During the 1970s, MBA graduates outnumbered advanced-engineering graduates 36,600 to 16,100 a year. The opposite was true during the 1950s, a period of middle-class prosperity. On average, 4,700 advanced degrees in engineering were awarded each year, compared with 3,800 MBAs.

In the 1980s, the gap expanded exponentially as business schools turned out 64,200 graduates yearly while engineering schools produced only 20,000. Many of the 20,000 were foreign nationals who received their diplomas in this country and returned to their native lands.

Let's summarize the degrees and the numbers. Advanced engineering graduates do the kind of work that leads to new technologies and products, which in turn lead to the creation of new manufacturing jobs that pay middle-class wages. MBAs do the kind of work that leads to new financial products—including assorted credit instruments like junk bonds—which in turn lead to the creation of a few high-paying professional positions, a lot of

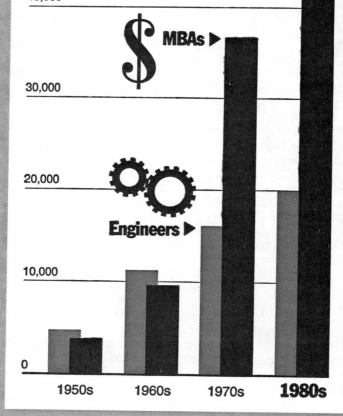

American academic emphasis: Money over engineering

In the 1950s, more graduates were awarded master's degrees in engineering than in business management.
In the 1980s, MBAs outnumbered engineers by more than 3 to 1.

Average number of degrees per year:

64,200

MBAs ▶

Engineers ▶

40,000

30,000

20,000

10,000

0

1950s   1960s   1970s   **1980s**

SOURCE: National Education Association

low-paying clerical jobs and, quite often, the elimination of manufacturing and other jobs.

So, from the 1950s to the 1980s, the number of advanced engineering graduates rose 326 percent, from an annual average of 4,700 to 20,000. During the same time, the number of MBAs spiraled 1,589 percent, from an annual average of 3,800 to 64,200.

It was a trend the Japanese did not rush to copy. In 1989, Japanese universities awarded nearly 12,000 advanced degrees in engineering, compared with 1,000 MBAs.

Akio Morita, the chairman of the Sony Corporation and one of Japan's most innovative corporate leaders, understands the competition well: "Americans make money by playing 'money games,' namely, mergers and acquisitions, by simply moving money back and forth . . . instead of creating and producing goods with some actual value."

Global Moneymen—Beyond the Law

For Marc Rich, there are no national loyalties. He is a member of an army of global moneymen who with the touch of a computer keyboard move money, commodities and information around the world at the speed of a blinking eye, erasing traditional boundaries among nations.

The crude oil in a supertanker bound from the Middle East to the United States, for example, may change owners a half-dozen times before it ends up as gas in your car. Each change in ownership is accompanied by a change in price—and the final price in the chain is the price you pay at the neighborhood gas station.

More important, Rich and other electronic financiers have insulated themselves from regulation by the United States government, have exempted themselves from the official government rule book. From abroad, they have more opportunities than deal-makers on United States soil to escape payment of taxes either by legal or illegal means; engage in business practices that otherwise would be considered harmful to the best interests of American consumers and workers; avoid prosecution for financial crimes; and continue to do business with the United States government.

So it is that, although Marc Rich most likely has never set foot in Ravenswood, West Virginia, he has had a powerful impact on the town of 4,100, which is embroiled in a bitter labor dispute.

The trouble dates from 1989, when the town's largest employer, the aluminum smelting plant, was purchased in a leveraged buyout—the third change of ownership in the 1980s. On Feb. 7, 1989, the plant was acquired by Ravenswood Aluminum Corporation, a newly formed company whose stock was owned by Stanwich Partners, Inc., a Stamford, Connecticut-based investment company. Under Charles E. Bradley, Stanwich had acquired interests in a wide range of companies in the 1980s, from steel distribution to metal fabrication.

But Ravenswood was not a typical leveraged buyout, one financed by junk bonds or bank loans. The money came from a mysterious source in Switzerland—Ridgeway Commercial, AG. According to loan documents filed in a West Virginia courthouse, Ridgeway provided $260 million in loans for the buyout.

Ridgeway's official address was in Hergiswil, a scenic hamlet of 2,400 people on the shores of Lake Lucerne. Its United States address was "Clarendon, Ltd. . . . Stamford, Connecticut." "Clarendon, Ltd." is the United States office of Marc Rich's international trading company, Clarendon, Ltd., based in Zug, Switzerland.

The fine print of the loan documents disclosed yet another Rich connection. The preferred stock in Ravenswood Aluminum was held by a Dutch company, Rinoman Investment, BV. Netherlands corporate records list Rinoman's president as Willy R. Strothotte. Strothotte is one of Marc Rich's closest lieutenants, an executive who has worked for the fugitive financier for years. Strothotte is president of Clarendon, Ltd., and his office is in the same Zug office building at 37 Baarerstrasse where Rich and his companies are housed.

Lastly, another Ravenswood tie to Rich shows up in Delaware corporate records. Ravenswood Aluminum's chairman, R. Emmett Boyle, and Stanwich's Bradley are directors of two other United States–based companies with Edward Creswick, who also works for Rich in Zug.

When a telephone call was placed to Creswick in Zug to ask about his association—as well as Rich's—with Ravenswood, Creswick responded: "Where have you got my name from? And my phone number?"

Told that his name appears on corporate records as a director with Boyle and Bradley, he replied: "I would prefer not to comment on that."

Just months after the Ravenswood plant was sold, Strothotte, the Rich executive, and Boyle acquired a majority of the stock in the company from Stanwich Partners, with Strothotte picking up the larger share. The ownership change set the stage for a labor dispute that would turn family member against family member in Ravenswood. In the spring of 1990, months before negotiations were to begin on a new labor contract with the steelworkers union, the Ravenswood company implemented procedures that made a labor showdown seem inevitable.

The plant was encircled with a ten-foot-high fence topped with barbed wire. Security cameras were installed. Office windows were boarded up. An armed security force was employed. Boxcars of food and mobile homes were brought into the plant, and salaried employees were drilled in security procedures. And ads began to appear in out-of-state newspapers for replacement workers. Not surprisingly, little progress was made toward a new contract that fall, and on Nov. 1, 1990, when the agreement expired, employees were turned away when they came to work. The company called it a strike; the aluminum workers call it a lockout.

The National Labor Relations Board (NLRB) agreed with the union and formally charged Ravenswood Aluminum on July 18, 1991, with refusing to bargain in good faith and for illegally locking out its employees. But, while the case worked its way through the administrative-hearing process, the company hired 1,100 workers to replace the locked-out employees, a move that led to scores of incidents of violence.

The shutdown was a financial disaster for the 1,700 employees of Ravenswood, many of whom, like Toby Johnson, were employed there all their working lives. The son of a Ravenswood Aluminum retiree, Johnson went to work at the plant in 1966 straight out of high school. He worked in the finishing department, where aluminum is cut into sheets for cans, automotive components or other products. Like other Ravenswood workers, Johnson exhausted his unemployment benefits in July 1991. After that, he and his wife and thirteen-year-old son existed largely on $35 a week in food vouchers from the United Steelworkers Union and provisions from the union-run food bank.

"Basically, we eat what they give you instead of going out to the store and buying what you want . . . which you can't afford," Johnson said. "We have had to cut a lot of corners." When they have needed cash, they have dipped into savings or been helped by relatives.

The hardest part for Johnson and other employees is what the shutdown has done to the community and to their own families. Ravenswood Aluminum hired many replacement workers from the town, putting neighbors and family members on opposite sides of a bitter issue.

"It's put a real strain on the community and individual families," Johnson said. "It's wrecked homes. There is brother out against brother. There is a father who's locked out and the son is working. It has worked on everybody emotionally and physically."

Johnson said the issue had touched his own family. A niece is married to a replacement worker. He said his father allows the man to visit the home.

"He keeps letting him come to his house, which I disapprove of," said Johnson. "He still comes there so I don't go there to my own parents' house. So it has really messed us up in our relationship."

As might be expected, officials of Ravenswood Aluminum and Clarendon are reluctant to talk about Marc Rich and his ties to the aluminum company. When the United States office of Rich's Clarendon, Ltd. was asked about the source of funds to acquire Ravenswood Aluminum, a spokesman for the company in Stamford declined to answer, referring questions to Ravenswood. "I think it would be more appropriate from them," the spokesman said.

When Ravenswood officials failed to respond to requests for information, telephone calls were placed to Willy Strothotte at Rich's Zug headquarters. He, too, failed to return the calls.

While Rich's ties to Ravenswood Aluminum are shrouded in secret

Swiss loan agreements and corporate arrangements, his ties to you are quite direct. Take a look in your pocket. Those pennies? They may have been minted from copper that Rich's Clarendon, Ltd. sells to the United States Mint. Or those nickels in your pocket? Yes, indeed. They, too, may have been minted from nickel that Clarendon, Ltd. sells to the mint. Over the years, the mint has awarded millions of dollars worth of contracts to Clarendon for metals.

When the authors asked about the United States government's business relationship with Clarendon and Rich's association with the company, a spokesman for the mint said: "The information that the United States Mint has on Clarendon comes from Clarendon. So what we would prefer you to do is to go to them and inquire. Is that fair? Because we would just be recounting to you what they have told us."

Let's make the Rich–United States government associations perfectly clear: Rich sells copper to the United States Mint, a branch of the Treasury Department, while the Internal Revenue Service, another branch of the Treasury Department, and the Department of Justice, are, in theory, seeking to bring him to trial on tax-evasion charges.

But not seeking too hard.

In fact, Rich, now in his eighth year on the run, seems to have faded from the memories of law enforcement officials. When a telephone call was placed to the FBI in Washington to ask if there was a "wanted" poster for Marc Rich, the following exchange took place with a specialist on fugitives:

FBI representative: "I've heard the name before. I don't believe so. Is he wanted in this country?"

Author: "Yes."

FBI representative: "Are you trying to get a hold of the poster?"

Author: "Yes, exactly."

FBI representative: "I know the name. It's right on top of my head. It's not coming to me what he's been involved in and where he's wanted."

CHAPTER SIX

THE HIGH COST
OF DEREGULATION

WHAT WENT WRONG

Thousands of firms gone. 200,000 jobs lost.
Deregulation has been costly to workers and
consumers alike.

In the case of the savings and loan industry,
the cost to taxpayers will be staggering:
the equivalent of every penny of tax paid
by every resident of
Ohio, Vermont, Washington,
South Carolina and New
Mexico earning up to
$50,000 — for the next
33 years. That's until the
year 2025.

THE YEAR
2025
2010
1995
1992

Now, the push is on to
deregulate the banking
industry.

SOURCE: Projections from U.S. government tax data

Wrecking Industries and Lives

Since deregulation of the trucking industry in 1980, more than 100 once-thriving trucking companies have gone out of business. More than 150,000 workers at those companies lost their jobs.

Since deregulation of the airlines in 1978, a dozen airline companies have merged or gone out of business. More than 50,000 of their employees lost their jobs.

Since deregulation of the savings and loan industry in 1982, about 650 thrifts have folded, with at least 400 more in serious trouble. The bailout will leave taxpayers stuck with a half-trillion-dollar tab.

Now, the people who rewrote the government rule book to deregulate airlines, trucking and savings and loans are about to rewrite the rules on banks. They call it banking reform. President Bush spelled out the plans in February 1991: "Regulatory reform is long overdue. Our banking reform proposals . . . address the reality of the modern financial marketplace by creating a U.S. financial system that protects taxpayers, serves consumers and strengthens our economy."

Sound familiar? It should. The arguments for deregulating banks are much the same as those that were made in the 1970s and 1980s for the other industries: Removing government restrictions on the private sector would let free and open competition rule the marketplace. Getting rid of regulations would spur the growth of new companies. Existing companies would become more efficient or perish. Competition would create jobs, drive down prices and benefit consumers and businesses alike.

That's the theory. The gritty reality, as imposed on the daily lives of the men and women most directly affected, is a little different.

For Christopher E. Neimann of Fort Smith, Arkansas, deregulation meant the loss of health insurance as he was battling cancer. Neimann, who worked for a trucking company, was diagnosed with a rare bone cancer in November 1987. He went on medical leave two months later. In August 1988 his company, Smith's Transfer Corporation, entered bankruptcy, a victim of deregulation's rate wars. Its checks began bouncing, including ones paying for Neimann's treatments at the M.D. Anderson Cancer Center in Houston.

On Apr. 11, 1989, the hospital sent Neimann a stern letter asking him to pay his bill, which totaled $30,128. When the bedridden, gravely ill Neimann couldn't make payments, the hospital began pressuring his wife, Billie.

"The hospital called me one night and told me they were going to dip into the estate," she said. "And he wasn't dead. He was still alive. I knew he was going to die. And they knew he was going to die. I just cried and I said, 'I beg your pardon. Could I ask you what estate are you talking about?' And they said, 'Well, his estate.' And I said, 'Ma'am, at thirty-one years old, you don't have an estate. You don't have anything to go into an estate. At this age, we're just starting out.' I said, 'You can dip all you want. Dip right in and get some of the bills, too. Because there won't be anything left.' "

After a battle of a year and a half, Neimann died on June 6, 1989, aged thirty-one, leaving behind a young wife and an infant daughter. The calls from M.D. Anderson's collection department continued.

"They kept calling and told me that I was still liable," said his wife, who has since remarried. "I was so upset that eventually I talked to my lawyer and he told me to give them his name. I don't know what's happened, but lately they haven't called."

For Leslie Wagner of Flower Mound, Texas, deregulation meant seven years of relentlessly shrinking paychecks—and, ultimately, no paycheck. At twenty-three, she went to work as a flight attendant for Braniff International Airlines. That was in 1969, when the Dallas-based carrier was the nation's eighth largest airline. By 1982 her base salary was $19,300 a year. That year, the fourth year of airline deregulation, Braniff asked workers to accept wage cuts and other concessions.

Even after employees agreed to reductions, Braniff still could not pay its bills and the airline was forced to seek protection in United States Bankruptcy Court in May 1982. The action grounded Braniff and put 9,000 employees, including Leslie Wagner, out of work. Two years later a scaled-down Braniff, Inc., under new owners, emerged from bankruptcy court and resumed service. Former employees were offered jobs, but at reduced pay. When Wagner returned to work in 1985, her new base pay was $15,600 a year—19 percent less than she earned in 1982.

By 1989, with Braniff still in financial trouble, employees were asked to take another pay cut. Wagner's base pay went down again—to $14,400. On Sept. 28, 1989, Braniff was forced into bankruptcy court for the second time in seven years. Its assets were auctioned off to pay creditors, and the airline's remaining 4,800 employees were let go. After absorbing pay cuts of 25 percent during the years when the cost of living rose 28 percent, Leslie Wagner was out of work. The company resumed limited service in July 1991, but Wagner was not recalled. It didn't matter. Braniff was back in bankruptcy court a month later, for the third time in a decade.

For Joyce D. Heyl of Sioux Falls, South Dakota, deregulation also meant the loss of a job. Heyl worked nineteen years in the accounting department of an interstate trucking company, American Freight System, Inc., until it went out of business in August 1988.

"When you work for a company a long time and you like your job, you always think it's going to be there and then suddenly one day it's not," she said. "I loved my job. I was very upset when the company went down." Her standard of living went down with it. "I'm fifty-nine years old and I thought to go back into the job market with a lot of young people was something I wouldn't be able to do," she said.

To supplement the family income she works part time at various jobs. At American Freight, she earned $410 a week, or $21,320 a year. Afterward, she was lucky if she earned half that.

For Barbara Joy Whitehouse of Salt Lake City, deregulation meant a devastating financial blow, on top of a personal one. Her husband was killed in a 1986 Montana highway accident while driving a truck for a company called P-I-E Nationwide, Inc. After his death, Barbara Whitehouse, fifty-four, began receiving $299 a week under Montana's workers' compensation law, which makes payments to spouses of workers killed on the job.

Because P-I-E was a large company and appeared to have considerable assets, Montana authorities permitted it to pay claimants directly, rather than contribute to the state's workers' compensation fund, which disburses benefits in most cases.

That was a mistake. P-I-E was not as solid as Montana officials thought. Deregulation was helping drive it, like many other interstate trucking companies, out of business. After huge losses, P-I-E filed for bankruptcy in October 1990 and is being liquidated. After the bankruptcy filing, the company ran out of cash and Whitehouse's biweekly checks stopped. P-I-E's last check to her, on Oct. 10, 1990, bounced.

Whitehouse has filed a claim with the bankruptcy court for $466,440—the amount due her under Montana law if she lived to be eighty-four and didn't remarry. But Whitehouse will see little, if any, of that money. Hers is one of more than 7,000 unsecured claims against P-I-E—meaning she'll collect, at best, a few cents on each dollar owed.

"P-I-E knew they owed me $299 per week for life and should have put aside a safe fund to meet this debt," Whitehouse wrote to the bankruptcy court. "They didn't, so now the court wants me to go at the bottom of the list to see if they can offer me what's left after the big guys get their fair share. I am as important as any big company. . . . This is wrong. My husband dies, the law says they pay me for life and now I have nothing."

And finally, for you, the American taxpayer and consumer, deregulation has meant fewer airlines and higher air fares, more unsafe trucks on the highways, and more of your tax money diverted to pay for the savings and loan debacle. That last one is going to cost you for years to come.

For this, and all the other costs associated with deregulation, human and economic, you can thank the people in Washington who wrote the government rule book, the collection of laws and regulations that provide the framework for the United States economy. Changes in the economic rules by a succession of presidents and Congresses have propelled federal, state and local taxes ever higher while forcing middle-class job holders into lower-paying jobs. So it is with deregulation, which has meant lost jobs or pay cuts for employees in the airline and trucking industries, and, ultimately, higher taxes for everyone to rescue the savings and loan industry.

Backers, to be sure, predicted a rosy future for airlines and trucking when those industries were deregulated. Few of the benefits they foresaw have come about. Advocates of airline deregulation claimed that it would stimulate competition, reduce fares, open up air travel to more Americans. And in the beginning it seemed as if that would happen.

Freed from government restrictions to set fares and schedules, the industry eagerly embraced deregulation. New airlines began service and existing carriers extended routes to new points. Fares went down. Service went up. Competition increased. But it didn't last. In an unregulated market, those who had the financial muscle to dominate soon did—the big airlines gobbled up the little airlines. New airlines soon found they lacked the financial resources to compete.

Today, there is less competition in the airline industry than before deregulation. In 1978 the ten largest airlines accounted for 88 percent of the revenue passenger miles flown by United States flag carriers. By 1990 the ten had increased their share of the miles flown to 94 percent. In many markets, there is virtually no competition, and prices reflect it. In 1977 it cost $86 to fly from Philadelphia to Pittsburgh, round trip; in 1983 the cost had gone up to $124. By 1992 it cost $460.

Even on routes where competition developed after deregulation, ticket prices soared. A one-way ticket on the Eastern shuttle from Washington to New York cost $38 in 1977. By 1991 a ticket cost $142—nearly four times what it had in 1977. If the price of a gallon of unleaded gasoline had gone up at the same rate, it would have cost $2.33 in 1991. As for competition, the Washington–New York route is served by two carriers, Delta and the old Eastern shuttle, which was sold to Donald Trump as Eastern was collapsing, and which Trump subsequently turned over to his creditors when he encountered financial hard times.

For many air travelers, ticket prices are irrelevant. They are the people who live in small towns across America that were once served by airlines but no longer are. Paul Stephen Dempsey, a University of Denver law professor who has studied the impact, estimates that more than 130 small communities were dropped from scheduled air service after deregulation.

In summary, under airline deregulation, fares have gone up, not down. Competition became destructive, not productive. Service was cut back. The increase in air travelers was lower in the decade after deregulation than in the decade before it. Cities once served by multiple carriers are now served by one or none. And the airline industry is in shambles.

Nonetheless, the people in Washington have a different view. In January 1991, Samuel K. Skinner, when he was secretary of Transportation, offered this assessment: "Airline deregulation . . . ushered in a decade of competition and consumer savings unsurpassed in the history of the industry. With deregulation having accomplished so much throughout the 1980s,

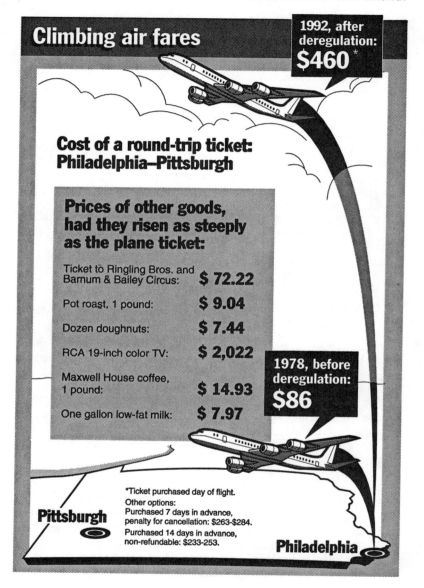

Climbing air fares

1992, after deregulation:
$460 *

Cost of a round-trip ticket: Philadelphia–Pittsburgh

Prices of other goods, had they risen as steeply as the plane ticket:

Ticket to Ringling Bros. and Barnum & Bailey Circus:	**$ 72.22**
Pot roast, 1 pound:	**$ 9.04**
Dozen doughnuts:	**$ 7.44**
RCA 19-inch color TV:	**$ 2,022**
Maxwell House coffee, 1 pound:	**$ 14.93**
One gallon low-fat milk:	**$ 7.97**

1978, before deregulation:
$86

*Ticket purchased day of flight.
Other options:
Purchased 7 days in advance, penalty for cancellation: $263-$284.
Purchased 14 days in advance, non-refundable: $233-253.

Pittsburgh

Philadelphia

we must stay the course in the coming decade as the industry continues to restructure. Every credible analysis of airline competition in the 1980s has declared deregulation a success."

Judge for yourself. The year 1990 was the worst financial year in American aviation history as airline losses soared to $3.9 billion. By 1992, Pan American, the flagship of United States carriers, founded in 1927, was in bankruptcy court and on the verge of liquidation. Eastern Airlines, founded in 1927, was in bankruptcy court and was being liquidated. Braniff, founded in 1934, was in bankruptcy court for the third time and was on the verge of liquidation. Continental Airlines, founded in 1937, was in bankruptcy court. Midway Airlines, founded in 1979, was in bankruptcy court and was being liquidated. Trans World Airlines, founded in 1928, was in bankruptcy court.

And then there's America West Airlines of Phoenix—once considered deregulation's success story. From a modest regional carrier with three jets and 280 employees in 1983, it grew into a nationwide airline with ninety-two planes and 12,000 employees. With revenues of $1 billion, it moved onto the list of the nation's top ten airlines in 1990. In June 1991 it moved into bankruptcy court.

Indeed, most United States carriers have been left so weakened by the airline industry's increasingly grave financial condition that they have been unable to invest in new aircraft to replenish their aging jet fleets. As a result, United States airlines are flying jets that are considerably older than the planes of major European competitors, which are clamoring for permission to enter the United States domestic market and compete with American carriers. The average age of the United States fleet in 1990 was 13.5 years, according to data compiled by the Boeing Company. By contrast, the average age of aircraft flown by airlines in Europe and Asia was 10.4 and 8.7 years, respectively.

Ten years ago, in 1980, the average age of the United States fleet was almost half what it was in 1990—7.56 years, according to the Federal Aviation Administration (FAA). The data on the planes of one air carrier, Trans World Airlines, illustrate what has happened. In 1978, the year of deregulation, TWA's fleet of 224 planes had an average age of 10.5 years. By the end of 1990, the fleet's average age had risen to 15.52. But even that sharp increase did not tell the full story. Many of TWA's planes are much older than 15.52 years. Its entire fleet of Boeing 727–100s are on average twenty-five years old, the oldest having rolled off the assembly line in 1964.

If all the news from the skies appears bleak, the authors of the government rule book—the people who brought you airline deregulation—have another solution: They have already invited foreign airlines to invest in the remaining American carriers. And they are thinking about opening the United States domestic market to foreign carriers, so that Air Japan, for example, might one day fly between Los Angeles and San Francisco or between Dallas and Houston.

So it is that the government, which revised the rule book to spur competition among United States airlines, is contemplating encouraging foreign airlines—many of which are subsidized by their governments—to compete against the few remaining United States carriers.

Struggling to Survive

In trucking, it has been a similar story. Rather than making the industry stronger, as congressional backers predicted, deregulation triggered price wars and cutthroat discounting that have destroyed many of the largest companies and weakened others. More trucking companies failed in the 1980s than in the entire forty-five previous years that the Interstate Commerce Commission (ICC) regulated the industry.

Part of the reason, of course, was that there were many more companies scrambling for work. In 1979, the year before deregulation, 186 companies went out of business. Eleven years later, in 1990, the number had soared to 1,581, the most trucking failures ever recorded in a single year. For the decade, a total of 11,496 failed. Of the thirty largest motor carriers of 1979, only ten are still in business. The others either went bankrupt, merged or were broken up and their pieces acquired by one of the surviving companies.

A decade into deregulation, trucking appears to be following a variation on the airline-industry pattern. That is, after an initial burst of competition has come a shakeout, with widespread failures that eventually could leave control of the industry in fewer hands. Meanwhile, though, small, mom-and-pop operators continue to come in, keeping the pressure on.

Trucking industry data show that consolidation already is under way. Before deregulation, the three largest trucking companies accounted for one-third of the operating revenue of the top twenty-five companies. In 1991, those three—Roadway Express, Consolidated Freightways and Yellow Freight System, Inc.—accounted for about one-half. Nevertheless, advocates of trucking deregulation, like their airline counterparts, contend that it has been an unqualified success. Darius W. Gaskins, Jr., former chairman of the ICC, told a House committee in 1989: "The trucking industry has saved billions of dollars through more efficient operations allowed and stimulated by deregulation. . . . The benefits to consumers from deregulation exceeded our fondest dreams."

A 1990 study by the Brookings Institution, a Washington, D.C., think tank, echoed this view: "Surface freight deregulation (trucking and rail) has been extremely beneficial to shippers and to their customers. Total annual benefits from rate and service changes amount to $20 billion."

While companies that hire truckers have profited from lower rates, there are no economic data showing that the cost savings have been passed

The collapse of the U.S. trucking industry

Most of the top 30 trucking firms of 1979 are gone

1.	Roadway Express	Operating
2.	Consolidated Freightways	Operating
3.	Yellow Freight System	Operating
4.	Ryder Truck Lines	**Folded**
5.	McLean Trucking	**Folded**
6.	Pacific Intermountain Express	**Folded**
7.	Spector Freight System	**Folded**
8.	Smith's Transfer	**Folded**
9.	Transcon Lines	**Folded**
10.	ETMF Freight System	**Merged**
11.	Interstate Freight System	**Folded**
12.	Overnite Transportation	Operating
13.	Arkansas-Best Freight Sys.	Operating
14.	American Freight System	**Folded**
15.	Carolina Freight Carriers	Operating
16.	Halls Motor Transit	**Folded**
17.	Mason & Dixon Lines	**Folded**
18.	Lee Way Motor Freight	**Folded**
19.	TIME–DC	**Folded**
20.	Wilson Freight	**Folded**
21.	Preston Trucking	Operating
22.	IML Freight	**Folded**
23.	Associated Truck Lines	**Merged**
24.	Central Freight Lines	Operating
25.	Jones Motor Co.	Operating
26.	Gateway Transportation	**Folded**
27.	Bowman Transportation	**Folded**
28.	Schneider Transport	Operating
29.	Delta Lines Inc.	**Folded**
30.	Garrett Freightlines	**Merged**

SOURCES: Commercial Carrier Journal, The Philadelphia Inquirer

along to consumers. There are substantial economic data, however, showing that the cost savings to shippers have come at workers' expense.

Indeed, what has happened to those workers provides a glimpse into the future for employees in other industries, both blue-collar and white-collar. Already, corporate restructuring and downsizing have led to layoffs and the elimination of benefits. But the most pervasive trend—one that is growing—is the one that forces workers into lower-paying jobs.

Sometimes it happens across a broad industry. Three jobs that pay, say, $30,000, are eliminated and six jobs that pay $15,000 are created. The government statistics show a gain in jobs, but often fail to disclose the decline in wages. Similarly, workers in other companies are compelled to accept pay cuts in return for keeping their jobs.

Consider the pay of flight attendants. In 1983, according to data compiled by the Association of Flight Attendants, the average annual salary was $28,847. Six years later, in 1989, it had declined to $27,160. That represented a pay cut of 6 percent at a time when living costs shot up 24 percent.

During those same years, the people who write the government rule book—and who revised the laws that, ultimately, led to lower salaries for airline employees—increased their own salaries 48 percent. The pay of members of Congress went from $60,662 in 1983 to $89,500 in 1989. The $28,838 increase alone exceeded the full salary of flight attendants. In 1992, congressional salaries are $125,100.

For truckers, the 1980s were a dismal time, even though government statistics suggest that all is well. According to the Bureau of Labor Statistics, employment and wages in the trucking industry have increased since 1980. Between 1980 and 1990, the number of employees increased 248,000, rising from 1.242 million to 1.490 million. Average yearly earnings went from $18,400 to $23,400, the government says.

What those figures fail to disclose: During the years when total employment rose, more than 100 of the big, established trucking companies folded. With them went more than 150,000 jobs. These were the higher-paying trucking jobs—held by drivers with seniority and providing company-paid benefits, such as health insurance and pensions. Many of those truckers earned solid, middle-class wages—$30,000 or more in recent years.

Deregulation brought an influx of one-owner, shoestring trucking operations, which cut into the business of established companies. Jobs at these small operations paid less. So it was that deregulation eliminated two jobs that paid, say, $30,000, and created three jobs that paid $20,000 or less.

Just as misleading are the earnings reported by the government. In 1990 trucking industry workers earned, on average, $23,400 a year, according to the Bureau of Labor Statistics (BLS). But the government excludes one major category of truckers from its figures—self-employed drivers. And their earnings generally are lower than those for drivers employed by major companies.

"We don't really have any data on how many there are," said a BLS official. "An individual in business for himself is technically not covered by our study." A spokesman for the ICC said that the agency does not know how many owner-operators exist. "I'm not sure we have ever had an accurate count," he said.

The Owner-Operators Independent Drivers Association, the largest trade group representing individual drivers, estimates there are 350,000 to 400,000 owner-operators. Based on surveys by its magazine, *Landline*, the association estimates the annual income, after expenses, of owner-operators at $20,000 a year, or $385 a week, according to Sandi Laxson of the drivers' group.

"Deregulation has been a nightmare for our people," said Laxson. "I remember my uncle was a truck driver twenty years ago and, wow, he made a lot of money. He was on the road all the time. But his wife drove a nice car and they had a nice house. Now, drivers are struggling to survive."

The source of the upheaval in the trucking industry is the Motor Carrier Act of 1980, which changed the rules that had governed trucking for half a century. Responding to criticism that the ICC's rules had frustrated competition and discouraged new companies from entering the business, Congress scaled back the agency's powers, making entry easier and giving truckers more freedom to set rates.

President Jimmy Carter summed up the high hopes when he signed the law in July 1980: "The Motor Carrier Act of 1980 will eliminate the red tape and the senseless overregulation that have hampered the free growth and development of the American trucking industry."

Undoubtedly, the ICC, like its counterpart in the airline industry, the Civil Aeronautics Board (CAB), had stifled competition and discouraged innovation. Rather than correct the defects in the regulatory system, Congress chose instead to throw it out, thereby ushering in an era of economic anarchy for which no one was prepared. It was somewhat akin to eliminating the referees in a football game because of flawed calls, instead of merely replacing them.

As promised, the law unleashed new competition—on a scale unforeseen and with an intensity that became destructive. New trucking companies surged into the industry by the thousands. Most were one-person operations. By 1979, the year before deregulation, the ICC had granted operating licenses to 17,000 interstate carriers. By 1990, that number stood at 45,000. The ICC granted more operating certificates in the 1980s than in the previous forty-five years of its regulation of the industry. From being an agency that exercised tight control over truck licensing, the ICC became one that essentially rubber-stamped applications.

Yet while the number of companies more than doubled, there was no corresponding increase in the volume of freight hauled. Too many trucks were suddenly chasing too little freight. Total intercity tonnage increased just 11 percent, from 2.26 billion tons in 1980 to 2.5 billion tons in 1989.

Thus, more than twice as many ICC-approved companies were competing for roughly the same amount of freight.

The trucking glut led to desperate rate wars as truckers scrambled to survive. With each round of rate cuts, many longtime companies found themselves awash in red ink. As losses mounted, companies whose trucks had long been familiar names on American highways began to vanish. Even companies that initially thought they would benefit from deregulation were, in the end, destroyed by it.

When the parent corporation of American Freight System, Inc., one of the nation's largest trucking companies, based in Overland Park, Kansas, in 1987 acquired another old-line interstate carrier, Smith's Transfer of Staunton, Virginia, it sought to allay concerns of Smith employees about being absorbed by another company. In an Oct. 2, 1987, letter, American Freight welcomed the Smith workers into the new company, citing numerous fringe benefits—profit-sharing, pension and health and welfare plans—to which they would be entitled.

"Your economic security has been made more certain," the letter said. "American Freight System is a financially viable carrier with a secure future in the deregulated motor carrier industry." Nine months later American Freight filed for bankruptcy court protection. The action threw 9,300 people out of work, closed 258 trucking terminals across the nation and idled 17,000 trucks and trailers. The company has since been liquidated.

For trucking companies still in business, the outlook is also grim. Many that have survived deregulation's rate wars are just getting by. Profit margins have been squeezed. Equipment is neglected or pushed to the limit.

So many carriers are entering and leaving the industry that the Federal Highway Administration has been unable to keep pace with safety inspections of interstate carriers. The inspections are required by the Motor Carrier Safety Act of 1984, which was aimed at reducing trucking accidents. A January 1991 report of the General Accounting Office noted: Federal Highway Administration "workload data show that the number of carriers entering the marketplace in any one month can exceed the number that underwent safety reviews." For those vehicles that the highway agency did inspect, the GAO said, "Seventy percent . . . received a less-than-satisfactory rating."

That comes as little surprise to DeWayne Snow. The owner of Snow's Welding and Truck Repair Inc., in Tyler, Texas, 100 miles east of Dallas, Snow does repair work for both large and small trucking companies.

"It's real tough on them right now," Snow said. "They don't fix anything they don't have to. . . . They'll bargain over everything. They even say to you, 'Can I bring in some used parts?'"

As companies fought to stay in business after deregulation, they struggled to cut costs. Usually that meant reducing the wages and benefits of workers. This was sometimes accomplished, curiously enough, through a program intended to broaden ownership—Employee Stock Ownership Plans, or ESOPs.

Created by Congress in 1974, ESOPs have become more and more popular with a wide spectrum of American corporations. Proponents say that ESOPs give workers a voice in their company's operations and make them feel committed to its success. In the trucking industry, though, ESOPs were used as a device to persuade employees to accept pay cuts. In return for wage reductions of up to 15 percent, workers received stock in the company. If the firm prospered, they were told, their stock would appreciate in value and they would earn back what they had given up. That was the theory, anyway.

Contrary to the image of American labor as uncompromising on bread-and-butter issues, trucking industry workers went along—usually overwhelmingly so—with virtually every request of financially strapped employers for wage cuts in exchange for ESOPs. Since 1980, more than two dozen ESOPs financed by worker wage cuts have been adopted by large trucking companies. With few exceptions, the companies failed anyway.

The first major trucking company to adopt an ESOP was Transcon Lines, Inc. of Los Angeles, a carrier with terminals in forty-five states. The plan, approved at Transcon in 1983, was widely hailed as an example of labor and management cooperation. A remarkable 88 percent of Transcon's 4,000 employees agreed to reduce their wages by 12 percent for five years in return for 49 percent of the company's stock.

Financial analysts loved the deal. Said William H. Legg, a transportation analyst with Alex Brown and Sons, Inc. of Baltimore: "Without the ESOP, Transcon wouldn't have been able to put enough capital into the company to stay even with the more well-heeled carriers."

The Transcon example soon spread through trucking, as one carrier after another secured wage cutbacks from workers in return for stock in the company. In the spring of 1989, amid much fanfare, Transcon distributed 2.5 million shares of stock to its workers, signaling the successful conclusion of the plan. Calling the ESOP an "unqualified success," Orin Neiman, Transcon's chairman, paid tribute to the workers who now owned almost half of the company's stock.

"The ESOP helped the company through years of fierce price competition and saved Transcon and 4,000 jobs that otherwise would have been lost," Neiman said. One year later, Transcon was out of business. With the ICC's approval, the company was sold in the spring of 1990 to a Florida-based real estate company. Three weeks later, Transcon closed its doors and entered federal bankruptcy court in Los Angeles. Its trucks, trailers and terminals were later sold.

Virginia Oates, who worked for Transcon in Charlotte, North Carolina, remembers the last day. "The company I worked for, Transcon Lines, was involved in a hostile takeover on Apr. 20, 1990," she wrote the ICC. "The takeover transpired at 4:50 P.M., Friday, Apr. 20, 1990, without any advance notice to the employees of Transcon Lines from anyone. All personnel, except the salesmen, were advised to take all their personal things with them as they left that day." A Transcon employee for fifteen years, Oates—and 4,000 Transcon workers nationwide—were suddenly out of work. The stock they had bought with $50 million of their wages was virtually worthless.

"It is hard for me to believe that the ICC has done their public duty in this case," wrote Oates.

The Deregulation Bandwagon— and Its Victims

Trucking deregulation was the product of a broad-based political movement for regulatory reform that gathered steam in the 1970s. While the perception exists that deregulation was Ronald Reagan's idea, it actually predated his arrival in the White House. In fact, airline and trucking deregulation were pushed through by Reagan's predecessor, Jimmy Carter.

The legislative coalition that brought about those changes and the subsequent deregulation of the savings and loan industry in 1982 had broad support in both parties.

It seemed that everyone in Washington was caught up in deregulatory fever from the mid-1970s on. It was a new concept that backers said would yield enormous economic benefits for the nation.

When President Carter signed the airline deregulation bill in 1978, he said: "It will also mean less government interference in the regulation of an increasingly prosperous airline industry."

When Congress adopted trucking deregulation in 1980, Herbert E. Harris II, a Democratic congressman from Virginia, hailed it as a victory over red tape: "The reform of trucking regulations will significantly reduce the current excesses of government regulation that prevent free market conditions from guiding the trucking industry toward more efficient pricing decisions that benefit shippers, carriers and consumers."

When President Reagan signed the law deregulating the savings and loan industry in 1982, he said it would make thrifts a "stronger, more effective force." He added: "This bill . . . represents the first step in our administration's comprehensive program of financial deregulation. It provides a long-term solution for troubled thrift institutions."

Such political opposites as Senator Jake Garn, the conservative Republican from Utah, and Senator Edward M. Kennedy, the liberal Democrat from Massachusetts, were both on the deregulation bandwagon. And it was Kennedy, more than any other senator, who led the charge for passage of the airline and trucking deregulation bills.

When Carter signed the Motor Carrier Act on July 1, 1980, at a ceremony in the White House Rose Garden, he singled out Kennedy for special attention: "It's particularly gratifying to me to welcome Senator Kennedy

. . . because he's done such a tremendous job . . . in helping the whole nation understand the advantages to be derived from this trucking deregulation bill."

Using language that sounded very much like the speeches that Reagan administration officials would make later in the 1980s, Kennedy described the Motor Carrier Act as "a significant victory" in the "ongoing battle to . . . reform and reduce needless federal regulation of business. . . . It means less government interference with industry . . . and more freedom for individual firms to conduct their business in the way they think best. It'll mean new opportunities, new jobs."

Kennedy was half right. New jobs were created—at low wages. But many jobs that paid middle-class wages were eliminated. Ask Charles D. Wright, Jr.

For twelve years, Wright was a dockworker at a sprawling truck terminal in Hagerstown, Maryland, a distribution hub that received and rerouted freight across America. After completing high school in Hagerstown, Wright went to work at the terminal on a plain north of the city where he had hunted groundhogs as a boy. He felt fortunate.

"Trucking was a good job in those days," he said. "The pay was good. It was steady work." And Ryder Truck Lines, which owned the terminal, was a good company, he said.

"I was proud to work there," he said. "People would ask you where you worked. I'd tell them, 'Ryder Truck Lines.' Big smile."

Ryder was one of the nation's oldest trucking companies. Founded in the 1930s, it was owned by IU International, Inc., a Philadelphia-based conglomerate that had diversified into the interstate trucking business. In addition to Ryder, IU owned another old-line trucking company, Pacific Intermountain Express, Inc. (P-I-E), based in the West. As separate divisions of IU, Ryder and P-I-E long were profitable operations. Deregulation turned the profits into losses.

To try to stem the losses, IU merged Ryder and P-I-E in 1983, creating Ryder/P-I-E Nationwide. But the red ink still flowed. The trucking operations lost $42.5 million in 1984. Another change was also beginning. Charles Wright and fellow workers at the Hagerstown terminal watched the company, once a solid, well-run organization, gradually deteriorate into a chaotic operation.

"They kept on hiring more management, more supervisors," he said. "When it was Ryder, there were just two supervisors a shift, and some nights only one. And then after deregulation, we had more superintendents and more managers than we ever had before. There was a lot of turnover among those guys. When it was Ryder, the same guys were supervisors for years."

The Ryder/P-I-E merger didn't work. In 1985 the company lost $86.4 million—the largest one-year loss ever recorded by any trucking company. In the fall of 1985, to keep afloat, the company proposed an Employee Stock

Ownership Plan. In exchange for giving up 15 percent of their wages for the ESOP, employees would receive stock in P-I-E. A prospectus spelling out the benefits was mailed to employees, saying: "The purpose of the plan is to enable employees . . . to acquire stock ownership in and thereby to share in the future of and to provide employees who participate with an opportunity to accumulate capital for their future economic security."

Over the five-year life of the ESOP, employees would give up about $250 million in wages in exchange for 49 percent of the company's stock.

Victor Anderson, another Hagerstown dockworker, recalled the day the ESOP was proposed: "They took everybody off the dock and brought us down to our break room and said, 'Hey, we've got this ESOP program. We're in financial difficulty and if you all don't decide to get into this—now we can't force you to get into this—but if you don't get into this, we're going to go out of business—next week.'"

Employees who signed up were sent buttons proclaiming "I'M AN OWNER," which they were urged to wear on the docks. The more workers who supported the ESOP, the lower the company's wage costs, so IU kept up a steady drumbeat of promotions urging workers to "keep those sign-up cards coming in" and to "get to 100 percent and top 'er off." Fearing that they would lose their jobs, more than 85 percent of P-I-E's 10,500 employees signed up. Charles Wright reluctantly agreed to go along, although he was convinced it was merely a device to get him to take a wage cut from $500 to $425 a week. In truth, most workers felt they had no choice.

"When you think about it, what are you going to do?" asked Anderson. "Are you going to take a 15 percent cut in pay or are you going to go out and try to get a job when it was hard to find one? So the majority of the people decided to get into the ESOP. . . . You were under a lot of pressure."

Eighty-five days after the stock plan was adopted, IU sold the company that it had spent months persuading employees to save by forfeiting their wages. On Dec. 31, 1985, the truck line, then renamed P-I-E Nationwide, Inc., was sold to a privately held Chicago investment partnership, Maxitron, Inc., which had no experience in the trucking industry.

Many employees were embittered by the sale, coming so soon after they had agreed to 15 percent wage cuts. Indeed, employees would later file lawsuits seeking to recover the money they had contributed to the ESOP. The lawsuits have since been settled and a fraction of the money returned.

"When they turned around and sold the company right after the ESOP, it left a bad taste in people's mouths," said Anderson. "They led us to believe that the company would not be sold, that it was going to turn around and that sometime our stock would go onto the open market."

Such was not the case. Under Maxitron, P-I-E continued to slide. Top management changed with each season. In the twenty months after adoption of the ESOP, P-I-E had four different chief executive officers. And the chaos at the top filtered down through the company.

"It seemed like anything that went wrong was your fault," said Wright, "and anything that went right was their idea."

"The equipment was neglected after deregulation," said Anderson. "Before, they had a regular program to replace so many tractors each year. That way you replaced your fleet every few years. But after deregulation . . . they had to do everything to keep their customers. One of the big things that suffered was the equipment.

"One way they could cut expenses was, if the truck needed brakes or tires, to run it one more trip. Or if the clutch was slipping on a tow motor, use it another week before you fixed it. There was a lot of neglect."

In the spring of 1990, the company changed hands yet again. The new owner was from Miami Beach and, like Maxitron, had no experience in the trucking industry. Olympia Holding Corporation, as it was called, had the same address, 1250 Ocean Drive, Miami Beach, and many of the same officers of a company that only three weeks earlier had acquired control of another old-line trucking firm, Transcon Lines of Los Angeles. Olympia's plan, its officers told the ICC, was to merge the troubled lines into one company. After applications were submitted, the ICC tentatively agreed to transfer the operating certificates to the new owners.

If the ICC had been guilty of overregulation in the past, its approval of the Transcon and P-I-E acquisitions showed just how far in the other direction the agency had swung. The central figure behind Olympia Holding and the Transcon and P-I-E deals was a controversial developer, Leonard A. Pelullo, who has operated from Chester County, Pennsylvania, to Miami Beach. About the time that the ICC approved Pelullo's control of the two trucking companies, he and his businesses were the subject of civil complaints and criminal investigations. Disgruntled investors, banks, the IRS, other government agencies and federal grand juries were suing or probing Pelullo's business activities, from Philadelphia to Miami, from Newark to Los Angeles.

Some of his difficulties grew out of his unsuccessful attempt to restore a collection of Miami Beach's historic art deco hotels. The real estate venture was undertaken by the Royale Group, Ltd., a publicly traded company that Pelullo controlled. After the Royale Group attracted millions of dollars from investors and banks to restore the hotels, the company collapsed.

While the ICC was considering the transfer of P-I-E's and Transcon's operating certificates to Pelullo's companies, his business empire was reeling, as a summary of the litigation and complaints against him shows:

■ His principal company, the Royale Group, and its affiliates were in bankruptcy court in Miami.

■ A bankruptcy court trustee in that case reported to the judge that Pelullo had transferred assets to family-controlled entities, with the apparent intent to "deprive creditors" of assets.

■ The Federal Deposit Insurance Corporation (FDIC) had filed a claim in Dade County, Florida, Circuit Court seeking to recover more than $30 million in principal and interest from a loan to a Pelullo company by a failed savings bank.

■ The IRS had filed a claim of $697,000 against Royale and seized company documents in an attempt to collect unpaid federal taxes for various Pelullo corporations.

■ A federal grand jury in Cincinnati had indicted Pelullo for allegedly bribing an officer of an Ohio savings and loan. A jury later acquitted him of the charge.

■ A federal grand jury in Philadelphia was investigating charges that Pelullo had defrauded a savings and loan association in Stockton, California, from which the Royale Group had borrowed $13.5 million in 1984.

■ A civil complaint filed in New Jersey accused Pelullo of raiding the pension fund of Compton Press, Inc., a Morris Plains, New Jersey, printing company the control of which he had acquired in 1987, and of siphoning off millions of dollars from the company's retirement plan for his personal use. A federal judge in New Jersey later sent Pelullo to jail for three weeks when he failed to pay back the fund.

This, then, was the background of the new owner of two longtime trucking companies, whose certification the ICC approved in April 1990.

Pelullo's Growth Financial Corporation acquired Transcon for $12 on Apr. 1, 1990. That's right. Twelve dollars.

In the next few weeks, liquid and real assets of Transcon were diverted to other Pelullo entities, according to a bankruptcy trustee. The trustee asserted in bankruptcy court in Los Angeles in 1990 that Growth Financial appropriated to itself $1.655 million in cash belonging to Transcon. The trustee said the transfers were only the first of many transactions that would reduce Transcon to a "debt-ridden shell, all in an attempt to move all of Transcon's assets beyond the reach of its creditors."

What happened to the cash that disappeared from Transcon's accounts remains a mystery, but the trustee contended that perhaps $400,000 was diverted to P-I-E, as were tractors and trailers owned by Transcon. If they indeed were diverted to P-I-E, none of these assets helped that company either. It just prolonged the inevitable.

Victor Anderson and his fellow P-I-E workers at the Hagerstown terminal saw it coming. "It just became so obvious the last month they were going to go down," he said. "When you run out of toilet paper and soap, you know it's the end."

Then the company ran out of cash. "It got to the point none of the banks would cash our checks," Anderson recalled. "We had two or three checks bounce and . . . after two weeks none of the banks would cash our checks because the company's checks were bouncing." To solve the problem, P-I-E issued the checks and cashed them in the office at the terminal.

The end came quickly. On Oct. 16, 1990, P-I-E filed for protection from creditors in bankruptcy court in Jacksonville, Florida. Pledging to reorganize and stay in business, the company closed terminals and slashed its work force. It was too late. In early December of that year, the bankruptcy reorganization was converted to a liquidation. P-I-E's few remaining assets were to be sold off.

December 17 was the last workday for Charles Wright at the Hagerstown terminal. After twelve years of steady employment, he was out of a job. To support his wife and two children, he began drawing $215 a week in unemployment compensation. Along with his wages, Wright lost his health benefits. The Teamsters Union offered to provide coverage but he would have to pay the cost. It was an offer he had to pass up.

"When we left, we were told we could pay into the health and welfare program for $432 a month," he said. "But who has $432 a month when you are laid off? How is anybody who's laid off going to afford that? So we don't have any health coverage."

And what of Leonard Pelullo, the man the ICC approved to take over P-I-E? In a criminal case involving events that occurred before Pelullo acquired Transcon and P-I-E, he was convicted in July 1991 of defrauding a Stockton, California, savings and loan and the Royale Group, the company that he controlled, of $2.2 million. In that case, a United States District Court jury in Philadelphia found him guilty on fifty counts of wire fraud and racketeering. Judge Robert F. Kelly sentenced Pelullo to twenty-four years in prison—jailed him immediately and ordered him to pay a fine of $4.4 million and restitution of $2.2 million.

At the sentencing hearing, Judge Kelly posed a rhetorical question concerning Pelullo's control of a public company—a question the ICC might easily have asked at the time of the P-I-E/Transcon merger:

"Why would any public corporation ask him—let him—ever get control of their assets?"

CHAPTER SEVEN

PLAYING RUSSIAN ROULETTE WITH HEALTH INSURANCE

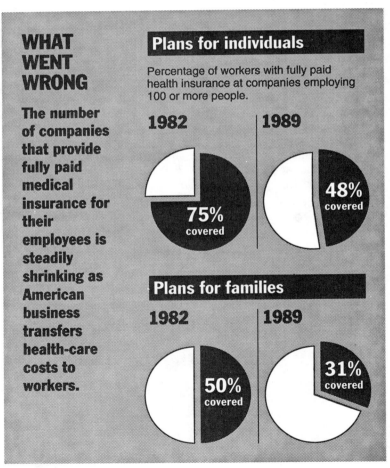

WHAT WENT WRONG

The number of companies that provide fully paid medical insurance for their employees is steadily shrinking as American business transfers health-care costs to workers.

Plans for individuals

Percentage of workers with fully paid health insurance at companies employing 100 or more people.

1982

75% covered

1989

48% covered

Plans for families

1982

50% covered

1989

31% covered

SOURCE: Bureau of Labor Statistics

End of the American Dream

Bobby Jean McLaughlin of Charleston, West Virginia, mother of six and grandmother of six, is a multiple statistic in America's new economic order. Mrs. McLaughlin lost it all. She lost her job, her health insurance, her pension, her savings and, in the end, her husband.

She lost her job as a $6.20-an-hour department store manager, after eighteen years, as a result of the prevailing corporate financial craze. With it, she lost the health insurance that had paid the family medical bills. And she lost her pension when she took the lump sum payment set aside for her retirement and was obliged to use it instead to pay hospital and doctor bills.

She had little choice. Her husband of more than thirty-five years, Joseph, worked in a small bakery in Charleston that did not provide health insurance for its employees. He was suffering from emphysema, his condition deteriorating with each passing day. When he could no longer breathe without the aid of a ventilating machine, he was forced to quit.

Recalled Mrs. McLaughlin: "It just wiped out my savings. I couldn't tell you the amount of money we put out. He was using those tanks of oxygen. And it was just breaking us up, cause they were $38.50 every time they came with one. "I tried to get help with the medical bill, but they look at you like you are dirt under their feet. We were always kind of independent. He worked at the bakery thirty years. He worked even after the doctor told him his lungs were bad enough he could get disability."

In December 1990, Joseph McLaughlin died.

No one, not in the federal government, not in private industry, keeps an accurate count of the Bobby Jean McLaughlins. But their numbers already are in the millions. They are the anonymous middle-class health-care casualties of high-stakes corporate finance in America, the victims of a government rule book that looks after the demands of deal-makers and ignores the needs of ordinary citizens.

They are not poor enough to qualify for state or federal health-assistance programs. They are not affluent enough to be able to afford the cost of private medical insurance.

And so they go without—joining the ranks of an estimated forty million Americans who have no medical insurance. That does not take into account more millions who are underinsured.

Those numbers are bound to grow—unless the United States government reverses policies. Consider:

■ United States Labor Department surveys of large and medium-size companies that offer health insurance for thirty-one million employees

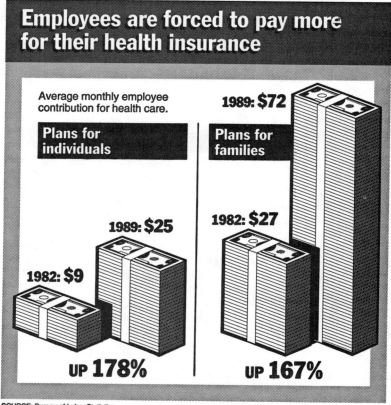

Employees are forced to pay more for their health insurance

Average monthly employee contribution for health care.

Plans for individuals

Plans for families

1982: $9

1989: $25

1982: $27

1989: $72

UP **178%**

UP **167%**

SOURCE: Bureau of Labor Statistics

show that the percentage of those employees with fully paid coverage for themselves alone fell from 75 percent in 1982 to 48 percent in 1989, the latest period studied. (Large and medium-size companies are those with 100 or more employees.)

■ At those same companies, the percentage of employees with fully paid coverage for themselves and members of their families fell from 50 percent in 1982 to 31 percent in 1989.

■ The average monthly employee contribution for individual health-care protection rose from $9 in 1982 to $25 in 1989—an increase of 178 percent. During that same period, the average weekly paycheck went up 25 percent.

■ The average monthly employee contribution for combined individual and family health-care protection rose from $27 in 1982 to $72 in 1989—an increase of 167 percent.

- Because part-time workers seldom receive fully paid fringe benefits, such as health insurance and pensions, their numbers are growing exponentially. Companies like this arrangement because it reduces costs. At Wal-Mart, now the nation's largest retailer, 40 percent of the work force is part-time. At Kmart Corporation, it is 47 percent. At Sears, Roebuck and Company, it is 55 percent.

- As a result of the largest increase in corporate bankruptcies since the Great Depression, millions have lost their health insurance protection. The bankruptcy surge is continuing unabated.

- Faced with steadily rising expenditures for the health-care costs of retirees, companies are curtailing or eliminating a benefit once promised for life. Millions of future retirees will see their coverage disappear. The government's General Accounting Office estimates that companies paid $9 billion in retiree medical costs in 1988, but should have set aside $32 billion for future payments. They did not.

- The number of workers losing their health-care protection grows daily as one company after another dismisses employees to trim expenses, eliminates jobs while seeking to reorganize in bankruptcy court, or goes out of business.

For a lucky few workers across the country in that situation, the government rule book offers some relief. Call it the hospital legal lottery. If you win, your medical bills are paid. If you lose, you pay your own medical bills. But very few win.

Here is how it works: Let's say the company where you have been employed so many years decides to restructure itself to cut its costs. As a part of the realignment, your job is terminated. Suddenly, you lose the health insurance that has been paying your medical bills. You hire a lawyer and sue the company. If you are like most workers, you will lose, which means you will be responsible for all those medical bills. If you are among the lucky few, you will win and recover, if not your health, at least the money you lost.

But the process can be expensive and time-consuming. Ask Roy Mahon, Jr. In 1984 Mahon went to work as a salesman in Garden City, Kansas, for Massey-Ferguson, Ltd., the Canadian company that was one of the world's largest manufacturers of agricultural tractors, combine harvesters and other farm equipment.

"I was a salesman for six months," Mahon recalled, "then I was moved up to store manager."

A year later, Massey-Ferguson executives followed a course charted by so many United States corporations. They reorganized the business, as they put it at the time, to "achieve profitable growth through acquisition." First, in May 1986 they created a new company called Massey Combines Corporation, which took over the money-losing combine operations, including the dealership that employed Mahon in Kansas. The rest of the business operations stayed with the old Massey-Ferguson, which gave itself a new name, Varity Corporation, and sold stock. The proceeds were earmarked for the acquisition of businesses. To soften the impact of the change, Massey-Ferguson executives came up with a name to describe the corporate realignment. They called it "Project Sunshine."

The new Massey Combines got more than just the depressed combine business. It got: About $200 million in debt; about 1,500 employees, including Roy Mahon, and the financial obligation to pay the medical claims and other benefits of retirees and the widows of retirees of the original Massey-Ferguson.

The result was predictable. On Mar. 4, 1988, Massey Combines Corporation went into receivership in Canada, the equivalent of bankruptcy court. The company fired all its employees and notified retirees that their health and other benefits were being terminated.

Roy Mahon remembers that time well. Earlier in the year, he said, "I was working on a new parts counter in our building. I stood up and I thought I had sprained something real bad. Turned out I had an aneurysm and it gave way. That night I was in the hospital. Two days later I had my leg taken off. Consequently, they found out I had an aneurysm in each groin and my aorta was about to blow. . . . So basically the operations were the amputation of the left leg, then aorta surgery, and they went in and rebuilt the area on the right leg. . . . The surgeon spent seven and a half hours on that leg."

Soon after Mahon returned home to recuperate, he discovered something amiss at Massey Combines. "I was wondering what was happening because one of my claims went to the administrator and they sent it back not paid," he said. "The next thing I knew I got a telephone call from my former boss who said the company went belly up. They were bankrupt and everything was gone. . . . That was it. I was left hanging with about $65,000 to $75,000 in hospital bills."

Eventually, Mahon said, Kansas Medicaid paid all but $18,000 to $20,000 of the bills. He had to pay the rest. "I had to cash in my IRA account to survive," he said. "I sold one of my cars. In August 1988, I sold my house to get what I could get out of it because I had to have funds to live on. I had to get these bills down. But consequently I have absolutely no credit whatsoever. . . . Financially, I'm now at the bottom."

A philosophical Mahon—the assets he accumulated over a lifetime parceled out to pay his bills—summed up his situation: "I found out very quickly if you are fifty-six or fifty-seven and have one leg and are trying to get a job, forget it. I had an extensive sales background. But no one was interested after I had the leg removed. I am sorry to say it but it's the facts of life."

That was early in August 1991. Days later, his situation—at least his economic condition—changed. He won the health-care legal lottery. Not long after Mahon and the other Massey Combines employees and retirees lost their health insurance, they retained a law firm to file a class-action lawsuit against Varity. They argued that the creation of Massey Combines was a sham transaction intended to allow the company to escape its obligations to provide health insurance for current and retired employees.

As the case was about to go to trial in United States District Court in Des Moines, Iowa, Mahon and several other more severely disabled workers reached an out-of-court settlement. Mahon, who has since moved to Fort Worth, Texas, said he was uncertain of the exact amount of the settlement, but that his remaining hospital bills were to be paid and he was to be reimbursed for other expenses and losses.

He added: "I just wish this had never happened. If they had done what they said they were going to do, this would have been a lot easier on us. I would probably have come out in a lot better shape. . . . I have no credit. Nobody would probably give me credit now. If I went down to buy a house today they would laugh at me."

As for the other nearly 100 employees who were part of the class-action litigation, a jury, after a trial in September, 1991, found Varity liable for $10 million in actual damages and $36 million in punitive damages. But it could be years before those employees see any money. Varity immediately announced its intention to appeal the verdict, saying that it would "move to set aside the verdict based on its view that the verdict is inconsistent with the law and facts and, if necessary, would vigorously pursue an appeal of the decision." Varity, which was created out of the same Canadian parent company as Massey Combines, contends that it has no responsibility for Massey Combines' former workers.

The workers in the class-action lawsuit fell into several categories. Some, like Mahon, incurred medical expenses after the new Massey Combines was established. Others had disabilities that went back to the old Massey-Ferguson. And then there were the retirees, who maintained that the old Massey-Ferguson had made a commitment to provide health insurance until they died, a commitment that workers in many businesses are led to believe is irrevocable. It is not.

In any event, the economics of it all puzzles Mahon. "Can you imagine," he asked, "what this whole thing is going to cost, all the lawyers' fees? It's unreal. The odd part of it is that Massey-Ferguson had a reputation for taking care of their people. If you said a bad word about Massey-Ferguson, the fight was on. They had that kind of loyalty. But you won't find that any more."

Varity, for its part, is prospering. In March 1988, the same month that Massey Combines went into receivership, Varity reported that it "achieved its highest earnings from operations since 1976." That was $50.6 million. In 1990, it did better: $92.1 million in profits.

The rising profits, though, had a down side: corporate income taxes. But just as the old Massey-Ferguson came up with a solution for its failing combine business that was also a solution to its burdensome benefit commitments, Varity came up with a solution to its tax problem. On July 31, 1991, the Canadian company, which could trace its corporate ancestry to the first Massey manufacturing plant in 1847, reincorporated in Delaware and became a United States company, relocating its world headquarters from Toronto to Buffalo.

So what's the tax advantage for a Canadian company to become a United States company? Remember the net operating loss deduction? The one that has soared out of control, going from $9.4 billion in 1980 to $51.4 billion in 1988—an increase of 447 percent? That is the deduction that allows companies to subtract prior-year losses from their taxable income for up to fifteen years in the future—and avoid paying corporate income taxes.

Listen to how Varity, in reports filed with the Securities and Exchange Commission, explained the benefit of its new American home: "The amount of the United States net operating loss is significantly larger than the net operating loss for Canadian tax purposes. The period that the net operating loss may be carried forward from the year of incurrence for Canadian tax purposes is seven years, whereas for United States tax purposes it is fifteen years."

What kind of money is at stake here? Varity has a net operating loss left over from past years of more than $1 billion. More than half of that sum is in the United States, meaning the company can escape payment of $170 million or so in United States income taxes.

Let us summarize: A Canadian company divides in two, with the slumping business operations and the obligation to pay health-care benefits to one group of workers and retirees dumped into one company (Massey Combines) and the thriving business lines folded into another (Varity). After Massey Combines goes into receivership, leaving its American workers and retirees to fend for themselves, Varity moves to the United States to escape payment of income taxes by taking advantage of the United States net operating loss deduction.

Losing Health Benefits in Bankruptcy

For a growing number of retired people, and future retirees whose ranks will swell by the millions during the 1990s, the rule-makers are playing a kind of health-insurance roulette. It's a game of now-you're-covered, now-you're-not.

The supplemental coverage that companies provide their retired employees is growing in importance because the gap between what Medicare pays and does not pay is steadily increasing. These rising out-of-pocket medical expenses are placing an added burden on people living on fixed incomes.

But corporate promises of lifetime health insurance are vanishing along with the corporations. Depending on the health of your company, you could, after you retire, lose your benefits if the company declares bankruptcy. This could happen the day the company folds, or months or years later. You may lose all of your medical-insurance protection or only a portion of it. You may have to pick up the full tab or only a portion of the bill. All this depends in part on the vagaries of bankruptcy law and whether the company you worked for is being reorganized or liquidated.

Under bankruptcy law, a company can cut off health benefits to retirees almost immediately after it files for bankruptcy protection, if it files under Chapter 7, the liquidation section, of the bankruptcy code. If, however, the company files under Chapter 11, the reorganization section, it must continue payment of benefits and can only terminate them with court approval. The distinction between the chapters stems from the Retiree Benefits Bankruptcy Protection Act, which was passed amid great fanfare in 1988 with lawmakers claiming that retiree health care benefits would henceforth be protected when a company sought bankruptcy court protection.

As Senator Howard Metzenbaum, the Ohio Democrat, told the Senate on May 23, 1988: "[This] legislation is a major reform of our bankruptcy laws. It protects retiree health and life insurance benefits when companies go into bankruptcy. This measure sends a strong and powerful message to companies which make promises to their workers—you cannot use the bankruptcy courts as a way of reneging on retiree promises."

But if the company is in weakened financial condition with few assets, the distinction between Chapter 7 and 11, and the protections that Senator Metzenbaum said the 1988 act afforded, are meaningless.

Retirees of Garfinckel's, Inc., Washington, D.C.'s, once-premier department store chain, learned that lesson the hard way in 1991. They also learned that, however sincere the motives of lawmakers, there is a difference between Capitol Hill rhetoric and reality. Following a dizzying series of events in which Garfinckel's was bought and sold five times in ten years, Garfinckel's entered bankruptcy court in 1990 under Chapter 11 and shortly afterward closed all its stores and began liquidating assets. In addition to putting 800 people out of work, the shutdown led to the cancellation of health benefits for retired employees.

In May 1991, Judge S. Martin Teel, Jr., of the United States Bankruptcy Court in the District of Columbia, responding to a request by Garfinckel's attorneys, approved an order terminating payments to the retiree health plans. The retired employees have since filed claims with the court, calculating the value of their lost health benefits based on their years of life expectancy. But they will receive, if anything, only a fraction of the value of their claims. As Judge Teel noted when he approved the order: "All indications are that there's likely to be very little for unsecured creditors."

For most of the retirees, cancellation of benefits meant they went without the additional coverage provided by a lower-cost group plan such as Garfinckel's. "They had been part of a larger group so they benefitted from the costs associated with that," said John Noble, a lawyer who represented them. "For them to go out into the market and get coverage was simply impossible. Many were probably uninsurable because of preexisting conditions."

Much the same kind of process was underway, though on a much wider scale, in the Eastern Airlines bankruptcy case. One group of Eastern retirees, those sixty-five years old or older, lost its company-provided health care in 1991 after the airline filed for bankruptcy. Another group, those under sixty-five, has twice postponed the cutoff of its benefits. After Eastern sought bankruptcy court protection in 1989, it tried to reorganize, but after that failed the airline in January 1991 shut down operations and began liquidating assets. Five months later, in May 1991, the trustee overseeing Eastern for the bankruptcy court applied for permission to terminate the health benefits of 11,000 retirees.

"The trustee recognizes that numerous retirees will suffer hardship as a result of the termination of the retiree benefits," the trustee wrote in a petition to the court. "However, inasmuch as the liquidation of Eastern's estate will generate barely enough funds to satisfy the costs of liquidation and make a token distribution to creditors, the continued payment of retiree benefits can no longer be justified given the trustee's obligation as a fiduciary to Eastern's estate and its creditors."

When a committee of Eastern retirees asked the court to block the move, a compromise was struck in which coverage was dropped for those over sixty-five in return for providing benefits for the under-sixty-five group until the end of 1991. William G. Bell, a lawyer representing the retirees, said the decision was made to give up the coverage of those over sixty-five and try to preserve benefits for those under sixty-five, who were not covered by Medicare. Those under sixty-five also had to kick in $75 a month toward their own coverage. In December 1991, a United States Bankruptcy Court judge extended the coverage through 1992, instructing Eastern to pay an additional $20.4 million—an amount equal to the cost of providing the retiree health benefits program in 1991.

"We got a year's extension," said Bell. "But who knows? We could be back in six months or nine months asking for more. There are a lot of variables."

What will the Eastern retirees do when that money runs out? "We have been living with this ever since Eastern went down," said Vito Borrelli, a vice president of the Eastern Airlines Retirees Association in Miami. "We'll cross that bridge when we come to it. Who knows what will happen."

Exactly how soon the Eastern retirees get to that bridge depends on the success of the airline's program to sell off its assets. The company still has $250 million in assets to dispose of, including a sizable number of mothballed aircraft. With the collapse of so many airlines in recent years, the used airplane market is glutted. With a large inventory and few buyers, prices are depressed. Over the long term all the Eastern retirees will lose their benefits, as almost all retirees eventually do when a company goes bankrupt.

When the retirees' lawyer, Bell, was asked the solution to the health benefits crisis affecting retirees at Eastern and other bankrupt corporations, he said: "I hope it's a Congress that gives us a national health plan. I told the judge in bankruptcy court 'Just give us two years. Then maybe both parties are going to have to act on this.'"

Whatever the future holds, the present is abundantly clear: Many corporations are systematically scaling back the health-care coverage they provide. At large companies, workers are being forced to assume a growing share of the costs, through higher deductibles or increased copayments. At small companies, the coverage is being eliminated.

The people who write the government rule book have a solution. Congress, which wrote the rules that encouraged the corporate restructuring that led to the collapse of many businesses, the realignment of others—and in the process the elimination of health-care benefits for millions of workers—is at work on legislation that it promises will guarantee medical insurance for everyone: Compel all employers—large and small—to provide health insurance.

But employers say they can't afford it. Neither can Bobby Jean McLaughlin. For eighteen years, Mrs. McLaughlin had worked for Heck's, Inc., a regional discount department-store chain based in Nitro, West Virginia, near Charleston. She began as a clerk at the Charleston store on Oct. 23, 1967, worked her way up to become manager of the toy department, and, for the last six years of her employment, was manager of the cosmetics department.

The retailer was prospering, growing from a single store in downtown Charleston to a regional chain with more than 120 stores scattered across the Middle Atlantic states. Then the new management took over. That was 1983. And the business went awry.

The layoffs came first, as the jobs of a select number of employees were eliminated. Next came individual store closings. And finally bankruptcy and the death of a retailer and more than 7,000 jobs.

The layoffs began in October 1985. On Tuesday, Oct. 15, 1985, just twelve days short of her eighteenth anniversary at Heck's, Mrs. McLaughlin and another employee were summoned to a meeting with the store manager and district manager. "They told me that my job was eliminated," she said. "They eliminated two department managers in each store. . . . You go all your life thinking something like this couldn't happen."

Mrs. McLaughlin wondered whether she could work as a clerk instead of a department manager. "I even asked them if they had any kind of job in that store that I could do," she said. Their reply: "No, ma'am."

"And I said, 'After all these years you can't find a job for me in this store?'" The answer: "No, ma'am."

Mrs. McLaughlin, fifty-seven, once described her years at Heck's this way: "I was at work every day and was never late. . . . I was never disciplined. I received good evaluations. . . . I was never reprimanded or told that my work was unsatisfactory." Nevertheless, the firing was swift and immediate. She was told to get her things "and leave the store," she said.

"They treated you like . . . you done something wrong after working for them all those years. . . . It hurts you when you work in a place for . . . years and they treat you like that."

Not only was Mrs. McLaughlin out of work, but the health insurance that paid her husband's costly medical bills was gone. Private insurance was unaffordable. Eventually, he had to quit his bakery job and was hospitalized twice, in 1988 and 1989. "I think he was in there about seven days the first time," she said, and "it was about ten or eleven days the last time." On the second stay, he spent about five days in the intensive care unit. "There was one test they run on him," she said, "it was close to $1,000."

In August 1990, when the couple was interviewed in their home, McLaughlin, who despite his serious illness was given to quiet witticisms, was tied to an oxygen machine by an umbilical cord. It was long enough that it allowed him to walk slowly through the rooms of their one-story house.

He was disconnected from the life-support system only when his wife had to drive him to the doctor's office. "It's really hard on him," she said at the time. "It's just gotten that bad in the last year or two. I've been trying to pay the hospital a little at a time. The guy from the hospital calls every month if I'm late. . . . The medicine runs me a fortune. It just wiped out my savings."

Three months later, Joseph McLaughlin returned to the hospital for cataract surgery. "He did real well with it," his wife said. The following month, on Dec. 7, he died at age fifty-nine.

Now Bobby Jean McLaughlin works full time at the bakery—the same bakery where her husband spent his working life. The pay is at the minimum-wage level. And she is confronted with a hospital bill that she said has "something like a balance of $24,000." It was turned over to a collection agency.

The bill collector "was calling me quite a bit," she said. "And he would call and ask to speak to Joe. After I told him my husband had died, he would still call me and ask to speak to Joe. I do okay, you know, just paying my utility bills and paying my property taxes and stuff like that. But I just can't pay this hospital bill."

She added: "It has made a nervous wreck out of me."

Death of a Department Store

In March 1987 Russell L. Isaacs, the chief executive officer of Heck's, Inc., the department store chain where Bobby Jean McLaughlin had worked, received a singular honor. He was selected by the Horatio Alger Association as one of ten people from across the country to receive its annual Distinguished American Award.

The fifty-four-year-old Isaacs that month joined a prestigious roster of previous award-winners. They included Bernard M. Baruch, adviser to seven presidents; Raymond A. Kroc, the founder of McDonald's Corporation; Dr. Michael E. DeBakey, the pioneering heart transplant surgeon; and Sam Moore Walton, the cofounder of Wal-Mart Stores and one of America's ten wealthiest individuals.

Intended to recognize rags-to-riches success stories, the awards are given, in the association's words, to show young people that "opportunity still knocks in America for anyone willing to work." The association and its awards are named for the author of the popular nineteenth-century novels— *Ragged Dick* and *Luck and Pluck*, among others—that recounted the tales of young boys who achieved success, fame and wealth through hard work, perseverance, honesty and luck. The association described the 1987 winners in general as "role models who give others a different kind of inspiration to succeed."

In Isaacs's case, the association related the rise of the store executive from an impoverished West Virginia family—his father was a coal miner and his mother "suffered an apparent stroke" during the birth of her seventh child—to become chairman and chief executive of Heck's, a discount department-store chain. The association said it was most fortuitous that Heck's directors had selected Isaacs, who once had been the company's chief financial officer, to run the entire operation: "Giving Isaacs free rein has proven to be a wise decision. . . . His previous knowledge of the company gave him an advantage in implementing changes he thought most beneficial to the company."

Well, not exactly. Actually, Russell Isaacs had just overseen three consecutive years of losses adding up to $31 million. He had directed the closing of three dozen stores scattered across several states. He had fired hundreds of employees, including Bobby Jean McLaughlin and many others who had worked at Heck's for ten or fifteen years or more. And he had presided over the company's relentless downhill decline—a decline that in time would lead to the elimination of thousands of jobs.

In fact, on Mar. 5, 1987—the week before Isaacs was inducted into the Horatio Alger Association at a dinner in Washington—Heck's, Inc. filed for bankruptcy protection. The irony is not an isolated one. For Russell Isaacs, the $300,000-a-year chief executive, is little different from thousands of other executives and investors who have assumed control of American corporations—from retailing businesses to manufacturing plants.

He is a financial officer by training. And by all accounts a good one. But aside from a grasp of the numbers, his critics say, he had little understanding of the business he was running, or what made it work.

Listen to Douglas R. Cook, one of the founders of Heck's who left when Isaacs took over: "Russell is a certified public accountant and a good financial man. Unfortunately . . . there's a difference between a financial man and a hands-on manager." Cook, who with three other men built Heck's from a single department store in Charleston to a chain of more than 120 stores across the Middle Atlantic states, added: "I always tell people, if you started out to destroy a company, you couldn't have done as good a job as Russell Isaacs did. . . . He . . . tried to make a lot of changes, tried to fix a lot of things that weren't broken."

Isaacs has a different explanation. When Kmart and Hills built stores "two or three times the size of ours, you know it doesn't take a rocket scientist to figure out you can't compete with that size store," he said. "Just picture a 40,000-square-foot store beside a 120,000-square-foot store. Where's the customer going to go? He's going to go where the selection is the greatest and prices are the best."

While Heck's no longer exists and thousands of employees lost their jobs, there were a few notable financial success stories. One was that of Russell Isaacs. As was the case with many corporate executives and investors, Isaacs, his managers and those who followed him received millions of dollars, collectively, in generous compensation packages, pensions and severance contracts.

By contrast, Patsy J. Perry of Teas Valley, West Virginia, one of the many longtime Heck's workers dismissed by Isaacs and his successors during a string of failed reorganization efforts, received little more than $1,000. The money represented her pension for twelve years' work. There was no severance pay for Perry, fifty-six, who lives alone and supports herself. There was no interim allowance to tide her over until she found another job.

More important for Perry, a diabetic who takes insulin daily, the medical insurance that Heck's provided was terminated. For two years, Perry said, she could not afford regular medical checkups. Her vision deteriorated because of the diabetes.

Still, she recalled fondly the early years at Heck's. "We were just like one big family," she said. "In fact, that's what they called it, Heck's family." To understand how that family was born and prospered, and then withered and died, it is necessary to turn back the clock to 1959.

The place is downtown Charleston, in an empty building that had housed a Kaiser-Fraser auto dealership. It was there that Fred Haddad, brothers Tom and Lester Ellis, and Douglas Cook opened their first discount department store. Haddad and the Ellises had operated competing stores in nearby Madison, West Virginia. Cook was working for a wholesale distributor.

The new store, called Heck's after the letters in the names of the founders and two friends, proved an instant success. A second was opened in 1960 in St. Albans, West Virginia, Cook recalled, "and about a week or two later we opened our third store in Huntington." Fred Haddad was Heck's chairman and president, a hands-on executive who wandered through the stores and knew his employees by name. Cook was in charge of merchandising and advertising.

By 1963 they had expanded beyond West Virginia, opening stores in Kentucky, Maryland and Virginia. From the very beginning, according to

Cook, the company was profitable: "We showed a good profit. And it was profitable every year up until, say, 1984."

By 1983, when Haddad retired and sold his Heck's stock, the company had grown to 122 stores with annual sales of $435 million. Although net income trailed off in 1983 to $10 million from a peak of $15 million in 1980, Heck's still had posted twenty-four consecutive years of profits. Then it all unraveled.

Haddad was replaced by Russell Isaacs, who had worked for Heck's in the 1960s and 1970s before becoming executive vice president of Wheat First Securities, Inc., a Richmond, Virginia, brokerage firm. Haddad was a retailer by instinct. Isaacs was a trained certified public accountant. *Discount Store News,* a trade publication, related this account of the differences between the two men: "Unlike Fred Haddad, his predecessor, who was described by one Heck's executive as a hip-pocket entrepreneur, Isaacs is seen as a professional executive who has taken the entrepreneur's room at the top and made it big enough to hold a management team."

Isaacs recruited new managers, introduced new marketing concepts, redesigned store layouts, and added a new computer system. In a report to stockholders, Isaacs recited the achievements for his first full year in charge: "Cramming into one year an effort that normally requires three to five years to achieve, Heck's in 1984 reset, or relaid, the floor plans of 105 of the company's 125 discount department stores in nine states. Accompanied in many cases by partial or full remodeling, the reset stores were made to conform to highly successful prototype retail units tested over the past years."

As part of the sweeping overhaul, Isaacs told shareholders, "each store was planogrammed, a photo-optical process that allocates product space uniformly . . . according to a master plan based upon sales." He explained: "Hence, fast-moving products were given greater shelf space and a better position than slower-moving items. In addition, low-profit and marginal products were dropped from Heck's product mix, an important step in improving store productivity."

The rearranged layouts, Isaacs said, included "one or more racetrack aisles leading shoppers to prominent departments through the store. The racetracks were dotted with speed tables featuring fast-moving and desirable merchandise to attract shoppers." Isaacs concluded that "though the overall effort was massive and frequently caused dislocation to shoppers, the initial results indicate a positive response."

Well, not too positive. Despite—or perhaps because of—the racetrack aisles, photo-optical process and upscale merchandise, Heck's celebrated its silver anniversary in 1984 by recording its first loss ever: $8 million. Along the way, veteran Heck's employees heard a mounting chorus of complaints from customers who were irked when they were unable to buy products the chain had stocked for years but no longer carried.

Like Lucite paint. Perry said it was one of the biggest sellers in the store where she worked, but the new management "did away with it and went to another brand. . . . I know the other paint didn't sell."

Douglas Cook agreed. "We had a big following in that," he said. "We had regular customers. . . . We did a terrific amount of Lucite business. . . . The first thing that Russell Isaacs's new management team does is throw out Lucite paint. . . . That's a good example of why . . . the customers get upset."

The ever-changing store layouts also caused confusion. "Every time you turned around," Perry said, "they were changing something. All the customers complained because they never could find anything." In any event, Russell Isaacs, fresh from the experiences of his own investment firm and a satellite Wall Street investment house, plunged ahead—with more changes.

He next did what so many other executives were—and still are—doing when confronted with an ailing business: He sought to acquire other businesses. In 1985 he bought another retailer, Maloney Enterprises, Inc., which operated thirty-four discount department stores in Heck's marketing area. The selling price was right. That's because Maloney's had filed for reorganization under the United States Bankruptcy Code in 1982 and was just emerging from court protection. The acquisition, completed in August 1985, brought the number of Heck's stores to 166.

That same month Heck's picked up a quick $9 million from the IRS by applying its 1984 net operating loss against taxes paid in earlier years when the company was profitable. Even so, Heck's was sinking fast.

On Sept. 4, 1985, the company borrowed $4 million from Algemene Bank Nederland N.V., a Netherlands bank. Two weeks later, on Sept. 17, it borrowed an additional $1 million. Next, it began firing dozens of workers. On Friday, Oct. 11, 1985, Heck's management sat down to decide who would go. It later seemed to some that many employees selected for termination were those with the most experience—and the most pay and benefits.

There was S. Pearl Lovejoy, who was earning $6.61 an hour as a supervisor after sixteen years with Heck's. That gave her a base salary of under $14,000 a year. There was Bobby Jean McLaughlin, who was earning $6.20 an hour as a department manager after eighteen years with Heck's. That gave her a base salary of less than $13,000 a year. And there was Patsy Perry, who was earning $5.60 an hour as a supervisor after twelve years with Heck's. That gave her a base salary of under $12,000 a year.

All three women were in their fifties. Each worked at a different store in the Charleston area. Each got the word on her termination during individual meetings around lunch time on Tuesday, Oct. 15. As Mrs. Lovejoy later described her abrupt dismissal in a court document: A district manager said there were going to be cutbacks in each store, that another employee "and I were the two to go. He said the quicker you get to the unemployment office the quicker you will receive your checks. You will receive your vacation pay for 1986 plus any retirement due you in one lump sum. You can check out and leave now."

In an interview, Mrs. Lovejoy recalled that "they told me they were paying me too much money."

Perry recounted her dismissal in an interview: "They just came in one morning, the store manager and the supervisor, and called me and another lady and told us as of today we were being laid off. And she had worked longer than I had. . . . She was in cosmetics. . . . I was over all the [cash] registers. . . .

"I was so upset. I asked them if we could work in a different part of the store if they were doing away with our jobs. And they said no, they weren't doing it that way. . . . They were just letting us go. . . . I was fifty and I think Inez must have been about fifty-seven, the lady that got laid off when I did. They called it laid off, but then later they called it terminated. . . . They had us to go home as soon as they told us. They thought it would be better if we leave the store immediately, they said."

The employees were stunned. "It was a shock," Perry said. "My mother was here visiting. . . . When I came home, I cried and cried. She nearly thought I was going to have a stroke. That night, the girls from the store kept coming over to the house. It was like a funeral."

The timing of her firing had a bitter twist for Perry, who had lived for years in her own home in St. Albans, West Virginia, about fifteen miles from the store. "I sold it in September," she said, "and bought me a little trailer and a lot . . . so I'd be close to work and I could be here till I retired . . . about five minutes away. And then I got laid off the next month."

Fifty Years Old and Out of Work

Other former Heck's employees, particularly those over forty, found themselves unable to obtain a job that paid comparable wages or benefits. Betty Jean Thompson, a widow, was terminated as a $6.09-an-hour department manager after eleven years. Thompson, who turned sixty in 1991, eventually was hired by another retailer—but for only twenty hours' work a week. Her new salary: $3.50 an hour. That represented a 43 percent pay cut. There was no health insurance. No life insurance. No pension.

For a brief time, the firings of people such as Betty Jean Thompson and Bobby Jean McLaughlin and Patsy Perry and Pearl Lovejoy appeared to stem the tide of red ink at Heck's. Indeed, company executives forecast a return to profitability by year's end.

The optimism was unfounded. As it turned out, Heck's new management team had failed to detect data errors in yet another of its fresh merchandising and cost-control innovations—a new computerized accounting system. The computer, it seemed, abetted by human error, ran amok. Price markdowns on merchandise went unrecorded, thereby creating fictitious profits. Invoices were incorrectly marked, which led to the reordering of unneeded goods. A company spokesman was quoted as saying: "When you have computers and people messing up, you have a big problem." By the time all the bookkeeping errors had been corrected, Heck's had posted a $5 million loss for 1985.

The longtime employees had seen it coming. Recalled Bobby Jean McLaughlin: "I would order six eyebrow pencils. Two or three dozen would come in. . . . They had people who didn't know what they were doing." That was none too surprising, given the stream of new management recruits. "That's all you saw," she said, "were people from different places. They brought people in to show us how to set the shelves and all that stuff, like we weren't smart enough. They brought all those big shots in."

Isaacs labeled the accounting breakdown nothing more than "a temporary setback in our efforts to return the company to a strong, profitable operation." Nevertheless, to shore up Heck's shaky finances, the board of directors in April 1986 embarked on another money-raising course: It voted to raid the company's pension fund.

On Oct. 30, 1986, Heck's informed the Pension Benefit Guaranty Corporation that it intended to withdraw $4.6 million of the $7.4 million in the retirement fund. Heck's management was going to take 62 percent of the fund's assets and use them to help bail out the business. That would leave 38 percent of the assets, or $2.8 million, to be distributed among 3,251 employees with vested pensions.

That worked out to an average of $861 for each employee. Isaacs and Ray O. Darnall, who had served as president and later vice chairman of the Heck's board, did a little better. According to records filed with the Securities and Exchange Commission, Isaacs collected $134,494 from the pension plan, and Darnall picked up $397,851.

The pension fund raid failed to shore up the company's shaky finances. Heck's ended 1986 with a loss of $18 million. On Mar. 5, 1987, four months after Heck's submitted the pension plan termination to the PBGC, the company filed for protection in United States Bankruptcy Court. As the year wore on, however, Isaacs expressed continued confidence in the plan to restore Heck's to profitability. To that end, in August 1987 he announced the appointment of a new president with a similar-sounding name. He was John R. Isaac, Jr., who had worked for several retailers, including Service Merchandise Company and a subsidiary of Federated Department Stores.

Russell Isaacs was enthusiastic about the new president: "We believe his extensive retailing background will be instrumental in helping Heck's effect the recovery it has been working so diligently to achieve. I'm just tickled to death with him."

John Isaac most recently had been president of Tradevest, Inc., a Florida mail-order company that attorneys general in several states had labeled a pyramid scheme. Tradevest peddled $789 subscriptions to a mail-order purchase club. Once people joined the club, they could sell subscriptions to others and collect a commission. In return for their fee, members were assured they could earn a rebate of 90 percent of what they spent buying products. The rebate would come as an annuity—to be paid twenty years after the purchase. Soon after John Isaac left the mail-order business to take over day-to-day operations at Heck's, Tradevest filed for protection under the U.S. Bankruptcy Code.

But John Isaac was confident about Heck's. A discount-store trade publication quoted him at the time as saying that "the company has been making good progress in redefining its basic core group of stores and in re-evaluating its future direction. I'm very optimistic about our prospects." Once more, the optimism proved unfounded. Heck's ended 1987 with another loss. In fact, the loss of $61 million was almost double the cumulative losses of the preceding three years.

John Isaac, who recruited new management, including former employees at Tradevest, ended the year by closing eight more stores and dismissing scores of employees. By June 1988 John Isaac had a new plan: He would sell off or close forty additional stores, fire hundreds more employees. A company news release used all the catch phrases that have become so much a part of corporate jargon to justify eliminating businesses. John Isaac said, "The restructuring would enable the company to dispose of assets which have not provided an adequate return on investment . . . and which the company believes provide only limited growth potential for the future."

It was to no avail. The losses continued to pile up. Heck's stores continued to disappear. From a high of 166 stores, the retailer shrank to fifty-five stores. Employment plummeted from more than 7,000 workers to 1,700. By January 1990 the name Heck's had vanished; the remaining stores were renamed the Take 10 Discount Club—as in pay $5 to become a member and take 10 percent off everything. Total Heck's losses for 1988 and 1989: $85.5 million. In February 1990 the management of Take 10 Discount Club sold the business to a subsidiary of Jordache Enterprises, Inc. The sale price: $1 and the assumption of $22 million in debt. The remaining stores scattered across the hills of Appalachia were relabeled L.A. Joe Department Stores. One year later, L.A. Joe was in bankruptcy court. The stores have since been closed.

Two footnotes to the collapse of a once-successful regional retailer: John Isaac, who earned $360,000 a year in the top job at Heck's, and four associates who managed the final dismantling of the company, collected more than $1.5 million in severance pay. And about two dozen lawyers who oversaw the formal breakup of the company in bankruptcy court collected additional millions of dollars. The top lawyers, paid at the rate of $200 an hour, collected in less than four hours the amount of money the average Heck's employee—whose job was eventually terminated—received for his or her lifetime retirement.

By the way, the lawyers also got a piece of the proceeds from the terminated pension plan. It happened this way: By the time Heck's completed the paperwork on ending the retirement system, the company already was in bankruptcy proceedings and the more than $4 million removed from the fund got tied up in the process.

The bankruptcy court eventually approved a plan that called for 20 percent of the money to go to Heck's for operating the business, and the remaining 80 percent to go into a cash pool. That cash pool was used to pay the administrative costs of bankruptcy, including attorney's fees, and unsecured creditors such as Pittsburgh National Bank, Algemene Bank of Nederland N.V., General Electric Company, International Business Machines Corporation, Black and Decker Corporation and Eveready Battery Company, Inc.

In any event, there were no million-dollar severance packages for employees who were thrown out of work when the stores closed, or who, like Patsy Perry, lost their jobs in the earlier failed restructuring.

Although she subsequently found work in a convenience store, Perry said that she did not make as much as she did at Heck's. What's more, two years went by before she qualified for medical insurance. During that time, her eyesight deteriorated and she had laser surgery on both eyes. She also underwent a hysterectomy. As for the medical bills run up during the time she had no health insurance, Perry said: "I still owe almost $4,000 to them people which I can't begin to pay. So I don't know what's going to happen."

When she was off work for an extended period, she lost her job at the convenience store. She later found another job working about thirty hours a week for minimum wage. It provides some insurance. The job is at a Value City discount store housed in an old Heck's building.

CHAPTER EIGHT

SIMPLICITY PATTERN— IRRESISTIBLE TO RAIDERS

WHAT WENT WRONG

Simplicity Pattern Co. was sitting on tens of millions in cash and investments in 1981. It was too good to pass up.

Over a decade, six moneymen made runs at the dowager company. When they were done, the money was gone. And Simplicity was drowning in debt.

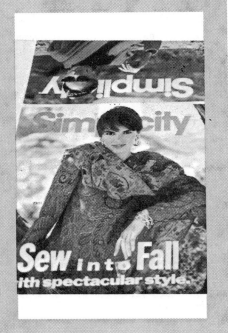

The Raiders Attack

It was the fall of 1979 when the first of the moneymen descended on the Simplicity Pattern Company. By the time they were finished a decade later, a company that once had $100 million in the bank was more than $100 million in the hole.

For more than half a century, Simplicity was as much a part of the American home as the radio and the sewing machine. It helped dress generations of girls and boys, women and men, through the sale of billions of patterns for the home-sewing market. Decade after decade, the company's revenues grew. It enjoyed good relations with a loyal work force at its plant in Niles, Michigan. But, as with many mature companies, the earnings from Simplicity's major business, the sale of patterns, had begun to trail off in the late 1970s, a problem the company's management had yet to deal with.

Then came the moneymen.

They were men like John Brooks Fuqua, an Atlanta investor who made so much money swapping corporations like cards in a poker game that he once earned a spot on *Forbes* magazine's list of the 400 richest Americans. And Victor Posner, another onetime member of the *Forbes* 400, a Miami Beach wheeler-dealer who led Sharon Steel Corporation into bankruptcy court and was convicted of filing false income tax returns to evade more than $1 million in taxes. There was Graham Ferguson Lacey, a British takeover artist and born-again evangelist who prayed with Jimmy Carter at the White House. And Charles E. Hurwitz, a Houston investor whose business associates included former president Gerald R. Ford and Michael Milken, who went to prison for securities-law violations.

There were others, and throughout the 1980s they all worked their managerial and financial wizardry on Simplicity Pattern. When they were done, they had turned a venerable, money-making business, which paid federal income taxes, into a money-losing business that paid no federal income taxes. They had, in fact, driven Simplicity to the edge of bankruptcy.

In that decade, the moneymen:

■ Bought and sold the company four times and made tens of millions of dollars running up the price of Simplicity stock in threatened and actual takeovers.

■ Drained $100 million that Simplicity had in its bank account and investment portfolio.

■ Raided the company's pension funds on two occasions, taking out $10.7 million.

- Issued bonds and borrowed from banks, sending the company's debt soaring from near nothing to $100 million.
- Sold off properties to raise badly needed cash after they had depleted the company's $100 million cushion.
- Created so much debt that Simplicity could no longer generate enough cash to make the interest payments.
- Defaulted on the interest payments on bonds and bank loans.

It was just one more American business success story—if you measure success by how much money assorted investors made buying and selling Simplicity stock and buying and selling the company itself. And they got help from the United States government rule book. Thanks to several provisions of the federal tax code, including the net operating loss deduction and the deduction for interest expense, they were able to build their empires on debt and write off the interest. So the raids that cost hundreds of Americans their jobs and made millions for the raiders were, in effect, subsidized by the American taxpayer.

Consider John Brooks Fuqua, who accumulated enough of a fortune that he earned the ultimate accolade, a business school named in his honor—the Fuqua School of Business at Duke University. Fuqua was the third of the four moneymen who acquired Simplicity in the 1980s. Fuqua, seventy-three, was chairman of Triton Group, Ltd., a Los Angeles company that in an earlier incarnation, under a different name and management, had been a failed real estate investment trust. In 1983, three years after the company emerged from bankruptcy proceedings, Fuqua and several associates took control of Triton, which was little more than a corporate shell.

For investors, Triton painted a cheery picture of a Fuqua-led future. In a report to stockholders, the company said: "The objective of the Fuqua group investors is to create value for all Triton stockholders. . . . Several years ago Fuqua took over the management of a similar publicly owned former real estate investment trust. Fuqua undertook a corporate restructuring comparable to that underway at Triton and in five years that company's stock increased fifteen times in value."

In any event, Triton purchased Simplicity Pattern for $65 million in late 1984 and sold it three years later for $117 million, for a profit of $52 million before taxes. That was good for Triton. It was not so good for Simplicity Pattern. The company, bought with borrowed money, was burdened with so much debt that it couldn't sell patterns fast enough to pay the interest on its bonds and loans.

And it definitely wasn't good for Simplicity's employees—people such as Charlotte L. Mitchell, a secretary at the plant since 1970. On June 8, 1988, six months after Fuqua's group sold Simplicity to Wesray Capital, Mitchell got a big surprise. It was on her birthday. "They [her co-workers] had a big party for me in the office," she remembered. During the party, she recalled, "My boss got back and he said, 'Charlotte, I've just been told you are going to be let go.'"

Others got the news equally abruptly. Mitchell told of a secretary who had been on sick leave. Her bosses called her at home and said they'd like to take her to breakfast. "After breakfast was over, they told her she didn't have a job to come back to," Mitchell said. However the notification, the reasons were the same: debt and declining sales.

That was the explanation given to Edgar C. Stanley, manager of the bindery and finishing department, who had been at the plant since 1971. He was dismissed the same day as Mitchell. In a "Dear Ed" letter, Charles E. DeWitt, a vice president and plant director, wrote: "As you know, the performance of the home sewing market has been weak and sales trends in the industry for the first five months of 1988 have been soft. These unit sales declines and our outstanding debt have created the need for Simplicity to reduce costs. . . . The decision was made that Simplicity must reduce its work force. . . . Thus, effective today, your employment with Simplicity will end."

At sixty-two, after more than seventeen years at Simplicity, Stanley was out on the street. His medical insurance was paid for three months, after which he was on his own. His life insurance was paid for two months, after which he was on his own. And he got a reduced pension. The new Simplicity executives had handled the layoffs with about as much skill as their predecessors had dealt with the company's underlying problems. Which is to say that Simplicity Pattern was hardly a model of a well-managed company.

The Trouble Starts

Simplicity had been founded in New York City in 1927 by an advertising man, Joseph M. Shapiro, and his son, James. It opened the Niles plant in 1931 and, through low prices and solid marketing, became the world's largest pattern maker. But in the mid-1970s, a disturbing trend began to emerge.

Although the company was financially healthy, it was making more and more of its money from its investments, less and less from the sale of patterns. Between 1976 and 1980, income from patterns dropped from $24 million to $9 million. During those years, income from investments rose from $3 million to $9 million. The explanation was simple enough. As more women left the home and moved into the work force, they had less time for sewing. Fewer women making clothes for their families meant the sale of fewer patterns.

While that trend had been clear for some years, Simplicity's longtime management seemed unable to develop other business lines to take advantage of the company's equipment and expertise. In short, Simplicity Pattern was a Harvard Business School case study of a stagnating company— an entrenched management unable to meet the challenges of a changing market. Simplicity was also a company ready-made for the corporate raiders.

By the early 1980s, the raiders were being glorified as the saviors of American business: MBAs flying about the country buying up companies, ousting unimaginative managers, installing tight spending controls, selling off or shutting down peripheral operations, restructuring businesses and putting them back on a solid foundation. That, anyway, was the image.

As Drexel Burnham Lambert, Inc., the Wall Street investment house, explained to a congressional committee in March 1985: "Drexel believes that corporations that have undergone restructuring as a result of acquisition activity or strategic change have evolved into stronger companies better equipped to compete in today's domestic and international markets. An unsolicited acquisition can also result in the replacement of management with a new team better able to realize the full potential of a target company. . . . Merger and acquisition activity results in a shifting of assets to more productive uses."

Not really. Drexel Burnham itself proved that. It filed for bankruptcy court protection in February 1990, a victim of its own philosophy. Simplicity Pattern was another victim of that philosophy. Its story, with variations, has been repeated at hundreds of businesses, with the same consequences for tens of thousands of workers.

It began in 1979, when corporate raiders started poring over Simplicity's financial documents, taking note of the more than $100 million parked in investments and pension funds. Among the early arrivals was Victor Posner, an investor described by one newspaper as a "corporation empire-builder." While empire building, Posner arranged for the publicly owned corporations that he controlled to pay personal and living expenses for himself and his family. Securities and Exchange Commission records show that corporate funds were used to redecorate his apartment, to buy jewelery, to pay for groceries and for the yachts that his Sharon Steel Corporation—based in the landlocked western Pennsylvania community of Sharon—owned and docked next to Posner's home in Miami Beach.

Posner began acquiring Simplicity stock in earnest in August 1979. Over the next four months, his holdings grew to more than one million shares, or 7 percent of the stock. The four-month cost: $7.1 million. Drexel Burnham fanned the speculative fever after Simplicity postponed its annual shareholders' meeting in 1980. In a report to its clients, the investment firm suggested that Simplicity management had delayed the meeting because it feared it might lose control of the company. That fear was good reason to speculate in Simplicity stock. As Drexel Burnham put it: "Such a change in management is, in our judgment, a valid reason for speculating in the shares for those who are inclined to a short-term philosophy."

Meanwhile, Posner continued to add to his Simplicity holdings. By the end of 1980, he owned 1.2 million shares, or nearly 9 percent of the company.

In Niles, Simplicity's management was trying to cut costs and threatening to move the company to a part of the country where wages and costs would be lower. Under the headline, "Simplicity considers abandoning Niles plant," the South Bend (Indiana) Tribune on Nov. 8, 1980, quoted Kenneth James, the company's director of employee relations, as saying: "We've got to look at the alternatives of getting out of here."

Company officials kept the pressure on in the weeks that followed, saying at one point that they were looking at possible sites in Kansas where the Niles plant could be moved. In the end, Simplicity's unions agreed to concessions that would cut the manufacturing payroll by 10 percent over the next four years and the company agreed to stay in Niles, at least through September 1985. With the labor concessions in hand in Niles, the takeover action began to heat up on Wall Street.

In a friendly deal initiated by Simplicity's management, NCC Energy, Ltd., a little-known oil and gas company out of London, in the spring of 1981 bought up 15 percent of Simplicity's stock. NCC Energy was controlled by the British financier Graham Ferguson Lacey and boasted of having oil, gas and mineral properties in Australia, Asia, Ireland and the United States. Its investment adviser was Drexel Burnham Lambert, and among those touting the deal was Peter Ackerman, the right-hand man of Drexel's junk-bond creator, Michael Milken.

Drexel liked the deal so much that it picked up 5 percent of Simplicity's stock for itself—a transaction that it kept secret. Additional Simplicity stock had been acquired by another member of the Milken-Drexel family of investors, an inner circle of financiers that traded stocks, bonds and companies among themselves.

That was First Executive Corporation, a Beverly Hills, California, life insurance holding company that later, in May 1991, sought protection from its creditors by going into United States Bankruptcy Court, thereby earning the dubious distinction of becoming the largest insurance company to be brought down by junk bonds.

NCC Energy bought out Posner, paying him $22 million for his holdings. That gave Posner a profit of $10 million. This set the stage for the world's largest pattern maker to go into the oil and gas business, a field in which it had no experience. NCC Energy's intention, a Simplicity spokesman said at the time, was to use millions of dollars of Simplicity's reserves to explore for oil and gas. This would be good for Simplicity, the spokesman said, because NCC's oil and gas exploration was thriving, and pattern-making was declining.

But before the NCC-Simplicity business combination could be completed, another raider appeared on the scene. In August 1981 companies controlled by Carl C. Icahn reported they had acquired 1.6 million shares of Simplicity, or 11.2 percent of the stock outstanding. By November, Icahn controlled 13.3 percent and had made a tender offer to buy an additional 18 percent—effectively blocking the NCC-Simplicity deal. To fend off Icahn, NCC Energy enlisted the help of an Australian company, Waltons Bond, Ltd., to make a counteroffer for Icahn's holdings. A month later, in December 1981, Waltons Bond paid Icahn's companies $26.5 million for their 1.8 million shares.

That transaction was especially lucrative for Icahn, whose businesses picked up a quick $15 million profit on the turnaround in Simplicity stock. Now the scorecard read: Investors Posner and Icahn: $25 million. Simplicity, its employees and customers: reduced earnings and higher pattern prices.

While Icahn was selling his stock to Waltons Bond, another company, Cook International, was buying Drexel Burnham's 5 percent of Simplicity shares for $6.8 million. Cook later sold the stock to NCC Energy. There was but one problem with the roughly $60 million in Simplicity stock purchases made by NCC Energy, Waltons Bond and Cook International: None of the companies had the cash to pay for the securities. Not to worry. Once NCC Energy assumed control, it would merely take the money out of Simplicity to pay for buying Simplicity.

A new management team took over in January 1982. Graham Ferguson Lacey, thirty-three, chairman and chief executive officer of NCC Energy, took on the same titles at Simplicity. Six of Lacey's allies also joined the board of directors. Among them was R. Cecil McBride, an aging Ulster millionaire who had bankrolled a teenage Lacey in his first ventures.

Lacey brought to his new job as chief executive of a venerable American business a reputation—at least in the British news media—for having carved out a "phenomenal business career." It began with McBride and real estate dealings in Northern Ireland during the 1970s and was followed by trading in large blocks of stock in British companies and finally the acquisition of companies. There were some setbacks along the way. A structural engineering company that he headed collapsed in 1978. A textile company that he headed went into receivership in 1980.

But, befitting his growing reputation as a fast-moving entrepreneur, Lacey began making acquisitions as soon as he assumed control of Simplicity. Interestingly, Lacey's Simplicity made the acquisitions from Lacey's NCC Energy. There were a pair of buildings in New York City, including a townhouse in which Lacey lived; an interest in a regional airline that had yet to get off the ground; oil and gas exploration; and common stock in an unidentified company—$10 million in all. This was good for NCC Energy, because its parent company back in England, Birmingham and Midland Counties Trust—also controlled by Lacey—was on the verge of bankruptcy. It was not so good for Simplicity.

Lacey's Simplicity also decided to pour cash into a gold-mining project in Australia—a Waltons Bond venture—and to buy $25 million of notes issued by a Waltons Bond–controlled mining company. This would be good for Waltons Bond, which needed cash. It would not be so good for Simplicity.

Simplicity's top officers that spring spoke enthusiastically about the acquisitions and the company's future as an energy producer. In an April 1982 report to stockholders, Lacey and two members of the old Simplicity management, Harold Cooper, vice-chairman of the board, and Lilyan H. Affinito, president, wrote:

"The board has embarked on a program designed to provide the company with both capital and earnings growth through . . . acquisitions in oil and gas opportunities in the United States, acquisitions in energy and mineral opportunities in Australia, and other acquisitions, primarily in the United States, that will not be energy-related."

Then, the deals unraveled. Simplicity's small stockholders, worried about the drain of assets, filed a lawsuit on Apr. 30 of that year to block the board's actions. The lawsuit alleged that NCC Energy, Waltons Bond and Cook International had "failed to disclose that they intended to use the cash assets of Simplicity in order to finance their acquisition of Simplicity stock" and that they "intended to use the cash assets of Simplicity to prevent Birmingham [NCC's parent company] from being forced into receivership." This was self-dealing, served only the personal interests of the defendants and constituted fraud, the lawsuit said. The board had been checkmated.

NCC Energy's parent company could no longer meet its debts. Birmingham and Midland Counties Trust was forced into receivership in England. Waltons Bond announced it was severing ties with NCC Energy and Simplicity, and was returning a $10 million Simplicity mining deposit. And four months after gaining control of Simplicity, NCC Energy announced it would sell its 20 percent interest.

No problem. Another moneyman, Charles Hurwitz, a forty-two-year-old Houston financier, was standing by. In May 1982 a pair of Hurwitz companies, MCO Holdings, Inc. and Federated Development Company, announced the purchase of Simplicity stock from NCC Energy and an agreement to buy the Simplicity stock held by Waltons Bond. Total purchase price for the 33 percent interest: $48 million.

MCO Holdings, based in Los Angeles, had investments in oil, gas and geothermal resources. Federated was a New York holding company. Perhaps more important, Hurwitz had access to an unlimited supply of cash. His banker was—surprise—Michael Milken.

Now Simplicity had another chairman and chief executive officer—Charles E. Hurwitz. And Hurwitz's allies, naturally, joined him on the Simplicity board. They included George Kozmetsky, a director of the Institute for Constructive Capitalism and immediate past dean of the College and Graduate School of Business of the University of Texas, and Barry Munitz, former chancellor and professor of business administration at the University of Houston.

In the beginning, Hurwitz's Simplicity abandoned the oil and gas business and gold-mining ventures. Instead, the pattern maker began buying stock in a New York company called Twin Fair Holdings, Inc., which owned properties that it leased to major retail chains, such as Gold Circle and Hills department stores. By the end of 1983, Simplicity Pattern owned 96 percent of Twin Fair. Simplicity also began buying stock in Amstar, Inc., a century-old company best known for its Domino-brand sugar. And, while Simplicity's new managers were spending money to buy sugar refineries and real estate, they were seeking to cut the pay and benefits of employees in Niles.

Hurwitz also initiated the paperwork required by the Internal Revenue Service that would lead to the removal of $2.9 million of $7 million from one of the pension funds covering Simplicity workers in Niles. Federal law allows companies to remove money from a pension fund if they certify that there are sufficient assets to meet pension obligations.

As 1983 turned to 1984, Simplicity's management continued to look for business investments unrelated to its pattern-making and pattern-printing operations. In April 1984 Twin Fair Holdings, Inc., now a subsidiary of Simplicity Pattern, began buying stock in another sugar refiner, Holly Sugar Corporation, and acquired a golf and tennis development in Naples, Florida.

Hurwitz also decided to change the name of the business to Maxxam Group, Inc., and stockholders agreed. The proposal was put to the stockholders this way: "The name Simplicity Pattern Co., Inc. was chosen at a time when the company was engaged exclusively in the manufacture and sale of paper patterns for home sewing to retail merchants.

"The company's pattern business is now conducted primarily through the company's wholly owned Delaware subsidiary, Simplicity Pattern Co., Inc. With the acquisition of Twin Fair Inc., the company is now also engaged in real estate development. . . . By reason of these changes, management believes that the proposed new name will more appropriately identify the company."

In May 1984, Simplicity management renewed the pressure on the unions to reduce wages and benefits. A headline in the *South Bend Tribune* for May 30, 1984, said: "Simplicity wants pay cut to '82-'83 levels." The *Niles Star* reported that if the company could not reduce its labor costs by about $1.9 million a year, it would leave the city it had called home since 1931. The newspaper quoted Charles DeWitt, the manager of the facility, as saying: "Simplicity has already identified a plant site in the South where taxes, utilities, and labor costs are lower and where local communities are aggressively soliciting new manufacturing operations with whole packages of special incentives."

Both the city of Niles and Simplicity's workers responded. The city promised to help arrange financing for more modern equipment and to give Simplicity, the area's second-largest employer, a 50 percent property tax break on plant improvements. Working against a July 2, 1984, deadline set by the company, Simplicity's five unions agreed to trim 3 percent off wages, which averaged about $9.90 an hour. They also agreed to give up two paid holidays and to eliminate the jobs of about seventy workers. Some of those who were terminated had been at Simplicity for more than three decades. The savings added up to $1.5 million, or 79 percent of the $1.9 million the company sought.

Bruce Bracken, director of employee relations, was quoted in an area newspaper as saying: "We fell short of our goal, but management was willing to stay here anyway because of the proven work force and high risk of starting off fresh somewhere else."

In reality, management was not staying anywhere. Management, in fact, was about to move on. Now that Hurwitz had invested Simplicity money in sugar and real estate; now that the company name had been changed to Maxxam; now that Niles taxpayers were going to subsidize the purchase of equipment; now that workers had agreed to pay cuts—he decided to unload the business. For a hefty profit. Less than two weeks after the labor agreements had been sealed, Hurwitz announced that Simplicity would be sold to Triton Group, Ltd., a holding company controlled by John Brooks Fuqua.

The board of directors of Maxxam, Simplicity's most recent parent, explained the decision like this in documents filed with the Securities and Exchange Commission: "The primary goal of the board is to broaden Maxxam Group, Inc.'s economic base and enhance its potential earning power and underlying asset value. The board believes that the sale of Simplicity to Triton on the terms provided in the sale agreement provides an excellent opportunity to further this objective.

"As previously reported by Maxxam Group, Inc., Simplicity has experienced continuing decreases in net sales and income from operations since the mid-1970s, reflecting the decline in pattern unit sales, although Simplicity continues to be a profitable business producing substantial cash flow."

Maxxam also said that Simplicity would prosper under its new owners as a result of "Simplicity's recently strengthened management team and by the experience of Triton's principal shareholder, Fuqua Industries, Inc., in managing consumer product-based businesses."

The moneymen loved the idea. Especially the dealmakers at Drexel Burnham Lambert. "Simplicity Pattern is a cash cow," Drexel Burnham told its clients in a report extolling the benefits that Triton and its parent, Fuqua Industries, Inc. of Atlanta, would derive from owning Simplicity.

"Last year, pretax income and depreciation generated $12 million in cash flow and the pretax profit margin in 1983 was 14 percent," the brokerage house said. "Even though the pattern business has been going nowhere for years because of the declining interest in home sewing, nevertheless pretax margins in this proprietary business consistently ranged between 12 percent–14 percent. Pretax profits approximated $15 million in 1983."

And then, the real reason that the Simplicity-Fuqua-Triton marriage made so much sense: Triton possessed "a potential tax loss carryforward of about $200 million to shelter future earnings. In order to take advantage of the carryforwards, Triton obviously needs to acquire operating companies with good cash flow and a consistent record of profitability." Translation: The losses run up in earlier years by a long-dead company—the real estate trust from whose corporate shell Triton had been formed—would be used to offset the taxes owed by a profitable firm.

Tax Gimmicks and Givebacks

The losses had originated in a real estate business in Massachusetts called Chase Manhattan Mortgage and Realty Trust, which went into bankruptcy court in 1979. A year later, it emerged with a new name, Triton Group, Ltd. It was acquired by Fuqua Industries in 1983.

In a report to Simplicity shareholders after Fuqua asssumed control, he offered this glowing assessment: "Simplicity has a dynamic new management team which in only a few months has made innovative moves to more widely use the Simplicity name, which has become synonymous with sewing through many decades of consumer product use. . . . Simplicity is already beginning to pay off a significant amount of the debt incurred to acquire this fine company, and the outlook is indeed bright."

Did this mean that an innovative new management had made structural changes to turn around a declining company? Of course not. Simplicity's seemingly changed fortunes were attributable to three factors: the tax code, a raid on a company pension fund and concessions by Simplicity's workers.

Triton Group, Simplicity's new parent company, reported profits of $13 million for 1985, $11 million for 1986 and $76 million for 1987. For the three years that it owned Simplicity, profits totaled $100 million. Yet according to records filed with the SEC, Triton paid no federal income taxes on that $100 million.

How could that be? Remember all those losses run up by the defunct realty trust before it went into bankruptcy court and came out as Triton? Well, Triton merely subtracted the old losses from the taxable income of Simplicity and Triton's other subsidiaries.

Having made use of the tax code, Triton now took aim at the pensions of Simplicity workers. In December 1986, Triton tapped one of the pension funds covering hourly workers. It removed $7.8 million of the $8.5 million in the fund, according to records filed with the Pension Benefit Guaranty Corporation in Washington. This was the second raid on a Simplicity pension plan in three years. Before the money was removed this time, the pension of each Simplicity employee enrolled in the plan was backed, on average, by assets of $39,535. Afterward, the average per worker was $3,256.

In the footnotes to a financial report filed with the SEC, Triton explained where part of the $7.8 million in pension-fund money went: "Simplicity's retirement plan for salaried employees was terminated during the year. Refunds received from the termination . . . will be held for or applied to redemption of the Simplicity Series B preferred stock until all such shares are redeemed."

And who owned Series B stock? Hurwitz's Maxxam Group, Inc., the previous owner of Simplicity, which had received the stock as a part of the $65 million package of cash and notes it received when Triton bought Simplicity. In other words, Triton used the pension fund money of Simplicity workers to help pay for Triton's purchase of Simplicity.

But surely, you say, the change in ownership brought change to the production plant in Niles? Not exactly. Paul M. Borowski, who at the time was Simplicity's general accounting manager in Niles, recalls visits to the plant by the new California owners. "I can remember the guys coming, walking through," he said, "making their grand show. . . . It was one of those things, clean the place up . . . get rid of the trash, clean the factory, you know, get it the way it should be every day. I can remember those guys coming in a couple of times. Everybody was scared to death of them."

But what about all those advantages that are supposed to come with corporate reorganization? Surely, the new management introduced ways of making better use of existing equipment and expertise, of expanding into new but related fields of business, of opening up other markets? Not really. Douglas G. Wimberly, a former manager of computer services at Simplicity, said there was a lot of talk about diversifying, but it was all talk. There were discussions about printing national magazines. One salesman even brought in a $1 million printing order, but no decisions were made and the order was lost. "Rumor was that management could never make up its mind," Wimberly said.

Borowski agreed. "We'd bring up at staff review meetings different proposals. The managers would say, 'Yeah, we're going to look into that.' I'd sit there, I'd say, 'I thought we were going to look into that four months ago.'"

Not only did the Triton management not diversify, but Simplicity was actually losing ground in the business it once dominated. More than 50 percent of all the patterns sold in America had carried the Simplicity label in the 1970s. The figure had dropped to 43 percent by 1983, and to 37 percent in 1986.

The gloomy sales figures aside, Triton did very nicely with its investment in Simplicity, thanks to the tax advantages. But after three years, Triton decided it was time to dump the pattern maker and move on. To manage the sale, it turned to a familiar face—Drexel Burnham Lambert, always ready to collect another round of fees.

That was in November 1987. A month later, Drexel arranged the sale of Simplicity to Wesray Capital, a company that had established a reputation through the 1980s as the most successful get-rich-quick operation in the field of corporate takeovers. Wesray's name was derived from the letters in the names of its two founders, William E. Simon, former secretary of the Treasury, and Raymond G. Chambers, a tax accountant who became a buyout specialist. By the time of the Simplicity purchase, Simon had moved on to other corporate deals unrelated to Wesray. Although Simon continued as chairman of the board, Chambers ran Wesray.

Why did Triton want to sell? One reason was that control of Triton had shifted from Fuqua to Charles R. Scott of La Jolla, California, a stockbroker turned corporate raider. Like Fuqua, he had made millions buying and selling companies. Scott had amended, slightly, Triton's mission. As he described the philosophy in a report to stockholders:

"Triton is in the business of acquiring and adding value to promising American growth companies. . . . Simply stated, our aim is to build shareholder value by acquiring promising companies, guiding management in restructuring, refinancing and repositioning for accelerated growth and, ultimately, selling our interest in a well-timed transaction."

In the Simplicity sale, timing was everything. Wesray paid $117 million for Simplicity. Triton walked away with a $52 million profit before taxes. In the amazing world of American business, a company that was worth $65 million in 1984 was worth $117 million in 1988—even though its sales and market share had all declined.

How can the value of a deteriorating company grow? It can't. But in the world of corporate and financial paper-shuffling, it happens all the time. With disastrous consequences for workers, taxpayers and the overall economy.

Wesray purchased Simplicity with borrowed money, meaning that Simplicity would have to pay for itself all over again. As it did when Triton bought it. As it did when Hurwitz bought it before that. Only now the debt load topped $100 million. And the $100 million that Simplicity had squirreled away in cash and investments when the decade began had long since disappeared. Nonetheless, the people at Wesray thought they had engineered a good deal.

At Simplicity's plant in Niles, the people who ran the day-to-day business knew better. So did the company's suppliers. They were being paid very, very slowly. It was the sure-fire sign of a business—or an individual—in financial distress: The old check-is-in-the-mail ploy. Paul Borowski, the general accounting manager whose duties included issuing the checks, remembers those days well.

When a supplier would call and ask about payment, Borowski said, "As a good accountant, following directions, I'd say, 'We've got new internal auditors hired and they're reviewing all our payments.' I said, 'I will call him tomorrow morning and have him release your check.' . . . You know, give him the line." Borowski said he was disturbed by the practice. But he was even more disturbed when the corporate office in New York ordered him to send the checks to New York for mailing, further delaying payment. After the checks arrived in New York and were approved there, they would eventually be mailed back to the suppliers in Niles.

Borowski said he also was directed to take the discount that suppliers give if payment is made within a certain period, say ten days, but then delay the payment: "If I'm dealing with you, I negotiate with you in good faith for a discount. Then I take the discount. Then I don't even mail the check till about two weeks later. We had one vendor, a big paper company, they had done business with for fifty years, they refused an order until the check was certified in their New York office."

There was a solution to the cash crunch: more layoffs. About twenty Niles workers were dismissed in June 1988, when Charlotte Mitchell and Edgar Stanley lost their jobs. Douglas Wimberly, the computer services manager, lost his job as well. "The way it was put to me, it came down from New York that X amount of dollars were going to be cut from personnel," said Wimberly, forty-one.

Borowski survived the June 1988 cuts. But not for long. Late one week in mid-August, on very short notice, he was asked to have checks for suppliers printed by the following Monday.

"I called one of my clerks back from vacation, to come in at noon [that Monday] to work," he said. "We were running two systems to get it all done. . . . Came in Tuesday morning, had everything balanced . . . checks all signed, you know, through a machine. And the ones that needed two signatures all ready. All checks were stuffed in envelopes. And when I called New York—it must have been about ten o'clock or so—he says, 'Are they in the mail yet?' I say, 'Waiting for your okay to take them to the mail table.' He says, 'Give them to the mail table right away.'

"I did that myself. . . . Went down there at 10:15. About 10:30, I get a call: 'Checks out?' I said, 'Yeah, they're at the mail table.' 'Okay, thank you very much.'"

Twenty minutes later, Borowski was summoned to the plant manager's office. He was told his job had been terminated. So had the jobs of another dozen or so employees. But Simplicity now had so much debt that even reductions in the work force didn't free up enough cash to make the interest and principal payments.

In an effort to stay afloat, Simplicity in 1988 reached an agreement to merge with one of its main competitors, Butterick Holdings, Inc. based in Altoona, Pennsylvania. The plan called for closing either Simplicity's Niles plant or Butterick's Altoona plant. Each had about 550 employees. But the Federal Trade Commission blocked the merger, contending that a union between Simplicity, the largest pattern maker, and Butterick, the third largest, would create a monopoly.

After the aborted merger, conditions continued to deteriorate. Wesray's Simplicity failed to make $10.5 million in interest and principal payments due in June 1989. It failed to make $4.4 million in interest payments on notes due in October 1989. During the three months ending Apr. 30, 1990, Simplicity incurred a loss of $2.6 million. Its debt totaled more than $100 million.

The company stated the obvious in a report filed with the SEC: Simplicity "is highly leveraged as a result of the 1988 acquisition. . . . This high level of indebtedness results in significant interest expense and principal repayment obligations for the company." Past-due interest and principal on its senior debt now totaled $23.4 million. Past-due interest on notes totaled

$8.8 million. In a June 1990 report to the SEC, Simplicity painted a picture that was growing more grim with each passing month: "[These] conditions raise substantial doubt about the company's ability to continue as a going concern."

In the fall of 1990, Simplicity Pattern underwent yet another change in ownership, as the outstanding debt was restructured and new investors were brought in. There was a touch of irony. The corporate raids and restructuring of the 1980s that led to the loss of middle-class jobs, the elimination of health-care insurance and the decline of living standards had turned on those who had started it all. The process had become so destructive that the raiders—who once made so much money on takeovers that their exploits were chronicled in newspapers and magazines, on radio and television—now were losing millions of dollars.

As might be expected, those involved are reluctant to say exactly how much. In fact, they don't want to even talk about the company or its revolving ownership.

So who owns Simplicity Pattern now? They don't want you to know. Representatives of Wesray failed to respond to repeated requests for information. A spokesman for Raymond Chambers said he no longer was associated with the firm.

When Simplicity Pattern's executive offices in New York City were asked if Wesray still owned the company, a spokeswoman replied: "We can't really give out that information." Later, a man identified as a company official called and said: "You're not going to be able to get any information. We are presently a privately held company that operates in a small industry, that basically everybody keeps to themselves and we don't talk to our competitors and our competitors don't talk to us. And it's so small and tight-lipped that we don't want any information at all getting out about us.

"And so we just come across with big, flat 'no comments' any time we get any inquiries about what our current ownership is, our financial situation or anything along those lines."

Still later, in a second interview, the Simplicity officer had this exchange with one of the authors: Simplicity: "We would prefer not to be mentioned in the article at all. Are we still going to be mentioned, regardless of my request?"

Author: "Yes."

Simplicity: "Okay, if we're going to be mentioned, I am prepared to make a brief statement and I will not answer any specific questions, but I can at least tell you this: That the company has positively turned around its operations, is now doing well, very competitive in the marketplace. All of our bankers and creditors are happy with us. And we anticipate in both the near future and on a long-term basis to be successful. And that's basically it."

The raiding of Simplicity Pattern Co.

Before the takeovers: A stable firm

Assets

$100 million in cash reserves, investments

1980 net income: $ 7 million

Founded 1927 in New York City.

By 1981, the world's largest pattern maker.

Factory: Niles, Mich.

1927–1981

First raider

Graham Ferguson Lacey

Chairman/CEO NCC Energy Ltd.

Gains control of Simplicity, becomes chairman/CEO.

Investments with Simplicity cash

- Two New York City buildings.
- A regional airline.
- Oil and gas exploration.
- Gold-mining company bonds.

Jan.–May 1982

Second raider

Charles E. Hurwitz

Chairman/CEO MCO Holdings Inc.

Gains control of Simplicity, becomes chairman/CEO.

Investments with Simplicity cash

- Shopping centers.
- Sugar refineries.
- Golf and tennis resort.

Pension fund raid

- $2.9 million (42%) removed from fund of Niles workers. Originally $10,455 per worker, cut to $6,085.

Labor cuts

- Jobs eliminated, wages reduced, some paid holidays eliminated.

May 1982–Dec. 1984

SOURCES: Securities and Exchange Commission, Pension Benefit Guaranty Corp.

Third raider
J.B. Fuqua

Chairman, Triton Group Ltd.

Acquires Simplicity.

Erasing taxes

■ Corporate income taxes eliminated by deducting losses of a bankrupt real estate trust.

Pension fund raid

92% cut

■ $7.8 million (92%) removed from another fund covering hourly workers. Originally $39,535 per worker, cut to $3,256.

Dec. 1984–Jan. 1988

Fourth raider
Raymond G. Chambers

Chairman/CEO
Wesray Capital Corp.

Acquires Simplicity.

Increasing debt

■ Borrows $120 million to buy Simplicity.

■ By June 1989, Simplicity in default on its loans.

■ By April 1990, delinquent on more than $30 million in payments on interest and principal.

Jan. 1988–Fall 1990

Simplicity today: Who owns it?

$100 million reserve gone

We can't really give out that information.

$100 million in debt, July 1990

Manufacturing Plants Everywhere

Lest you believe that Simplicity Pattern was a sewing industry aberration, you may want to ponder the fortunes of two other companies. The first is McCall Pattern Company, a Simplicity rival. The second is the Singer Company, the company that makes the sewing machines that turn Simplicity and McCall patterns into clothing.

McCall, like Simplicity, had enjoyed a stable existence through most of this century. Until 1983, that is, when it became just another card in a deck of corporations that was about to be reshuffled. At the time, McCall was owned by Norton Simon, Inc., a New York consumer products and services conglomerate whose many and varied holdings included Avis rental cars, Hunt's catsup and Max Factor cosmetics. The moneymen had targeted Norton Simon for takeover, believing, correctly, that millions of dollars could be made by selling off Norton Simon's assorted operations. The process would result in the closing of plants, the elimination of jobs and the weakening of some companies, but it would create an instant windfall for those orchestrating the deal.

The opening bid was made by Norton Simon's own management. It was so low, though, that it was generally regarded as just a signal that the company was on the auction block. Kohlberg Kravis Roberts, the Wall Street investment firm on its way to becoming the premier buyout specialist, immediately made a counteroffer. But the winning bid came from yet another conglomerate, Esmark, Inc., the Chicago-based company once known as Swift and Company. Esmark's products already included STP motor oil, Playtex girdles and Swift ham.

As has been—and continues to be—the case with corporate restructurings, Esmark lacked the money to pay for what it had just purchased. So it began to sell off pieces of Norton Simon. One of the first to go was McCall Pattern. In January 1984 a New York investment firm called TLC Group, Inc., headed by an emerging entrepreneur by the name of Reginald F. Lewis, bought McCall. The buyers put up $1 million and borrowed the remainder of the $24.5 million purchase price. Like so many business deals of the 1980s and 1990s, it turned out to be a short-term investment built on long-term debt.

First, Lewis and his associates reaped a quick profit when they extracted $19 million from McCall through a recapitalization plan. Then, in 1987, three years after the acquisition, they decided it was time to cash in and sold McCall Pattern to the John Crowther Group, a British textile conglomerate. The sale price: $63 million in cash and $32 million in assumed debt.

A news release distributed by TLC Group at the time took note of the extraordinary return: "The sale enabled McCall's stockholders to realize a ninety-to-one profit on their initial investment in the home sewing company. . . . McCall's stockholders have received aggregate proceeds of more than $90 million on their initial equity investment of $1 million."

Too good to be true, you say? Well, it was very good for Reginald Lewis and his investors. It was not nearly so good for McCall Pattern, the company. Eighteen months after the sale, in December 1988, McCall Pattern—unable to pay its bills—went into bankruptcy court to seek protection from its creditors.

Finally, there is the sewing machine used by generations of families to turn their Simplicity and McCall patterns into dresses and suits and coats and other clothes. It was the Singer. And the company that manufactured it was much older than Simplicity, its origins dating from 1851. For part of the nineteenth century and most of the twentieth century, the Singer Company dominated the world sewing machine market, its name becoming synonymous with the product it sold.

In the early years, European countries railed against the huge imports of the American-made sewing machine, complaining that Singer, with its emphasis on mass production and its reputation for building low-cost, but high-quality machines and providing good service, was dominating the world market. Which it was. At one time, Singer employed as many as 5,000 persons at its sprawling production plant in Elizabeth, New Jersey, where sewing machines were manufactured and shipped to virtually every habitable section of the globe.

No more. The Elizabeth plant closed in 1982, more than a century after it opened. The Singer Company became a defense and aerospace contractor. The sewing machine business was given a catchy new name, SSMC, Inc.

By 1992, SSMC had changed its name back to the Singer Co., incorporated in the Netherlands Antilles for tax purposes. The company continued to manufacture sewing machines and related products everywhere in the world—Brazil, Taiwan, Mexico, Turkey, Pakistan, Malaysia, Germany, Sri Lanka, the Philippines, Indonesia, Thailand, and Bangladesh.

Everywhere, that is, except in the United States.

CHAPTER NINE
THE DISAPPEARING PENSIONS

WHAT WENT WRONG

Under federal law, a company may remove money from an employee pension fund if it certifies that enough remains to cover its pension obligations. On eight different occasions between 1983 and 1988, companies controlled by Victor Posner tapped employees' pension plans.

Money drained from the pension funds of 4,800 workers at Posner-controlled companies

Company	Amount removed from pension funds	Average assets per participating worker	
		Before raid	After raid
Graniteville Co. Graniteville, S.C.	$ 15.4 million	$ 26,642	$ 10,714
Pa. Engineering Corp. Pittsburgh	2.4 million	11,455	4,754
Royal Crown Cos. Miami	1.9 million	23,909	18,488
Nat'l Propane Corp. New Hyde Pk., N.Y.	1.1 million	12,500	9,444
Birdsboro Corp. Birdsboro, Pa.	4.4 million	42,286	17,143
Salem Corp. Pittsburgh	3.5 million	57,857	32,857
Enro Shirt Co. Louisville, Ky.	1.5 million	19,000	11,500
Fischbach Corp. New York	35.0 million	40,036	24,466

Total removed from pensions: $65.2 million

A Frightening Future

The lesson for today is the American pension system. It is subtitled: What to look forward to when you retire. The text is drawn from the government rule book, with its contradictory and often-overlapping laws relating to pensions.

Here are the highlights:

■ For the first time, the percentage of workers who will receive a fixed monthly pension is steadily declining.

■ Women who retire from jobs in businesses receive smaller pensions than men.

■ The percentage of workers who will receive reduced pension benefits is growing, and half of all workers have no pension plan at all.

■ Corporations removed $21 billion from their employees' pension plans during the 1980s; overall, nearly 2,000 corporations dipped into employee pension funds for at least $1 million each; and workers in the private sector receive far smaller pensions than workers in local, state and federal governments, which now employ 17 percent of the American work force.

■ Conscientious workers who establish their own individual retirement accounts—believing them to be insured by the federal government—may one day discover to their dismay that many are not.

■ And the people who made all this possible—members of Congress—will continue to receive the best pensions of all.

Label this pension chaos.

Then understand that, barring a massive revision of the rule book by Congress, these conditions will continue to deteriorate. In the meantime, watch for the coming war between those who work for government and those who don't. It will come when workers in private industry realize how much power public-employee pension funds wield.

For example, local and state government workers, teachers and community-college professors in Oregon benefited handsomely when their pension fund sold its stock in NI Industries, Inc. early in 1985. NI Industries, formerly Norris Industries, Inc., was a manufacturing company based in Long Beach, California, that made everything from plumbing fixtures to automobile wheels. The Oregon Public Employees Retirement System had invested $25 million with Kohlberg Kravis Roberts four years earlier to help underwrite the Wall Street investment firm's takeover of NI Industries. When the Oregon pension fund cashed in its chips in 1985, it walked away with a return of 268 percent.

In its annual report for that year, the pension fund pointed to the splendid results of its takeover investments, saying that its "leveraged buy-out investments . . . continue to do well. The sale of the $25 million investment in NI Industries resulted in cash proceeds exceeding $92 million."

That was good for Oregon's public employees. It was not so good for workers at NI Industries. After Kohlberg Kravis took over the company with the backing of Oregon's public-employee pension-fund money, it raided the pension plan of workers at NI Industries.

Documents filed with the Pension Benefit Guaranty Corporation show that, in December 1983, the company's new owners removed $23.3 million from a pension plan—or 61 percent of the plan's total assets of $38.3 million. That left the 2,908 workers covered under the plan with an average of $5,158 each to be invested for their lifetime retirement benefits. By comparison, workers in the Oregon Public Employees Retirement System had, on average, assets of more than $33,000 each to provide for their retirement years. To make matters worse for NI workers, the raid on their pension plan was followed in later years by plant closings and the elimination of their jobs.

Public pension systems across the country are reaping billions of dollars doing the same thing that the Oregon Public Employees Retirement System did. They invest in corporations and then encourage restructuring or other business decisions that lead to curtailed pension benefits for workers in those corporations, the elimination of jobs, or both.

As a result, workers in private industry who pay taxes that pay the salaries of public employees are losing their pensions and jobs because of investment decisions made by pension funds representing those public employees. To put it more bluntly, the textile worker who lives down the street from a county courthouse worker stands a good chance of losing a portion of his or her pension benefits, job, or both, to provide a better pension for the courthouse worker.

A generation ago, this would not have been possible. Public employee pension funds were bit players on the pension scene. The largest pension funds were those of corporations like General Motors and AT&T. While those companies still have big funds, the list of the twenty-five largest pension funds is dominated by the names of public agencies—entities such as California Public Employees, New York State Teachers, the Wisconsin State Board, Michigan Retirement Systems and Pennsylvania Public Schools. All told sixteen of the twenty-five largest pension funds are public-employee funds. The assets of public pension funds grew at a much sharper rate in the 1980s than those of private funds. From 1980 to 1989, the assets of private pension plans increased 122 percent—from $496.6 billion to $1.1 trillion. During that same period, public pension funds grew by 267 percent—from $198 billion to $727.4 billion.

With this has come a newfound power to influence corporate America. Indeed, the private and public-employee pension funds together represent the largest unregulated, untaxed pools of capital in the nation. Managers

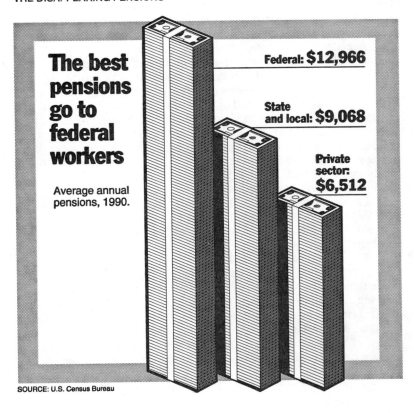

The best pensions go to federal workers

Average annual pensions, 1990.

Federal: **$12,966**

State and local: **$9,068**

Private sector: **$6,512**

SOURCE: U.S. Census Bureau

may invest the money almost anywhere they choose, from leveraged buyouts to the purchase of stock in foreign corporations, which may make products that compete with those made by American workers at home. Required by federal rules to maximize the return for the benefit of participants, their loyalty is to the bottom line of their balance sheets, as the NI Industries story illustrates.

In the future, pressure will mount on public-employee pension funds to increase their investment return. That is because most public pension plans are underfunded. Guaranteed, to be sure, but underfunded nonetheless. That means a pension fund does not have enough money to pay the benefits it has promised to the workers enrolled in the plan. As a result, fund managers will be called upon to produce ever greater returns.

In any event, the statistics tell the story of the difference between the retirement benefits paid by public and private funds. Take the average annual pensions for 1990: A retired federal worker received $12,966. A retired local or state government worker received $9,068. A retired private-sector worker received $6,512.

Actually, the situation is much worse than the numbers suggest. First, because public-employee pension plans are underfunded, taxpayers eventually may be called upon to provide the additional cash needed to pay the promised benefits. Second, nearly everyone who works for local, state and federal governments is covered by a pension plan that guarantees a fixed retirement check every month—long considered the best of all available retirement-plan options. But fewer than 30 percent of workers in private industry are covered by such defined-benefit plans. Third, many public-employee pension plans provide for mandatory inflation adjustment—that is, the retiree's benefit check is increased as the cost of living goes up. But mandatory inflation adjustments are rare in private pension plans.

Finally, the private pension system is deteriorating at the same time that there is a growing recognition—albeit grudging—that the Social Security system will lack the resources to provide for many of these same workers.

Welcome to the 1930s. Again.

Americans can expect little help from their government as they try to wade through the morass of laws, rules and regulations that govern pensions in this country. Consider the testimony of a top Labor Department official before a congressional subcommittee in April 1989. David M. Walker, assistant secretary of labor for pension and welfare benefits, told the members that when a company terminated a pension plan it was required to replace it with an annuity that would provide the retirement benefits that had built up.

"Annuity contracts must be purchased to secure the value of those accrued benefits," Walker said, adding, "The bottom line is that participants are fully protected with regard to their accrued benefits when there is a termination."

There is one problem with that last statement. It isn't true. Payment of so-called defined-benefit pensions is guaranteed by the Pension Benefit Guaranty Corporation, a quasi-federal agency. If a company reneges on its pension commitments, the PBGC issues the monthly pension checks to retired workers. That is not the case with annuity contracts. Annuities are not guaranteed by the PBGC or any other governmental agency.

For this, you can thank Congress, which wrote the rule book in such a way as to permit companies to terminate a pension plan, buy annuities for its workers that will pay the accrued benefits, and keep for themselves whatever accumulated money is not needed to pay for the annuities. It did not require them to guarantee, or insure, the annuities.

At the same time that growing numbers of employees are being asked to make sophisticated judgments on how to set aside their money for retirement, companies that have long provided fixed pension benefits are abandoning such plans in droves. Consider this: Each year, beginning in 1950 and continuing through the 1960s and 1970s, corporations spent a steadily growing amount of money on retirement plans, according to their federal income tax returns. In 1950 corporations claimed $1.7 billion in pension plan contributions. That rose to $4.6 billion in 1960, to $12.2 billion in 1970 and to $51.5 billion in 1980.

That is as it should be. Every year there are more workers. Every year there should be a larger sum set aside for their pensions. And so it went until 1983. That year, corporate pension contributions peaked at $54.4 billion. Then, while the number of workers in the country continued to rise, the money earmarked for their retirement began to go down. Corporate pension contributions dropped to $52.6 billion in 1984, dropped again to $48.2 billion in 1986, and dropped to $45.2 billion in 1988, the latest year for which complete tax statistics were available.

During that same period, the number of workers enrolled in a primary pension plan increased from 39 million in 1983 to 41.2 million in 1986. Of course, more than half of all workers are employed by companies with no pension plan at all. But that's another matter.

So what are corporations doing with the money that once went for pensions?

A large chunk of it is going to pay interest on the staggering debt incurred during an uncontrolled binge of borrowing in the 1980s. In 1950, for every $1 million that corporations contributed to pension plans, they paid out $1.6 million in interest on loans. As late as 1968, interest payments still amounted to just $1.9 million for every $1 million in pension contributions. But by 1986, corporate interest payments were consuming $5 million for every $1 million that businesses allocated for their employees' retirement.

Looked at another way, in 1986 corporations contributed to pension plans an average of $1,171 for every worker. They paid an average of $5,942 per worker in interest on corporate debt.

America's corporate pension system is especially grim for women, who have entered the work force in massive numbers during the last three decades. Labor Department statistics show that in 1988 the median private pension income for single women was $2,153. Half of all unmarried women received more than $2,153, half received less. The $2,153, of course, is for a full year. That's $41.40 a week.

More pointedly, the median pension income of single men was $3,820. Thus, single women received 56 percent of the pension income of single men. That was down from 74 percent in 1976, when the median pension income for men was $1,830, compared with $1,350 for women. Thus, in twelve years, the amount of single women's pensions fell from about three-fourths that of men's pensions to about half. This despite the fact that women live longer, that more women than ever are working, and that more women than ever are collecting pensions.

Married women in the work force are faring no better. Their median

Fewer workers with guaranteed pensions, and women retirees are worse off

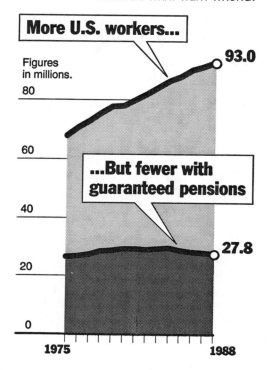

More U.S. workers...

Figures in millions.

...But fewer with guaranteed pensions

93.0

27.8

1975   1988

Women lagging behind men in private pensions

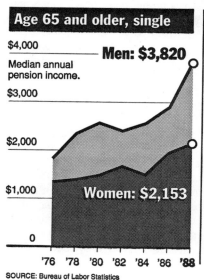

Age 65 and older, single

$4,000

Median annual pension income.

Men: $3,820

$3,000

$2,000

Women: $2,153

$1,000

0

'76 '78 '80 '82 '84 '86 '88

SOURCE: Bureau of Labor Statistics

Age 65 and older, married

$4,000

Men: $4,285

$3,000

$2,000

Women: $1,848

$1,000

0

'76 '78 '80 '82 '84 '86 '88

pension in 1988 was $1,848. For married men it was $4,285. That meant the pension of a married woman was 43 percent of the pension of a married man. That figure, too, is down from twelve years earlier. In 1976, married women got $1,310, or 61 percent of the $2,150 pension of married men.

From 1976 to 1988, the median pension income of single women went up 59 percent, rising from $1,350 to $2,153. The figure for single men shot up 109 percent—nearly double the women's rate, rising from $1,830 to $3,820. Since women outlive men, on average, by seven years, and since most private pensions are not adjusted for inflation, the pension dollars that women eventually receive are worth even less.

All the current evidence suggests that this pattern will continue. Why? Congress's tax-writing committees have heavily skewed the tax law against most women.

Women who work outside the home are most often employed in the service sector—in retail sales and clerical jobs—which generally provides inferior pension plans compared to manufacturing. But even women who work in manufacturing tend to be clustered in businesses with the poorest pension plans, such as the textile industry.

What is happening to women is just one of the ways people can be victimized by the lack of a coherent pension system. It began with the demise of the Studebaker.

The Studebaker Corporation dated from 1852, when the brothers Studebaker, Clem and Henry, built their first covered wagon. They equipped the Union army with wagons during the Civil War and turned out their first horseless carriage in 1904. For the next sixty years, Studebaker manufactured automobiles—sometimes with a styling flair, as with the 1950 Champion—at a sprawling plant in South Bend, Indiana.

The same year the Champion debuted, Studebaker established a pension program. In a booklet distributed to employees, H.S. Vance, the company president, said the plan "carried forward the Studebaker tradition—concern for the employees of the company and their family." The booklet, illustrated with a series of drawings depicting a life of leisure, began: "You may be a long way from retirement age now. Still it's good to know that Studebaker is building up a fund for you so that when you reach retirement age you can settle down on a farm . . . visit around the country . . . or just take it easy . . . and know that you'll still be getting a regular monthly pension paid for entirely by the company."

Reality fell far short of the promise. In 1964, after years of dwindling sales, Studebaker closed the South Bend plant. More than 5,000 workers lost their jobs. Those workers who had already retired, or who were sixty and eligible for retirement, received their promised pensions. Everyone else—more than 4,000 workers—divided up the $2 million or so that remained in the pension plan. That averaged out to lump-sum payments of $197 to $1,757, depending on seniority.

Seven years later, in 1971, when Congress began to seriously study the pension issue, Studebaker workers traveled to Washington to testify before the Senate Labor Committee. Lester Fox, one of those workers, summed up the issue:

"At the time of the plant closing, I was age forty . . . with twenty years of accredited service toward my pension. I received a lump-sum payment of $350 as my share of the residue of the pension trust. . . . The problem . . . is that in this instance, in excess of 4,000 workers who had a promise of a private pension plan witnessed it vanishing before their very eyes. . . . I commend those who are considering legislation that would provide for a public reinsurance of private pension plans, and I would view that as something similar to the Federal Deposit Insurance Corporation, which insures private savings."

More years of congressional wrangling slipped by, until 1974, when lawmakers enacted the Employee Retirement Income Security Act (ERISA). The act set standards for the first time that companies would have to follow if they maintained pension plans. A key provision established the Pension Benefit Guaranty Corporation, which would guarantee payment of pension benefits if a company failed to pay.

When President Gerald R. Ford signed the law on Labor Day 1974, he declared: "I think this is really an historic Labor Day—historic in the sense that this legislation will probably give more benefits and rights and success in the area of labor-management than almost anything in the history of this country.

"This legislation will alleviate the fears and the anxiety of people who are on the production lines or in the mines or elsewhere, in that they now know that their investment in private pension funds will be better protected. . . . It certainly will give to those thirty-plus million American workers a greater degree of certainty as they face retirement in the future."

So how goes it, eighteen years after the historic passage of ERISA? Again, some statistics: From 1975 to 1980, the number of workers participating in a pension plan insured by the PBGC rose to 29.7 million, from 26.8 million.

It has been downhill ever since. From 1980 to 1988, the latest year for which figures were available, the number fell from 29.7 million to 27.8 million. During that time, employment rose from 78.3 million to 93 million. Thus, while the work force grew 19 percent, the number of workers with insured pensions fell 6 percent. And the percentage of the work force covered by such plans is declining. Since passage of ERISA, the share of the work force enrolled in a pension plan guaranteed by the PBGC has fallen steadily from 39.4 percent in 1975 to 29.9 percent in 1988.

As those statistics suggest, the number of workers without guaranteed pensions, or with no pension coverage at all, has climbed sharply since Congress set out to protect the private pension system. One reason: Many companies pulled out of the guaranteed-pension program when their PBGC premiums soared. They were getting stuck paying for the insured pensions of the retirees of bankrupt companies.

The Pension Raiders

While tens of millions of workers have fared poorly under the existing system, corporate managers and takeover artists have profited handsomely from it. They did so by raiding pension funds—a practice made possible by the way the federal government wrote the rule book.

During the 1980s, nearly 2,000 businesses dipped into their pension funds and removed $21 billion. That is enough to provide pensions of $800 a month to a quarter-million retired workers. And their spouses. For the rest of their lives. The $21 billion does not count the billions that businesses diverted to other uses after substituting inferior pension plans for the plans that had been in place for decades.

How does a company go about extracting money from its employees' retirement bank? To withdraw money, a company must certify that the pension plan has more assets than are needed to meet its retirement obligations.

As noted earlier, Congress wrote the rule book in such a way as to permit companies to terminate a pension plan, buy for its workers unguaranteed annuities that will pay the accrued benefits, and keep what is left over. The losers in the transaction are the employees, who virtually always end up with smaller retirement checks than under the old plan. What's more, most companies that terminated their defined benefit plans— plans that promise a specified amount to a retiree—replaced them with defined contribution plans, meaning, in most cases, even lower retirement benefits in the future.

Under a defined contribution plan, an employer agrees to set aside a fixed amount of money for an employee's retirement. How much the employee eventually receives depends on how well that money is invested. In most cases, it is substantially less than what a defined benefit plan would provide. Most significantly, neither the annuities nor the defined contribution plans carry a government guarantee.

About 23,000 former and current employees at the Cannon Mills Company textile plants in North Carolina, South Carolina and Georgia learned that lesson the hard way. For years, workers at Cannon Mills, headquartered in Kannapolis, North Carolina, were covered by a pension plan that was insured by the PBGC. That changed in 1982 after a corporate raider by the name of David H. Murdock appeared on the scene.

Murdock now is chairman and chief executive officer of the Dole Food Company, whose products include Dole pineapples and bananas, and he is a member of the *Forbes* 400, the Who's Who of the nation's rich. Murdock, with a personal fortune that *Forbes* estimates at $1.3 billion, is involved in a number of businesses and is a major fund-raiser for the Republican party. In February 1988, he hosted a $10,000-per-person reception at his sixty-four-room Bel Air, California, home once owned by the late hotel baron Conrad Hilton. There, donors mingled and posed for photographs with his friend, President Ronald Reagan.

It was in 1982, during one of his takeover forays, that Murdock picked Cannon Mills. When Murdock launched his takeover of Cannon Mills, it was the last of the large family-controlled textile businesses. Cannon employed about 24,000 people at twenty-two plants, producing towels, sheets, other bedding accessories, kitchen products and rugs. The company was profitable, had extensive real estate holdings and no debt. It was run in much the same paternalistic way it had been in 1906, when it was founded. The company still owned 1,600 homes in Kannapolis, which it rented to workers for $20 to $85 a month.

As was the practice in the 1980s, Murdock bought Cannon Mills with mostly borrowed money and then used company revenue to pay the debt. To that end, he eliminated the jobs of 2,000 workers and sold the company houses. In January 1986, four years after acquiring Cannon Mills, Murdock decided to move on. Before selling the company, he terminated the pension plan covering 23,000 workers.

PBGC records show that the plan's assets at the time were valued at $102.8 million. Murdock removed $36.6 million, contending that the remaining $66.2 million was enough to guarantee pensions. He invested the $36.6 million in the stock of two companies that were potential takeover candidates and used the leftover $66.2 million to purchase annuities from an insurance company for Cannon Mills workers. But the annuities, unlike the pensions they replaced, weren't guaranteed by the PBGC.

And they were purchased from the Executive Life Insurance Company in Los Angeles—the same Executive Life that had sunk billions of dollars into junk bonds sold by Michael Milken of Drexel Burnham Lambert. The same Executive Life Insurance that was seized by California officials in April 1991 in what has become the nation's largest insurance company failure. The same Executive Life Insurance that has reduced the amount it pays each month to pensioners and other annuity holders, including retirees of Cannon Mills. They are now receiving only 70 percent of the pension benefits they had been promised before Murdock dipped into their plan.

As for Murdock, he converted the $36.6 million he had withdrawn from the pension plan into a handsome profit. When he sold the stock in the takeover companies, he reaped a $60 million profit on his investment.

While Murdock was raiding the pension fund of a single company, others were launching multiple raids. Among them: Meshulam Riklis of Beverly Hills, and Victor Posner of Miami Beach, the two elder statesmen of American business who were using borrowed money to make their fortunes long before the coining of the phrase junk bonds.

Riklis, at sixty-seven, may be best known for spending millions of dollars over the last decade to promote the singing-acting-entertainment career of his second wife, thirty-six-year-old Pia Zadora, whom he met when she was seventeen. He underwrote singing and acting lessons, orchestrated commercials and a nude layout in Penthouse magazine, arranged stage shows and movies. They included the 1982 Harold Robbins production

The Lonely Lady, which one critic dismissed as a "risible concoction designed to show off the nontalents of a nonstar in a film financed by her husband." Through a maze of interlocking companies, Riklis controls such familiar businesses as McCrory Corporation and J.J. Newberry, the variety stores that are a staple of small-town America; Samonsite Corporation, the luggage maker; and Culligan Corporation, the water-treatment company.

In October 1985, Riklis's Faberge, Inc. removed $6.2 million from its employee pension fund of $18.2 million. That same month, Riklis's McCrory Corporation removed $11.1 million from its employee pension fund of $87.5 million. And in March 1986, Riklis's Kenton Corporation removed $12.6 million from its employee pension fund of $18.9 million. Over a six-month period the three Riklis companies withdrew a total of $29.9 million from employee retirement plans. After the $11.1 million was extracted from the McCrory pension fund, the remaining $76.4 million averaged out to $5,045 to be invested for each worker covered under the plan.

Many of McCrory's 26,100 employees, though, were not eligible to participate in the pension plan. Among them were 9,360 workers who earned less than $4,000 a year. And nearly two-thirds of the 15,140 employees enrolled in the retirement plan earned less than $10,000 a year. As for Riklis, his compensation from the various companies ranged upward from $4 million a year. That was complemented by a retirement package of more than $100,000 a year for life. And then for his wife. For life.

Victor Posner, at seventy-two, is a Riklis contemporary. He works out of a fading, one-time hotel and apartment house in Miami Beach. Posner has maintained a lavish lifestyle. At various times, corporate funds have been used to pay for his yachts and horses.

PBGC records show that, like Riklis, he began raiding pension funds in the 1980s. First came the Graniteville Company of Graniteville, South Carolina. A textile company with a rich history dating to the mid-1800s, Graniteville was taken over by Posner in May 1983. That month, Posner's Graniteville removed $15.4 million from a company pension fund.

In July 1984, Posner's Pennsylvania Engineering Corporation, a Pittsburgh-based engineering and construction company, removed $2.4 million from a pension fund. In June 1985, Posner's Royal Crown Companies, Inc., a Miami soft drink distributor, removed $1.9 million from a pension fund. In April 1986, Posner's National Propane Corporation, a New Hyde Park, New York, liquefied-petroleum gas distributor, removed $1.1 million from a pension fund. In June 1986, Posner's Birdsboro Corporation, a Birdsboro, Pennsylvania, foundry whose corporate ancestors manufactured muskets for the Revolutionary War, removed $4.4 million from a pension fund.

In June 1987, Posner's Salem Corporation, a Pittsburgh industrial furnace and mining equipment manufacturer, withdrew $3.5 million from a pension fund. In December 1987, Posner's Enro Shirt Company, a Louisville, Kentucky, shirtmaker, withdrew $1.5 million from a pension fund.

Finally, in November 1988, Posner's Fischbach Corporation, a New York engineering firm, withdrew $35 million from a pension fund.

That brought to $65.2 million the total that Posner companies drained from the pension funds of nearly 4,800 employees.

In the case of one of his companies, Sharon Steel Corporation, Posner never put the money into the pension fund in the first place. In a report filed with the Securities and Exchange Commission in April 1986, the company said it had postponed $27.8 million in pension contributions that it was required to make for 1984 and 1985. At the time, Sharon Steel's pension plan was $105.6 million in the hole. And the hole was growing.

The Pension Benefit Guaranty Corporation reported in 1991 that Sharon Steel now ranks third among the fifty corporations with the largest percentage of unfunded pension liabilities. The PBGC report puts the steel company's employee-retirement obligations at $264 million and the pension fund's assets at only $86 million, leaving the pension plan short $178 million. That means all the other businesses that contribute to the PBGC will be obliged to pick up the tab for the retirees of Sharon Steel, which has been in bankruptcy court since 1985.

In the meantime, Posner was indicted on charges of tax evasion and filing false tax returns. In September 1987, Posner pleaded no contest to charges of filing false income tax returns. United States District Court Judge Eugene P. Spellman in Miami found him guilty, but delayed sentencing. Posner faced a maximum of forty years in prison and payment of fines, back taxes, penalties, interest and the cost of prosecution. In February 1988, Spellman ordered Posner to pay a fine of $75,000, back taxes and penalties of $2.1 million, and interest on that sum, which totaled about $2 million. He also ordered Posner to devote 5,000 hours to community service.

There is a historical footnote to this story: In 1977, the SEC cited Posner for diverting Sharon Steel pension fund assets to his personal use. He signed a consent decree promising not to violate the law in the future.

Government officials and corporate executives are fond of saying that most private pension plans are overfunded. That is, the plan's paper assets—the value of the stocks, bonds and other investments it holds—exceed the amount of money that will have to be paid to future retirees. Therefore, they argue, the extra money belongs to the company, not the employees—even though in some cases it was set aside for pensions in lieu of raises.

On the other hand, when a plan is underfunded, those same executives often refuse to make the additional contributions needed to make the plan solvent. It is the ultimate coin-toss game: Heads, the company wins; tails, the employees lose.

If a company terminates a pension plan and buys uninsured annuities, it gets to keep the leftover cash. But if the pension fund lacks sufficient cash to pay the promised benefits, it becomes the PBGC's problem. Or if the PBGC insurance fund goes the way of the Federal Savings and Loan Insurance Corporation insurance fund—broke—it will be the taxpayers' problem.

In other words, today's overfunded pension plan may be tomorrow's under-funded plan.

Witness the experience of the Boise Cascade Corporation. In 1984 assets in the Boise pension fund amounted to $522 million. Employee retirement benefits totaled $373 million. That meant the plan was over-funded. It had $149 million in what pension raiders like to call "excess cash."

Just seven years later, the Pension Benefit Guaranty Corporation released a list of fifty companies with the largest underfunded pension plans. Among those cited: Boise Cascade, which was $32 million short. Remember, too, that once upon a time the Chrysler Corporation pension plan was adequately funded. By 1991, according to the PBGC estimates, there was a $2.6 billion deficit.

And it's getting worse across the board. Testifying before the House Budget Committee in October 1991, James B. Lockhart III, the PBGC's executive director, warned that there was "at least $40 billion of unfunded liabilities in the defined benefit pension system." That is the amount of money the PBGC—already operating at a deficit—could be called upon to pay out in retirement benefits to employees of failed companies. If the PBGC runs out of money, taxpayers will be called upon to pick up the tab. Just as they are doing for the savings and loan bailout. Lockhart told lawmakers that 1991 "saw the two largest losses in the agency's history—Eastern [Airlines] with $700 million in underfunding and Pan Am with over $900 million."

Sometimes a company's pension fund serves as an early warning signal of corporate distress. An analysis by the authors documented scores of instances in which a company's decision to dip into the retirement fund of its employees was followed in a few years by bankruptcy court proceedings, corporate restructurings, the elimination of jobs, or all three.

Take SCOA Industries, Inc., a publicly owned, mini-retail conglomerate that in 1985 was headquartered in Columbus, Ohio. In December of that year, a Boston buyout firm, Thomas H. Lee Company, joined forces with Wall Street's money-raising takeover machine, Drexel Burnham Lambert, to take SCOA Industries private. The stock buyout cost more than $600 million—most of it borrowed. Drexel Burnham and the Lee company, headed by Thomas H. Lee, a nephew of SCOA's chairman, picked up millions of dollars in fees, as well as nearly 50 percent of the stock in the new company.

At the same time, SCOA Industries dipped into a company pension fund and removed $43.7 million. Soon afterward, the company began selling off some of its holdings to pare down the debt incurred in the buyout. The $43.7 million extracted from the pension fund amounted to 57 percent of the fund's assets. That left $33.3 million, or an average of $3,299, to provide lifetime retirement benefits for each of the 10,102 employees covered under the plan. Two years after taking SCOA Industries private, in

April 1987, Drexel Burnham and the Lee company announced plans to take the successor business, Hills Department Stores, public. They sold more than four million shares of stock and issued $40 million of debt that could be converted into stock.

From those transactions, Drexel Burnham and the Lee company picked up additional millions of dollars in fees, as well as millions of dollars in profits from the sale of stock they acquired when taking the company private.

In October 1987, Drexel Burnham issued a report touting the Hills stock to investors, saying that Hills's pricing strategy, "coupled with a strong management team, has produced one of the highest operating margins in the industry." Drexel Burnham forecast a "15 percent annual sales growth over the next five years" and dismissed concerns that the outstanding debt would pose serious obstacles: "While some investors may be concerned about the company's high financial leverage, it appears to be well covered. This risk should be minimized by the company's history of twenty-nine years of consecutive increases in operating profits and sales. . . . We feel Hills will be able to generate the earnings growth and cash flow necessary to pay down debt and deleverage the balance sheet, while expanding the operation at a faster than historic pace."

Two more years slipped by and Hills was not faring especially well. Nonetheless, Drexel Burnham remained bullish in a report issued to investors in September 1989: "Hills results have been below expectations since going public two years ago, but profits appear to be on the verge of a turning point." Gazing into Wall Street's crystal ball, Drexel Burnham analysts projected that "going out past 1991, we expect earnings per share to grow by nearly 25 percent annually. This growth is a function of leverage created by paydown of debt and improving operating margins." As for all that debt still outstanding, Drexel Burnham continued to exude optimism: "We believe Hills can generate excess cash flow from earnings growth to pay down debt and slowly deleverage the balance sheet."

Once again, the wizards of debt at Drexel Burnham had guessed wrong. In February 1991, Hills Department Stores, burdened with a crushing debt arranged by Drexel Burnham and the Lee company, filed for bankruptcy protection in New York.

The 1985 raid on the company pension fund had been a precursor of what was to come, just as similar raids were at scores of other companies. Consider: In September 1982, Branch Motor Express Company, an interstate trucking company headquartered in New York City, removed $4.53 million from a company pension fund. That amounted to 52 percent of the pension fund's total assets, leaving $4.23 million, or an average of $5,221, to provide lifetime retirement benefits for each of the 810 employees covered under the plan. Two years later, in August 1984, Branch Motor Express filed for protection from its creditors in United States Bankruptcy Court. The company's seventy terminals across the country were later closed and all employees dismissed. The company no longer exists.

Another: In June 1984, the owners of Ames Department Stores, Inc., the discount retail chain headquartered in Rocky Hill, Connecticut, removed $1.7 million from a company pension fund. That was 57 percent of the pension fund's total assets, leaving $1.3 million—or an average of $458—to provide retirement benefits for each of the 2,904 employees covered under the plan. Six years later, in April 1990, Ames filed for bankruptcy protection. The company that once operated nearly 700 stores under the Ames and Zayre names, mostly on the East Coast, closed 220 stores and dismissed 18,000 employees.

Another: In June 1985, Ohrbach's, Inc., the fashionable women's apparel chain headquartered in New York City, removed $9 million from a company pension fund. That amounted to 66 percent of the pension fund's total assets, leaving $4.7 million, or an average of $6,590, to provide lifetime retirement benefits for each of the 716 employees covered under the plan. One year later, in June 1986, the Dutch company that owned Ohrbach's, which was founded in 1923, announced it was discontinuing operations. Ohrbach's stores, concentrated in New York and Los Angeles, were closed.

Another: In December 1987, the owners of Morse Shoe, Inc., operators of the Fayva shoe store chain headquartered in Canton, Massachusetts, removed $8.3 million from a pension fund. That was 35 percent of the pension fund's assets, leaving $15.4 million—or an average of $5,477—to provide lifetime retirement benefits for each of the 2,812 employees covered under the plan. Three years later, in January 1991, Morse Shoe filed for bankruptcy protection.

Another: In September 1986, the owners of B. Altman and Company, the New York–based retailer, removed $10.9 million from a company pension fund. That amounted to 45 percent of the pension fund's total assets, leaving $13.1 million, or an average of $4,226, to provide lifetime retirement benefits for each of the 3,100 employees covered under the plan. Three years later, in August 1989, B. Altman's parent company filed for protection in bankruptcy court. A few months later, all B. Altman's stores were closed and 1,700 employees were out of work. The 124-year-old chain no longer exists.

To be sure, such pension-fund raids ran their course during the 1980s. After ten years and the removal of billions of dollars from retirement plans, Congress got around to rewriting the rules to take some of the profit out of the practice by imposing stiffer excise taxes. But that doesn't mean the pension-raiding era is over. Far from it. Last year, Congress quietly slipped a new provision into the government rule book that permits corporations to use their pension fund money for another purpose: to pay for employee health-care expenses.

As was noted earlier, corporations are already cutting back on health-care benefits as insurance premiums soar. Now, Congress has given them a way to attack that problem: to further drain pension funds.

What was left for workers after pension funds were tapped

Companies with funds drained, 1980-87	Avg. assets per participating worker		Reduction of assets
	Before raid	After raid	
American Greetings	$ 1,064	$ 277	74%
Hilti Inc.	917	323	65%
Ames Dept. Stores	1,033	458	56%
Household Merch.	2,213	577	74%
Gulf + Western Corp.	2,351	700	70%
Gino's Inc.	3,081	742	76%
Heck's	2,276	861	62%
Hospital Corp. of America	1,230	893	27%
Sea Coast Products Inc.	2,603	958	63%
Dan River Inc.	4,050	1,012	75%
Citizens Utilities	2,965	1,350	54%
Butler International	10,456	1,426	86%
Searle Medical Products	2,248	1,438	47%
Exxon	7,554	1,439	81%
Host International Inc.	2,897	1,512	48%

SOURCE: Pension Benefit Guaranty Corp.

The timing of the congressional action was fortuitous. For under a new accounting rule, businesses will be required to calculate the cost of retiree health care and enter that figure into their books each year. For many companies, that will translate into shrinking profits, drawing the ire of Wall Street. Corporations now will be able to soften the impact of the accounting change by using money set aside for employee retirement benefits to pay their health-care costs.

For corporations, the best part of the deal is that the retirement payments are guaranteed by the PBGC—and ultimately taxpayers—if the pension fund runs out of cash because money was diverted to health insurance premiums.

Junk Pensions

To better understand what the future holds for the retirement of millions of workers as a result of the way Congress writes the rules, let us return to the summer of 1986, to events that unfolded in two cities that are worlds apart—Seneca, Kansas, and Washington, D.C.

It was the week of July 13, 1986. On Friday of that week, in the sleepy town of Seneca (population 2,300), employees at the Community National Bank were processing paperwork for two self-directed individual retirement accounts for John G. Kass and his wife, Virginia. The Kasses lived in Topeka, about 75 miles south of Seneca. He was a painter for the Veterans Administration hospital; she worked in the accounting department of the Santa Fe Railroad. Their retirement accounts were among hundreds the bank was establishing for workers living in different sections of the country, but concentrated in the Midwest.

With the bank acting as trustee, John Kass invested $2,400 in senior subordinated debentures—a fancy name for a piece of paper that is a corporate IOU. His wife invested $2,500. The debentures promised a hefty interest rate of 12.5 percent a year. They were issued by the American Continental Corporation of Phoenix.

Actually, the Kasses had rolled over their IRAs from another small Kansas bank in yet a smaller Kansas town, the First National Bank of Onaga (town population 700). Like many others, the Kasses had opened their retirement accounts at the Onaga bank because it catered to the self-directed IRA business. With a self-directed IRA, future retirees tell the trustee—a bank, brokerage firm or insurance company—what stocks, bonds or other investments they want to put in their retirement account.

The Onaga bank encountered financial difficulties as a result of a portfolio of bad loans and was seized by federal regulators. Many of the IRAs, including the Kasses', were shifted to Seneca. The Onaga bank was quickly reorganized and continued to service its IRAs. Now it had competition from Seneca. As more people invested their retirement accounts in American Continental bonds because of the high interest rate they paid, processing the accounts became a sizable part of the work for both banks, which are in a region hard-pressed for jobs.

For the First National Bank of Onaga, the IRA business translated into jobs. "We are a town of 700 people," said Owen E. Duer, the bank's executive vice president, "and we employ twelve people in our IRA department who would not even be here if it weren't for that department. So we are pretty tickled that we have this so we can employ people in our town." In Seneca, the Community National Bank established a separate division, called the Retirement Plans Division, to process and monitor IRA investments.

During 1986, workers from around the country put more than a quarter-million dollars of their retirement money into American Continental bonds at the Seneca and Onaga banks. Today, the money that John and Virginia Kass, Duane Hudson, Janice Butterfield, Norman Kaufmann, Eleanor Fox, Myron Danielson, Bonnie Dahl, Gerald Hubert, Patricia Kasubaski, Mary Dulebohn and others set aside for retirement is largely gone.

American Continental, a financial services holding company, filed for protection in United States Bankruptcy Court in Phoenix in April 1989. When the reorganization is completed, investors will receive pennies for every dollar they put into their IRAs.

During that same week in July 1986 week when the Community National Bank of Seneca was processing the paperwork for what would turn out to be worthless retirement accounts, Charles H. Keating, Jr., was in Washington, doing what he did best—lobbying the people who write and revise the government rule book. Keating was a Phoenix homebuilder, fund-raiser for friendly members of Congress and presidential candidates, proprietor of one of California's largest savings and loan institutions, crusader for decent literature, and chairman and chief executive officer of American Continental Corporation. Back in the 1950s, when he was a Cincinnati lawyer, Keating had founded Citizens for Decent Literature, Inc. For years, he traveled the country identifying and denouncing smut.

On Wednesday morning, July 16, 1986, Keating was making the rounds of Capitol Hill, railing against government regulators and their efforts to impose some controls on financial institutions, such as his Lincoln Savings and Loan Association. Keating's American Continental had acquired Lincoln Savings and Loan, headquartered in Irvine, California, in 1984. He promptly abandoned the traditional savings and loan business of making home mortgages and opted for pouring hundreds of millions of dollars into junk bonds, luxury resort hotels, assorted real estate deals and foreign investments.

When the Federal Home Loan Bank Board, under chairman Edwin J. Gray, proposed a regulation limiting such investments, Keating mounted a banker's holy war against regulations in general and Gray in particular. He enlisted an army of supporters to lobby both the Federal Home Loan Bank Board and Congress. The army included Donald T. Regan and Alan J. Greenspan. At the time, Regan was White House chief of staff and Greenspan was a private consultant and member of the president's Economic Policy Advisory Board. That is the same Alan Greenspan who now, as chairman of the Federal Reserve Board, helps make policy decisions that influence the course of the economy and everyone's standard of living.

In a letter to the Federal Home Loan Bank Board on behalf of Keating's thrift, Greenspan wrote on Nov. 1, 1984: "I understand that Lincoln Savings and Loan Association has requested that the board allow me to meet with it or its staff in order to discuss my view that the proposed rule [limiting thrift investments] is unwarranted and could prove harmful if put into effect. I hope that the board will agree to such a meeting . . . at the earliest possible time."

The high-powered lobbying notwithstanding, Edwin Gray and the bank board issued the rule. By the summer of 1986, Keating was back in Washington, pushing for Gray's ouster, an end to the regulation on investments, and the appointment of more friendly regulators. He had come up with his personal nominee for a seat on the three-member bank board.

His candidate was Lee H. Henkel, Jr., an Atlanta lawyer and businessman. During the first administration of President Richard M. Nixon, Henkel had served as general counsel for the Internal Revenue Service and assistant general counsel of the Treasury Department. Henkel, who was active in Republican politics, had worked with Keating in 1980, when both men were backing John B. Connally's bid for the GOP presidential nomination. Henkel had also borrowed millions of dollars from Lincoln Savings and Loan to help underwrite some of his investments.

So it was that on July 16, 1986, Keating set off to the Senate to sell Henkel. First he met with Paula Hawkins, a Florida Republican. Then he met with Senator Donald W. Riegle, Jr., the Michigan Democrat. Then he met with Alan Cranston, the Democratic senator from California. Later Keating's forces would give Hawkins $8,000 in campaign contributions, Riegle $78,250—and Cranston $1.3 million. In the weeks that followed, Keating lobbied other lawmakers on behalf of Henkel. His perseverance paid off on Oct. 7, 1986, when President Reagan tapped Henkel for a seat on the board.

Henkel was no sooner in office than he proposed new banking rules that would have granted immunity to Lincoln Savings for some of its past lending practices. It seemed that Lincoln had put nearly twice as much money into risky investments as was allowed under the regulation still in effect. For months, federal bank examiners had been poring over Lincoln's books, asking annoying questions about the institution's investments and about missing paperwork.

Henkel's attempt to help backfired. When his financial ties to Lincoln were disclosed and Senator William Proxmire, the Wisconsin Democrat, demanded a Justice Department investigation, Henkel resigned from the bank board. But Keating's lobbying and incessant attacks on his nemesis, Edwin Gray, had had their effect. Gray left the bank board in June 1987 when his term expired. He was replaced by another Keating ally, M. Danny Wall, the former staff director of the Senate banking committee. Over the next two years, Wall's actions would protect Keating and his company from the federal auditors who correctly saw that Lincoln's investment practices would bring down the thrift.

But eventually it all unraveled. Lincoln Savings and Loan was seized by federal regulators. Its bailout will cost taxpayers $1 billion or more. American Continental went into bankruptcy court. The bankruptcy case is the largest in Arizona history and one of the half-dozen largest, in terms of paperwork, in United States history. And finally, in December 1991, a Los Angeles County Superior Court jury convicted Charles Keating himself on seventeen of eighteen counts of securities fraud in connection with the sale of the worthless bonds. Later that same month, a federal grand jury indicted him on fraud and racketeering charges.

In addition to the hundreds of people who put their retirement money in American Continental bonds, more than 20,000 others, most of them residents of California, purchased the bonds as a general investment. In California, where the debentures were sold at Lincoln Savings and Loan branches, many unsuspecting buyers thought the bonds, like their savings accounts, were insured by the federal government. So, too, did some of the people who bought the bonds for their retirement accounts, including the folks in and around little Seneca, Kansas. They were not.

Owen Duer, the First National Bank of Onaga official, said that a lot of people were confused, assuming that, because their IRA was in a federally insured bank, the account, too, was insured. Many IRAs are, indeed, backed by the government, but only when they are placed in accounts that are federally insured. After the American Continental bankruptcy filing, Duer said, "We had lots of phone calls. I can remember one gentleman who just swore up and down that he was insured by the [Federal Deposit Insurance Corporation], and I assured him that he wasn't, and that I didn't make that investment. He was only insured by FDIC if I made that investment for him. He chose to make that investment. He felt just because we were a bank, anything he did with us became insured."

Duer emphasized that the banks acted only as custodians: "We do whatever the customer or his representative says to do with the assets in his IRA. The only thing we do is the paperwork and the government reporting. We make no recommendations on whether to buy or sell. . . . That's the sum total of our involvement." Duer said it was possible that the people selling the bonds led the buyers to believe that, because a bank was acting as custodian, the IRA was insured. Or perhaps the salespeople did nothing to discourage a buyer who jumped to that conclusion.

But how was it, exactly, that people in Iowa and Michigan and Nebraska and Arizona opened IRAs in Onaga and Seneca, Kansas, and invested their future in a piece of Charles Keating's financial empire? Local and regional brokerage firms, among them the Offerman Company of Minneapolis, sold the bonds. The two Kansas banks acted as custodians.

John Kass, the Topeka painter who put his IRA money in American Continental bonds, remembers the broker's spiel well: "He said, 'John, I think this is pretty good. I think we ought to get into this. It's paying 13 percent . . .' or whatever it was. He said his boss had a lot of shares in it. He said it was a real good deal."

The broker's pitch notwithstanding, Kass might have chosen a different investment if he had heard the views a year earlier of the man in charge of the company issuing the bonds. During an appearance before a congressional committee in February 1985, Charles Keating, the American Continental chairman, spoke critically of subordinated debentures: "I do not happen to think [a] subordinated debenture is viable capital. I think it is a sham." Out in the heartland, the story was a bit different.

Another Topeka resident, Duane Hudson, a former telephone company lineman, said he was told that American Continental bonds were "as good as gold." "He [the broker] told me, 'This will be there when you retire.

You'll have your investment.' . . . The risk was never mentioned. It was just the same as though you had put it in a bank. He said that with institutions of that size, there is never any worry.

"I guess these were junk bonds, but they weren't sold to me as junk bonds," said an embittered Hudson. "These were sold to me as a security so when I retired I would have some money. I didn't want my IRA in anything that was risky. And that's why I'm bitter. I didn't know what a junk bond was from anything else, but I do now."

Dream Pensions

While all this may seem to suggest an unrelievedly grim picture of America's private pension system, there are, to be sure, a few bright spots.

Some pensioners are doing quite nicely. In 1990, H. Ray Roberts of Denton, Texas, collected pension checks totaling $56,520. Paul G. Rogers of West Palm Beach, Florida, picked up $60,480. Lawrence H. Fountain of Tarboro, North Carolina, received $58,992. And Bernice Frederic Sisk of Fresno, California, collected $53,700.

In each instance, the payments exceeded the average pensions received by most people after a lifetime of work—less than $7,000 a year. But then, all four men worked for the same generous employer—you, the taxpayer. All are retired members of Congress. That is the same Congress that, when it came to writing a law that would insure the pensions of millions of workers, set a limit on how much the government would guarantee. In 1991, it was $26,000.

Roberts, Rogers, Fountain, and Sisk are not unique. In fact, they don't even rank among Congress's top twenty-five pension collectors. That distinction goes to former lawmakers who collect pensions that exceed the salaries they received when they were working—by up to 275 percent.

Suppose you once earned $25,000 in your office or factory job. You retire. The years slip by. Now you collect $50,000. Or $93,750. Not likely. That is because about 99 percent of the labor force works for businesses that do not adjust pensions yearly to account for inflation. More typical is a pension that amounts to 25 percent, or less, of a worker's salary.

Unless you're in Congress. Then, the sky is the limit. Consider Eugene J. McCarthy, sometime-poet, Democratic representative and later senator from Minnesota for twenty-two years, and perennial presidential candidate. McCarthy retired in January 1971. His Senate salary the previous year was $42,500. In 1990, McCarthy's congressional pension totaled $68,268, or 161 percent of his salary.

Or take J. William Fulbright, the Arkansas Democrat who fashioned a reputation as a foreign policy expert during his thirty years in the Senate. Arkansas voters retired Fulbright in January 1975. His Senate salary the year before was $42,500. In 1990, Fulbright's congressional pension amounted to $82,224, or 193 percent of his salary.

J. Caleb Boggs, the former Republican senator from Delaware, has done even better. He served six years in the House and twelve years in the Senate, separated by two terms as governor. Delaware voters retired Boggs in January 1973. His Senate salary the previous year was $42,500. In 1990, Boggs's congressional pension reached $90,348—or 213 percent of his salary.

Finally, at the top of Congress's pension-income growth list is Frank M. Karsten, a relatively obscure Democrat from St. Louis who spent twenty-two years in the House. Karsten retired in January 1969. His House salary the year before was $30,000. In 1990, Karsten's congressional pension totaled $82,824—or 276 percent of his salary.

It should be noted that other onetime lawmakers draw heftier pensions, but their salaries were larger at their retirement, or they had more years of government service. Thus former Speaker of the House Carl B. Albert, an Oklahoma Democrat who retired in January 1977, collected a pension of $110,124 in 1990. That was 247 percent of his last salary. And Michael J. Mansfield, the longtime Democratic senator from Montana, received $149,508—or 167 percent of his final congressional salary.

In addition to their service-based congressional pensions, many lawmakers also have established supplementary pension accounts based on other income, most notably the money they made from giving speeches. Here again, they have amended the government rule book, time after time, to take care of themselves, while assuring workers everywhere they were merely strengthening the private pension system. The end result has been ever greater inequities: A system that provides extraordinarily generous pensions for some, meager pensions for others, guaranteed pensions for some, nonguaranteed pensions for others.

Overlying this chaos is another practice that Congress has elevated to an art form over the last two decades: Enacting specific legislative packages one year, then rescinding or amending them a few years later. This has been especially true in the area of taxes and pensions.

Take tax-deductible Individual Retirement Accounts, for instance. Congress passed the universal IRA program in 1981. In a report issued on Dec. 31 of that year, the Joint Committee on Taxation explained the reasoning: "The Congress was concerned that a large number of the country's workers, including many who are covered by employer-sponsored retirement plans, face the prospect of retiring without the resources needed to provide adequate retirement income levels."

In 1986, Congress took a different position and, depending on income levels, either limited or canceled the deductibility of IRAs. A Congress that five years earlier had said that IRAs should be expanded so everyone could have a retirement plan now said that IRAs should be curbed because people had too many retirement plans.

Bill Bradley, the Democratic senator from New Jersey, spoke for the revisionists: "Just giving a quick scan over the code, you find that it is

Congress is well cared for

❝You shouldn't have a double dip.❞

— Sen. Robert Dole (R., Kansas), who along with wife Elizabeth may have a *quintuple* dip.

Former members of Congress and the percentage of their last salary they receive in pensions:

SENATORS

J. Caleb Boggs (R., Delaware)

Salary: $42,500
Pension: 90,348   **213%**

J. William Fulbright (D., Ark.)

Salary: $42,500
Pension: 82,224   **193%**

Eugene J. McCarthy (D., Minn.)

Salary: $42,500
Pension: 68,268   **161%**

REPRESENTATIVES

Frank M. Karsten (D., Missouri)

Salary: $30,000
Pension: 82,824   **276%**

Carl B. Albert (D., Oklahoma)

Salary: $44,600
Pension: 110,124   **247%**

Paul G. Rogers (D., Florida)

Salary: $57,500
Pension: 60,480   **105%**

Bernice F. Sisk (D., California)

Salary: $57,500
Pension: 53,700   **93%**

H. Ray Roberts (D., Texas)

Salary: $60,663
Pension: 56,520   **93%**

Lawrence H. Fountain (D., N.C.)

Salary: $69,800
Pension: 58,992   **85%**

CONGRESSIONAL CONVICTS

Rep. John V. Dowdy (D., Texas)

Salary: $42,500
Pension: 66,612   **157%**

Rep. Frank M. Clark (D., Pa.)

Salary: $42,500
Pension: 64,068   **151%**

Rep. Cornelius E. Gallagher (D., N.J.)

Salary: $42,500
Pension: 58,368   **137%**

possible for a family to have six or seven different pension plans. For example, you could have a 401(k) plan. . . . If you have a spouse that works as a teacher or public employee, you could have a so-called 403 plan. . . . If you have a little self-employment income, you could have a Keogh plan. If you work for a company, you will have the company pension plan. If your spouse works for another company, you will have two company pension plans.

"If you are like an increasing number of Americans who, in their work life work for two companies, you could end up with two company pension plans. If your wife or husband worked also for two companies, you could end up in a family with four company pension plans. And that is all before we even get to the question of Social Security. So that you could find a family with a 401(k) plan, a 403 plan, a Keogh, two or three or four company pensions, and Social Security."

Such a scenario is indeed possible for about 17 percent of America's work force. The overwhelming majority are public employees—schoolteachers and college professors, local, state and federal government workers. For the remaining 83 percent of the population, the probability of multiple retirement checks is a fantasy.

Perhaps Bradley was talking about himself and his wife. Or about any number of other members of Congress—Robert J. Dole, the Republican senator from Kansas, for example. In 1986 Dole condemned IRAs for people who were already enrolled in a pension plan at work, saying, "You shouldn't have a double dip." Dole and his wife, on the other hand, could have a quintuple dip. Or more.

Dole will receive a guaranteed pension when he retires from Congress. He could contribute to a 401(k), and the federal government—make that the taxpayers—will match part of his contribution. He receives a tax-free military pension of $13,728 for injuries sustained in World War II. And he has established a Keogh account to accommodate his income from honoraria, speeches and writing. Dole's wife, Elizabeth, who held two cabinet posts, as secretary of transportation and as labor secretary, also could establish a Keogh account.

To understand how Congress has written the pension rules to favor the few, take a closer look at Senator Dole's Keogh account. From 1983 to 1986, Dole reported $663,857 in Schedule C income on his tax returns. That was business income—outside his Senate salary—on which the Keogh account was based. Of the $663,857 in income, $552,414 came from honoraria that Dole received for making speeches and writing articles. He retained $167,429 of the honoraria for his personal use, and donated the remaining $384,985 to charity, as required by law.

Over the four years, Dole set aside $133,442 in the Keogh account, with some of that money coming from honoraria and the rest from other sources, such as book royalties. According to a 1986 report prepared by E.F. Hutton and Company projecting the retirement benefits of the Keogh account, Dole will receive a yearly pension of $59,000 from that one retirement plan alone. Depending on when he retires from public office, Dole's congressional pension will top $90,000, giving him a minimum pension income of more than $150,000.

Now contrast that with the factory worker earning $25,000 a year, who has a wife and two children. If he's lucky enough to have a pension where he works, he may also establish an IRA, to which he may contribute a maximum of $2,000 a year. If his employer has no pension plan—a circumstance that is increasingly the case—he may contribute $2,250 to an IRA, but no more. His wife, who stays home to raise the family, is prohibited from having a retirement account.

This is not just to single out Senator Dole. Other members of Congress are doing just as well—or better. And some are already collecting pension checks in addition to their congressional paychecks. Senator Alan J. Dixon, an Illinois Democrat and one of the Senate's many millionaires, has augmented his $101,900 congressional salary with a $30,400 pension from his years of service in state government.

Even those lawmakers convicted of crimes have done quite nicely under the Capitol Hill pension system. Cornelius E. Gallagher, a Democrat, spent fourteen years in Congress as the representative of Hudson and Union Counties in northern New Jersey before checking into a federal penitentiary in 1973 after pleading guilty to income tax evasion. Gallagher's congressional salary in 1972, when he was indicted on charges of concealing more than $300,000 of income, was $42,500. His monthly pension checks in 1990 added up to $58,368, or 137 percent of his congressional salary.

Frank M. Clark, a Democrat, represented three western Pennsylvania counties—Beaver, Butler and Lawrence—for twenty years before voters retired him in January 1975. Three years later, Clark was indicted on charges of income tax evasion, mail fraud and perjury in connection with placing his housekeepers and campaign workers on federal payrolls. He pleaded guilty in February 1979 to income tax evasion and mail fraud and was sentenced to two years in prison. Clark's final congressional salary was $42,500. In 1990, he collected a pension of $64,068, or 151 percent of his salary.

And finally there is John V. Dowdy, a Democrat who spent twenty years in Congress as a representative of eighteen sparsely populated counties in east Texas before going to prison in 1974 after his conviction on bribery and perjury charges. Dowdy's congressional salary in 1973, the year before he went to prison, was $42,500. His pension checks in 1990 totaled $66,612, or 157 percent of his congressional salary. That is a weekly average of $1,281.

While Congress has guaranteed the pensions of its convicted felons, a few states have enacted legislation terminating the pension benefits of public officials found guilty of criminal acts. West Virginia's three-term Republican governor, Arch Moore, was sentenced to five years in prison in July 1990 after pleading guilty to federal charges of tax fraud, mail fraud, extortion and obstruction of justice. He is serving his time at a camp for white-collar criminals at Maxwell Air Force Base in Alabama. As a result of the conviction, Moore has lost his annual state pension of $20,864 and any survivor's pension for his wife.

But Moore didn't lose all his retirement benefits. He is continuing to collect his check from the United States Treasury for the years he spent in Congress.

CHAPTER TEN
THE POLITICAL CONNECTION

WHAT WENT WRONG

On Capitol Hill, it is the lobbyists who have the clout.
They speak for the vested interests, not the middle class.
And they have been extraordinarily successful in blocking tax-
law changes that would be detrimental to the privileged, as well
as in preserving tax breaks that benefit the few at the expense
of the many — such as the tax exemption for interest paid on
bonds issued by state and local governments.

52% of 1989 tax-exempt interest income — $20.1 billion — went to 800,000 individuals and families earning $100,000 or more.

That's less than **1%** of all U.S. tax filers.

48% of 1989 tax-exempt interest income — $18.7 billion — went to 3 million individuals and families earning less than $100,000.

That's **2%** of all U.S. tax filers.

108.5 million individuals and families received no tax-exempt interest income. They represent **97%** of all U.S. tax filers.

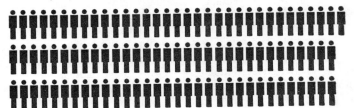

SOURCE: Internal Revenue Service

Investing in Capitol Hill

In Washington, where 11,000 organizations are lobbying Congress, there is an old adage: Successful lobbies are measured by the legislation they stop, not by the laws they get passed.

By that yardstick, the Alliance for Capital Access was phenomenally successful. Let's watch the Alliance in action in 1985, the year it stopped a big one. At the time, pressure was building on Congress to do something about the wave of hostile takeovers, leveraged buyouts and corporate mergers that were sweeping America.

Representative Timothy E. Wirth, the Colorado Democrat who was then chairman of a subcommittee of the House Energy and Commerce Committee, was concerned that "shareholders, companies, employees and entire communities have been harmed in these battles for corporate control." He wanted hearings to "assess the fairness" of the takeovers.

To schedule witnesses and set the agenda for the hearings, which were expected to lead to new legislation, Wirth turned to a close aide, David K. Aylward, the subcommittee's staff director and chief counsel. Aylward indicated that the hearings would go beyond a probe of the tactics used by raiders and explore the role that high-yield (junk) bonds were playing in financing corporate takeovers. "We really don't know where this money is coming from, and whether it could be better used for something else in the long term," Aylward told the *New York Times* on Feb. 18, 1985.

Shortly after the hearings convened, Aylward resigned from Wirth's staff and took a new job. He joined a lobbying company whose first clients would include the newly formed Alliance for Capital Access. Its sole aim: to block any legislation that would restrict junk bonds. Describing itself as an organization of high-yield bond users, the Alliance was in reality a Washington lobby for Michael Milken, Drexel Burnham Lambert, Inc.'s junk-bond chief, who helped create the group just as junk bonds came under mounting criticism.

Over the next few years, the Alliance became one of the capital's most successful lobbies—wining and dining lawmakers, passing out checks to House and Senate members to make speeches, testifying before congressional committees and extolling the benefits of junk bonds.

In the end, its success could be measured by a simple standard: Congress never enacted legislation to scale back the virtually unlimited deduction for interest on corporate debt—the engine that had driven the junk-bond movement. In 1991, the Alliance disbanded, its job done.

"I charge people money when there is something I can do for them,"

Aylward said. "There's no legislative activity on the horizon that would justify people contributing to that kind of organization anymore." That is good news for supporters of the Alliance.

But it's bad news for you—if you're a middle-class man or woman, family or single parent, child or senior citizen, factory worker or middle-level manager, homemaker or career woman. For successful lobbies like the Alliance for Capital Access have helped to frame the content of the government rule book, the agglomeration of laws and regulations that direct the course of the American economy.

That rule book is responsible for the decline of America's middle class, for the triumph of special interests. It determines whether you have a job that pays $15 an hour or one that pays $6; whether you have a pension and health-care insurance; whether you can afford to own a home. It governs everything from the tax system to imports of foreign goods, from the bankruptcy system to regulatory oversight.

But just as important as the laws and regulations that make up the rule book are the potential changes that are never enacted by Congress, never implemented by regulatory agencies—owing to the influence exercised by lobbies like the Alliance for Capital Access. It is because of such lobbies that Congress has failed to rewrite the laws that permit foreign-owned companies in the United States to pay taxes at a lower rate than American-owned companies.

It is because of such lobbies that Congress has failed to rewrite the laws that permit companies to escape their financial obligations to employees and retirees, suppliers and customers, by seeking sanctuary in United States Bankruptcy Court.

It is because of such lobbies that Congress has failed to rewrite the laws that permit wealthy citizens to pay combined income and Social Security taxes at a rate well below that paid by individuals and families earning less than $20,000 a year.

It is because of such lobbies that Congress has failed to do anything about forty million Americans who are going without health-care insurance and millions more who have insurance that provides only limited protection.

It is because of such lobbies that Congress has failed to rewrite the laws that permit wealthy foreign investors to pay taxes on their United States income at a rate well below that paid by individuals and families earning less than $30,000 a year.

It is because of such lobbies that Congress has failed to rewrite the laws that permit banks to deduct most of their bad loans, thereby shifting the cost of flawed business decisions from themselves to the American taxpayer.

And it is because of such lobbies that Congress has failed to even consider rewriting the laws to impose taxes on dealings that have long gone untaxed.

Like, say, a 1 percent excise tax on the trading of stocks, bonds, futures and options. That is the kind of tax that middle-class families pay every day. Look on your telephone bill. See that 3 percent excise tax added onto your charges? Look at the gas pump the next time you fill up the car. See the fourteen-cent federal tax? That is an excise tax—at a rate of 17 percent.

But the idea of an excise tax on securities transactions has been blocked each time it has come up in Congress. Lobbyists assert that such a tax would fall on pension funds—the largest pools of money that are presently untaxed. Listen to what a few members of the House Ways and Means Committee—the committee responsible for writing all tax legislation—had to say in response to a *Philadelphia Inquirer* survey about a 1 percent levy:

Bill Archer, a Republican congressman from Texas: "I would not support the enactment of such a tax. . . . A transfer tax would cause investors to shift financial transactions to foreign exchanges which do not impose them."

Dan Rostenkowski, the Illinois Democrat and committee chairman: "I am on record as being generally unsympathetic to such taxes in the past. . . . Given the globalization of financial markets and the international trading patterns that now exist, such a tax would raise serious questions about the ability of our nation to compete. Such a tax could reduce the price of shares, thereby increasing the cost of capital and actually discouraging investment and innovation."

And an aide to Charles Rangel, the New York Democrat: "He is against it. His reasons are very simple: He represents New York City, which represents the center of the securities industry. There have been a lot of studies which indicate the city would lose a lot of business. . . . It is a very simple, parochial, provincial view."

If Wall Street poured billions of dollars into leveraged buyouts, hostile takeovers and mergers in the 1980s, it invested just as enthusiastically in Washington. Witness the speech-making income of perhaps the most powerful member of Congress, the one lawmaker who more than any other determines the structure of America's tax system—Dan Rostenkowski.

From 1980 through 1990, Rostenkowski collected $37,000 in speaking fees from the Chicago Board of Trade. And $22,500 from the Public Securities Association. And $20,000 from Citicorp-Citibank. And $19,500 from the American Stock Exchange. And $18,000 from the American Bankers Association. And $15,500 from the Securities Industry Association.

He picked up $15,000 from the National Venture Capital Association. And $15,000 from the CL Global Partners Securities Corporation. And $14,500 from the Futures Industry Association. And $13,500 from the American Council for Capital Formation. And $13,000 from the Midwest Stock Exchange. And $10,000 from the Exchange National Bank of Chicago.

Add up the honoraria and the total comes to $213,500 for the eleven years. And that's just from twelve organizations—all with a direct stake in the Internal Revenue Code in general and the imposition of new taxes, such

Rep. Rostenkowski's plentiful honoraria

Top 20 contributors	Amount of honoraria, 1980 to 1990*
1. Blue Cross-Blue Shield	$ 42,500
2. Chicago Board of Trade	37,000
3. Public Securities Association	22,500
4. Hotel & Restaurant Employees' Union	20,500
5. Citicorp-Citibank	20,000
6. Wm. M. Mercer Meidinger Hansen	20,000
7. American Stock Exchange	19,500
8. American Society of Association Executives	18,500
9. American Bankers Association	18,000
10. AT&T	17,500
11. Joseph E. Seagram & Sons	16,500
12. Cosmetic, Toiletry & Fragrance Association	16,000
13. Securities Industry Association	15,500
14. Business International Corp.	15,000
15. Global Partners Securities Corp.	15,000
16. Chicago Research & Trading Group	15,000
17. National Association of Chain Drug Stores	15,000
18. National Automobile Dealers Association	15,000
19. National Venture Capital Association	15,000
20. Tax Executives Institute	15,000

*Lawmakers were allowed to keep only a percentage, giving the rest to charity.

SOURCE: Clerk, U.S. House of Representatives

as an excise tax, in particular. Over the eleven years, Rostenkowski pulled in $1.7 million in speaking fees or honoraria from businesses and organizations with an interest in tax legislation.

To put that sum in perspective, consider this: The $1.7 million that Rostenkowski received from groups seeking favored treatment was double the amount of money that he received for serving in Congress. He couldn't keep it all, of course. Federal law required that any amount above a fixed percentage had to be turned over to charity.

While Rostenkowski may have been the largest recipient of honoraria during the 1980s, the groups that contributed to him were also generous with other lawmakers. Throughout the period, investment bankers, banks, trade groups, stock exchanges, and brokerage houses gave millions in campaign contributions and speaking fees to senators and House members on crucial committees that write the rules by which the economic game is played.

Over the last six years, according to reports filed with the Senate Records Office, the Securities Industry Association, for example, gave $26,000 in speaking fees to nine members of the Senate Finance Committee. During that period, the American Stock Exchange gave $19,000 in speaking fees to seven senior members of the committee. Paine Webber Group, the Wall Street investment company, gave $18,500 to five senior members of the committee.

Congress has since banned honoraria. In exchange for a pay increase, to $125,100 a year, lawmakers are prohibited from accepting fees for speeches. But not to worry. There is a replacement: the personal congressional foundation or related tax-exempt organization. Now, contributions may be made directly to the Dole Foundation of Senator Robert J. Dole, the Kansas Republican. Or to the Derrymore Foundation of Senator Daniel Patrick Moynihan, the New York Democrat. Or to the University of Utah's Garn Institute of Finance supported by Senator Jake Garn, the Utah Republican.

However worthy the cause of the tax-exempt organizations, contributions to them, like the speaking fees, bring something beyond the reach of middle-class Americans—access to the people who write the rule book.

So, too, do campaign contributions. Many of the same lobbying groups that handed out speaking fees also contributed to the campaigns of members of the tax-writing committees.

Morgan Stanley and Company's political action committee, the Better Government Fund, made contributions in 1989–90 to Senator Max Baucus, a Montana Democrat; Senator Bill Bradley, a New Jersey Democrat; Representative Beryl F. Anthony, Jr., an Arkansas Democrat; Representative Thomas J. Downey, a New York Democrat; Representative Barbara B. Kennelly, a Connecticut Democrat; Representative Robert T. Matsui, a California Democrat; Representative Guy A. Vander Jagt, a Michigan Republican; and Representative Rangel, the New York Democrat.

The Public Securities Association's political action committee contributed to the campaigns of Senator Lloyd Bentsen, the Texas Democrat; Senator Thomas A. Daschle, a South Dakota Democrat; Senator Dole, the Kansas Republican; Senator Steve Symms, an Idaho Republican; and Representative Byron L. Dorgan, a North Dakota Democrat.

The Chicago Mercantile Exchange's political action committee gave to Senator Dave Durenberger, a Minnesota Republican; Senator Charles E. Grassley, an Iowa Republican; Representative Fred L. Grandy, another Iowa Republican; Representative Sander M. Levin, a Michigan Democrat; Representative Donald J. Pease, an Ohio Democrat; Representative Marty Russo, an Illinois Democrat; and Representative Donald K. Sundquist, a Tennessee Republican.

When Congress isn't busy taking care of such contributors, it's busy taking care of itself. In 1950, members of Congress received annual salaries of $12,500. That was six times the $2,065 salary earned by a department store clerk. Today, members of Congress, who have enthusiastically endorsed America's shift from a manufacturing to a service economy, are doing much better. By 1992, their annual salary of $125,100 was twelve times the $10,480 earned by a department store clerk.

But that higher salary is important because, without it, ordinary workers who would like a seat in the Senate would be unable to afford a life of public service. That, at least, is the way Senator Robert C. Byrd, the West Virginia Democrat, sees it. He said so in July 1991, when he introduced legislation providing for a 23 percent pay increase to bring the salaries of senators in line with that of representatives.

Said Byrd: "We must not perpetuate an arrangement which effectively shuts people out of serving in the Senate. To continue down this road means there will not be any welders that come out of the shipyards in Baltimore and stand in this place.

"There will not be any more meat-cutters that come out of the coalfields of southern West Virginia or Indiana or Illinois or Kentucky or Alabama to stand in this place. There will not be any garbage boys that come out of the hills of West Virginia, or produce salesmen or even small, very small, small business operators that will come here to give of their talents. . . .

"I feel that when it comes to this Senate floor, the poor boy or the poor woman may serve as well, may serve as industriously, as dedicatedly, as devotedly, as efficiently, as skillfully, as can the scion of the wealthiest sire in this country. That is what I am fighting for here tonight. . . . Let us open the doors to a few poor folks who may aspire to run for the U.S. Senate."

Caring for the Privileged

There was no talk during the debate on Senatorial pay about another pay gap—the widening pay gap between middle-class workers and the lawmakers themselves, a breach that happens to parallel the pay gap between factory workers and corporate executives—a gap that Congress has made possible.

Or about longtime inequities in the tax code that assure that the wealthy escape payment of taxes. For all the talk in the 1980s about repealing tax breaks benefiting the rich, Congress preserved some longstanding tax benefits that have been the special province of the wealthy for decades. Such as tax-exempt interest.

Tax-free income is everyone's dream, but only the very wealthy can make this fantasy come true. When former IRS commissioner Sheldon Cohen, now a leading Washington tax lawyer, told an audience that the Tax Reform Act of 1986 did not even "come close" to wiping out loopholes, he had tax-exempt bonds uppermost in mind: "We have a client who owned investment real estate, retired, and sold out for about $8 million. He invested every penny in tax-exempt bonds. He is a millionaire many times over. He did not pay any taxes before tax reform, and he still won't pay taxes after tax reform."

It was only fitting that tax reformers preserved this privilege of the very rich. Congress has kept it intact for more than half a century. The oldest loophole in the code, the exemption goes all the way back to the income tax law that was enacted in 1913.

The Sixteenth Amendment gave Congress all-encompassing power to tax income "from whatever source derived." But the first income tax law excluded interest from state and local bonds, ostensibly because of uncertainty over Congress's right to tax them. Under the Constitution, federal and state governments cannot tax each other, and so opponents argued successfully that it would be unconstitutional to levy a tax on state obligations.

Support for the idea came from the United States Supreme Court decision that overturned an earlier income tax law in 1894. The court held that the tax was invalid because it would tax municipal securities, which it regarded as "a tax on the power of the States and their instrumentalities to borrow money and consequently repugnant to the Constitution." The Sixteenth Amendment ratifying the income tax overrode the decision, but Congress refused to press the issue, and the exemption for state and local bonds continues.

Opposition arose at once and some of the most bitter battles in the income tax's early years were fought over this loophole. From the start, Republicans and Democrats, liberals and conservatives, presidents, secretaries of the Treasury, other political figures, and the press singled out exempt securities as one of the tax code's worst loopholes. On few tax questions has opinion been so consistent, so evenly dispersed through both parties, and so unified in its philosophical opposition. A sampling of comment through the years shows the range and consistency of the opposition.

Senator Philander C. Knox, a Republican from Pennsylvania, in 1918: "Exemption of the income from state bonds from taxation in the hands of their holders is against a sound public policy. It frees vast fortunes from taxation by the federal government without regard to the obligations or necessities of that government."

President Warren Harding in 1923: "I think our tax problems, the tendency of wealth to seek nontaxable investment, and the menacing increase of public debt, federal, state, and municipal, all justify a proposal to change the Constitution so as to end the issue of nontaxable bonds."

Representative Ogden L. Mills, a Republican from New York, in 1923: "Tax-exempt securities constitute, in my judgment, the greatest evil in the whole field of taxation—an evil so far-reaching in its consequences, both social and economic, as to be deserving of the most serious and immediate attention on the part of the people of the country. Of one thing I am perfectly sure: a progressive income tax at high rates and tax-exempt securities cannot exist side by side. Tax-exempt securities must inevitably destroy the progressive income tax, and I am by no means sure that the evil has not already reached such proportions as to make any possible action too late to save our present federal income tax."

President Calvin Coolidge in 1923: "Another reform which is urgent in our fiscal system is the abolition of the right to issue tax-exempt securities. The existing system not only permits a large amount of the wealth of the nation to escape its just burden but acts as a continual stimulant to municipal extravagance. This should be prohibited by constitutional amendment. All the wealth of the nation ought to contribute its fair share to the expenses of the nation."

Andrew Mellon, secretary of the Treasury, in 1924: "It is incredible that a system of taxation which permits a man with an income of $1,000,000 a year to pay not one cent to the support of his government should remain unaltered."

President Franklin D. Roosevelt in 1939: "It is difficult for almost all citizens to understand why a constitutional provision permitting taxes on 'income from whatever source derived' does not mean 'from whatever source derived.' ... A fair and effective progressive income tax and a huge perpetual reserve of tax-exempt bonds could not exist side by side."

John W. Snyder, secretary of the Treasury, in 1951: "The exemption of state and municipal securities is a long-standing barrier to the achievement of equity in the distribution of the individual income tax burden."

John Tunney, a Democratic Senator from California, in 1969: "The tax-exempt bonds that are owned by individuals are concentrated in the hands of the wealthiest 2 percent of the population. ... It will be possible for a select few to receive vast amounts of tax-free income, while persons with incomes of one-hundredth the size will be taxed at effective rates of 20 to 30 percent."

Stanley S. Surrey of Harvard Law School in 1976: "The tax-exempt subsidy is as inequitable as it is inefficient. ... Such a tax escape is distinctly unfair, and morally wrong. It is unfair to the millions of individuals who pay their federal income taxes and are often hard-pressed to do so."

Every attempt to revoke this tax break for the wealthy has failed. The first real effort came in World War I when the House Ways and Means Committee—supported by the Treasury Department—wrote a provision into the pending Revenue Act of 1918 to tax future state and local issues. With the nation fighting its first European war, the committee contended that "justice requires that at least in time of war the holders of these securities should share the burdens equally with the holders of Liberty bonds."

After the House gave overwhelming approval, the measure came under sharp attack in the Senate where Frank B. Kellogg, a Republican Senator from Minnesota, called the House provision a "doubtful and dangerous experiment" that could "destroy or render ineffectual state governments." That was all the encouragement the Senate Finance Committee needed to strike out the House attempt to tax the bonds. It also marked the beginning of what would become a long tradition in the tax-law process.

From then on, the Senate Finance Committee would play the role of spoiler both on tax-exempt-bond reform and other steps toward making the income tax more progressive. Through Republican and Democratic administrations, peace and war, prosperity and recession, the committee would seek to preserve tax privileges of the wealthy.

After the war, as the volume and the tax loss grew, a strong movement developed once again to end the exemption. Treasury Secretary Mellon charged that exempt bonds were diverting capital from private financing and channeling money into unproductive municipal make-work programs. In 1922 the House Ways and Means Committee adopted a resolution to amend the Constitution to authorize reciprocal taxation of state and federal securities. The House approved the resolution by a two-thirds vote in 1923, but the Senate rejected it.

Another attempt came the following year. It, too, failed, mainly because of opposition from states and local governments which contended that repeal would greatly increase their borrowing costs, a refrain that has been repeated over and over ever since.

The cause was revived in the 1930s, when no fewer than eighty resolutions were introduced calling for a constitutional amendment to end the exemption. After hearings in 1938 before a special Senate committee, the Public Bond Tax Act of 1940 was introduced in the Senate. While the bill would have taxed only future issues of federal, state and local securities—leaving outstanding bonds untouched—states and local governments campaigned successfully to kill the measure. In 1951, the Treasury again sought to eliminate the loophole, but states and local governments teamed up once more to kill the proposal before it even came to a vote.

The closest Congress has come in recent times to scaling back the break was in 1969, when the House version of the Tax Reform Act of 1969 proposed a surtax on some exempt bonds. Most state and local securities were to remain tax-free, but even that half-hearted swipe at the exemption proved enormously controversial. States and local governments attacked the "unwarranted incursion on state and local sovereignty." Municipal bond dealers painted a black picture of the bond market if the House bill carried the day. As before, the Senate Finance Committee opposed the measure, and when the bill emerged from conference, the section was gone.

There is no longer, if there ever was, any legal basis to support the tax exemption. Supreme Court decisions and subsequent legislation have stripped away the concept on which the exemption was originally based early in this century. Nevertheless, there is, if anything, even less interest in Congress in repealing this tax break than in the past.

When the tax reform bandwagon rolled around again in 1986, tax-exempt bonds were not even on it. Reformers pointed to outrageous tax shelters and other avoidance schemes, and attempted to show how such widely used middle-income deductions as Individual Retirement Accounts (IRAs), sales taxes, and consumer interest were really loopholes of the rich that should be repealed. Yet the most enduring income tax subsidy to the rich—tax-exempt bonds, which annually deprived the Treasury of more tax dollars than IRAs—was preserved.

It was not easy to overlook this loophole by the 1980s. The securities were more popular than ever. A surging demand had pushed the total outstanding ever higher, topping more than $625 billion by 1989, according to Federal Reserve Board data.

While states and municipalities are invariably the stalking horse to retain the bonds' tax-free status, wealthy individual taxpayers are the real beneficiaries. Donald Regan, President Reagan's first secretary of the Treasury, was fairly typical of many tax-exempt-bond buyers. As president of Merrill Lynch and Company, the large investment company, Regan invested in tax-exempts before joining the Reagan administration, where he soon oversaw drafting of the tax-reform plan that would lead to repeal of a wide number of deductions used by middle-income taxpayers.

Earning $550,000 a year in salary and bonuses, excluding investment income, Regan bought tax-exempt bonds from Middlesex County, New Jersey, the New Jersey State Housing Finance Agency, the Puerto Rico Water Resources Authority, the New Jersey Turnpike Authority, and similar state and local government units across the country. When he joined the Reagan administration in 1981, Regan's financial disclosure statement listed about $400,000 in tax-exempt bonds, which earned $27,500 to $50,000 a year in tax-free interest.

By Congress's decision to protect their special status in the tax code, tax-exempt securities looked even better after tax reform than before. What with all the publicity about the death of tax shelters, reductions in tax preferences and changes in other tax programs, tax-exempt bonds were one of the undeniable tax shelters left. Wall Street, appropriately, responded in breathless fashion, as in this advertisement from the Nuveen Bond Trust:

"Whew! What a relief.

"Isn't it like a breath of fresh air to know there is something simple in understanding the new tax law.

"The Nuveen-Tax Exempt Unit Trust is still tax-free.

"If you buy Nuveen today, you won't have to pay a penny in federal income tax on the interest you earn (not even the individual alternative minimum tax). Not today. And not when the law becomes effective either.

"So, as it's always been with Nuveen, what you earn you keep."

What, then, is the bottom line for this tax favor? You might want to look at it from a variety of perspectives. The statistics are for 1989, the latest year for which data are available.

Overall, 31.8 million individuals and families with income below $10,000 that year reported collecting a total of $15.4 billion in interest on which they had to pay taxes. At the other end of the scale, 809,000 individuals and families with income over $200,000 reported picking up $14 billion in tax-free interest. Let's review the numbers. That's 31.8 million people who had to pay taxes on $15.4 billion in interest. And 809,000 people who paid no taxes on $14 billion in interest.

More personally, 9.5 million individuals and families with income in the $30,000 to $40,000 range reported that, on average, they received $2,200 in interest on which they were required to pay taxes. At the same time, 59,300 individuals and families with income between $500,000 and $1 million reported that, on average, they received $51,600 in interest that was tax free.

From the standpoint of those who have a daily job, fifteen million individuals and families who work for a living reported that, on average, they received $22,800 in wages and salaries on which they had to pay taxes. Meanwhile, 37,300 millionaires reported that, on average, they received $135,500 in interest that was tax free.

Destructive Debt

If Congress was unable to bring itself to even suggest the repeal of tax-exempt bonds, it should come as little surprise that lawmakers throughout the 1980s also were unable to deal with the wave of buyouts, takeovers and corporate restructurings. This even though the tax code helped to underwrite, in part, the corporate restructuring that so often led to the collapse of companies, the shutting of plants and the wholesale dismissal of workers. For middle-class Americans, the process was wrenching.

Ask Robert Trent. Trent was born and raised in Clarksburg, West Virginia, served a stint in the military, and then followed the path of his father and uncles. In October 1962, he went to work at the Anchor Hocking Corporation glass-manufacturing plant, the largest employer in Clarksburg.

Over the next twenty-five years, Trent progressed through a series of jobs, eventually becoming a personnel supervisor at the factory, which turned out such familiar objects as the Star Wars and Camp Snoopy glasses distributed by McDonald's during promotional campaigns.

In the fall of 1987, when the Clarksburg plant was closed after an unfriendly takeover, Trent, along with 900 other men and women, found himself out of work for the first time in his life.

Trent likes to say that "just about every meal that I've ever had has come out of this plant." He worked there twenty-five years. His father worked there forty-four years. His brother worked there thirty-seven years. Even his mother worked there briefly. There were uncles and cousins, and all together, he said, "the Trent family's logged about 200 years in this plant. There were many families like that."

For Trent and 900 other workers, it all came to an end in 1987. In July of that year, Anchor Hocking (1986 revenue of $758 million) was acquired by a smaller concern, the Newell Company of Freeport, Illinois (1986 revenue of $401 million). A manufacturer and marketer of a variety of household products, Newell had been growing through acquisitions. In the process, Newell was fashioning a reputation as a takeover company which, once it completed an acquisition, moved swiftly to eliminate jobs, reorganize the operations it intended to keep and sell off or shut down the rest.

An unsuspecting Clarksburg discovered how swiftly Newell could move. On Aug. 10, 1987, just forty days after it acquired Anchor Hocking, Newell announced it was closing the West Virginia factory, eliminating the jobs of those 900 workers. It cited excess production.

Robert Trent remembers it well: "We were really excited about some Newell people coming down and looking at our facility, because we thought we were doing very well. They came in about ten in the morning. We saw them come in. They went to the plant manager's office . . . and told him they were closing this facility Nov. 1, 1987. And that was it. They were out of here by 10:30."

For the employees, it was painful. "One of our supervisors right now is working in a local store at minimum wage," Trent said. "It's a shame. He was one of our best supervisors. A very knowledgeable person. Again, in his mid- to late fifties, working for minimum wage now. That's a shock."

Victor M. Cunningham, the manager of the West Virginia Department of Employment Security office in Clarksburg, said many of the workers moved into "service and retail jobs, which are low-paid, short weekly hours and little or no benefits. It's so hard to convert someone who packed glass for twenty years to manage a convenience store," he said. "You don't know what kind of a struggle it is for them to think and apply themselves to something new. I don't know what the answer is."

More than 3,000 miles to the west, in another small town, in another industry, excessive debt produced a similar result. Ira G. March watched it happen. A husky, full-bearded outdoorsman, March spent most of his working life at a sawmill in Martell, California, in the foothills of the Sierra Nevadas. He rose from laborer to sawyer, the highest classification among the hourly workers.

During that time, the mill had four owners. The first was a lumberman, Walter Johnson, who founded the mill's parent company, American Forest Products, in 1925. "Johnson didn't care whether you were the clean-up guy or who you were," said March. "He would come into the mill and stop and talk to you. He knew all the old guys. That was the kind of guy he was."

Johnson's personal attention earned him the long-term loyalty of employees, many of whom went to work for American Forest Products out of high school and stayed until they retired. "We once had four generations of one family working at the mill," said Jerry Kirchgatter, the Lumber and Sawmill Workers Union representative at the mill. "People thought it was a good life, both for them and their kids."

The company, with more than a dozen sawmills, box factories and plants scattered throughout the Sierras, remained under Johnson's control for forty-five years, until 1970 when the Bendix Corporation, the defense and aerospace contractor, bought American Forest Products as part of a diversification plan. That was a time when Wall Street was profiting by putting together conglomerates.

In 1980, when Wall Street began profiting by taking apart conglomerates, Bendix sold the Martell mill and other American Forest properties to an investment partnership headed by the New York buyout specialists Kohlberg Kravis Roberts and Company.

March recalled an immediate change at Martell. Now, there was great pressure to work harder as the new owners struggled to cut costs to pay the interest on the debt. "The debt was the problem," said March. "It seemed to be known throughout the plant. That's why they were pushing the plant so hard. So we had to struggle, and we did struggle here for years trying to pay off that debt and make a profit."

But in vain. Even though American Forest Products posted a larger operating profit in 1987 than in the late 1960s when it was an independent company, it recorded a loss for the year. The reason: Most of the company's operating profits went to pay interest on its debt. Kohlberg Kravis began selling off pieces of the company. In 1988, it sold the mill to the Georgia-Pacific Corporation, a manufacturer of forest and building products.

Georgia-Pacific itself faced a corporate debt spiraling toward $2.5 billion, with interest due in 1989 alone of $272 million. To help raise cash, Georgia-Pacific, with annual sales of $8.6 billion in 1987, cut expenditures and dipped into the paychecks of workers at the Martell mill. It could do so because in the 1980s the National Labor Relations Board ruled that new owners could scuttle existing contracts, making it easier to reduce the pay of employees of companies being acquired. In the past, when one company bought another, it usually inherited the obligations of the selling company, including labor agreements.

But before the Martell mill changed hands, Kohlberg Kravis fired all the workers and sold the assets to Georgia-Pacific. This effectively terminated the labor contracts that had been in place, allowing Georgia-Pacific to reopen the mill and rehire some of the fired workers—at wage cuts of 10 to 15 percent.

For longtime mill workers at Martell, the wage cut was another setback in working conditions at a plant that had once been a good place to work. Ira March took early retirement. Pablo Iturri, a native of the Basque region of Spain who had worked at the mill for nearly three decades, stayed on briefly, but was disillusioned. "They cut everybody's wages," he said. "That was a big mistake. A lot of people had worked here their whole lives. This was no good."

While debt was undermining companies like American Forest Products, Anchor Hocking and hundreds of others, Congress stood by—watching and listening. It listened more often than not to financial experts who said that everything was all right—that the dizzying round of mergers, buyouts, takeovers and corporate restructurings was a healthy, natural process for the economy.

To turn back any challenge in Congress, the money industry relied on spokesmen to articulate the new values. One such value was based on the theory that debt was a positive force in corporate management. Advocates contended that debt forced executives to manage more efficiently and pay closer attention to the bottom line.

Among those who held this view was John A. Pound, an assistant professor of government at the Kennedy School of Government at Harvard University and a principal in a Cambridge-based consulting firm called the Analysis Group. It did work for a number of takeover artists, such as the Belzberg family of Canada. Among Pound's studies was a 1989 report he compiled for the Massachusetts Pension Reserves Investment Management Board, the state agency that oversees the pension funds of Massachusetts state employees.

Pound's Analysis Group extolled the benefits of leveraged buyouts in the report, calling them "part of the ongoing restructuring of corporations that is necessary for the economy to remain competitive." High debt levels were, in fact, a positive force, the report argued, because they made companies "more efficient." As proof, the report cited the Campeau Corporation, headed by Robert Campeau.

Campeau had run up more than $7 billion in debt in 1986 and 1988, acquiring a Who's Who of American retail establishments, including Bloomingdale's, Brooks Brothers, Jordan Marsh, Abraham and Straus, Ann Taylor, Garfinckel's, Bonwit Teller and Filene's. By September 1989, Campeau was unable to make a payment on its debt. With default looming, Campeau's financiers intervened and arranged what Pound described as a "fix for the credit crisis."

To Pound, the swift action of Campeau's financiers was proof of how high debt loads compel those holding the purse strings to step in before bankruptcy becomes inevitable. The result was a "more efficient and informal way to monitor corporate performance" than having to declare bankruptcy.

Pound wrote: "Default no longer necessarily means bankruptcy or even signals severe or prolonged financial distress. The Campeau liquidity crisis was resolved with a dispatch unimaginable a few short years ago. Most important, the resolution led to a significant shift of corporate control and corporate strategy.

"In the past, prior to LBOs [leveraged buyouts], such a shift in strategy and management would have been virtually impossible to accomplish until performance had slid to a terrible degree. This case demonstrates that high debt loads, and the default that they sometimes cause, cannot be measured by traditional yardsticks."

Pound's report on the Campeau rescue was dated Nov. 28, 1989. Forty-eight days later, on Jan. 15, 1990, Campeau's Federated Department Stores, Inc. and Allied Stores filed for bankruptcy protection. It was the largest retail bankruptcy ever and the sixth largest corporate bankruptcy in United States history.

Sometimes, the lobbyists extolling debt are the moneymen themselves. Men like Bruce Wasserstein, who with his partner Joseph Perella made a fortune buying, selling and restructuring businesses through their investment banking firm, Wasserstein Perella and Company.

In September 1987, during an appearance before a House Energy and Commerce subcommittee, Wasserstein discussed corporate debt and the unique abilities of sophisticated financial advisers to determine which companies are capable of carrying large amounts of debt. He cited as an example Harcourt Brace Jovanovich, Inc., the book publishing company that had expanded into other areas, including Sea World theme parks and insurance. In May 1987, Robert Maxwell, the late British publisher, sought to buy Harcourt for about $2 billion. To fend off the bid, Harcourt took on $2 billion in debt and distributed cash to stockholders.

Wasserstein approved: "The shareholders have every reason to be ecstatic over what happened at Harcourt because the offer that came in for the company was at something in the mid-$40s, and the total value of the package . . . shareholders received was something over $60 a share. We are confident that Harcourt will do very well, and that is reflected in the marketplace today."

Notwithstanding the sophisticated financial advice Harcourt received, the company was unable to meet the interest payments on a staggering $2.5 billion debt without selling off properties, closing certain operations and laying off employees. For 1987, the year it took on the new debt, Harcourt reported net income of $83.4 million. In 1988, the year after, the company lost $53.5 million. In 1989, Harcourt reported net income of $12.4 million. But that was due to the sale of its theme parks for $1.1 billion. Without the sale of assets, Harcourt would have lost $242.2 million on its operations.

As for the company's stock, in 1986—the year before the money industry moved in—it traded at a high of $104 a share. By late 1991, it was selling for as low as sixty-three cents. After the restructuring that Wasserstein oversaw, Harcourt had lost money, sold assets and scrambled to make ends meet.

Unable to manage its debt, the company in 1991 became a division of General Cinema Corporation, a Newton, Massachusetts, retailer and movie theater operator, in a $1.5 billion merger and disappeared as an independent company.

When Harcourt's final chapter is written, the casualty list will be long: There have been business casualties—of companies sold and jobs lost. There have been financial casualties, among them holders of Harcourt's stocks and bonds. There has been a corporate casualty, a once-strong company brought down by debt. And then there are the human casualties.

One of them, Robert L. Edgell, is worthy of special note. A charismatic man, Edgell headed HBJ Publications, the business-magazine and school-supplies division of Harcourt. Under Edgell, HBJ Publications grew from sixteen magazines in the early 1970s to more than one hundred in 1987, making it one of the nation's largest business-publication companies. But to pay off some of the debt it took on to defeat Maxwell, Harcourt in 1987 had to sell assets fast. One was HBJ Publications.

Long a steady source of income, HBJ was one of Harcourt's prized possessions. Fearful that an outsider might buy the company and split it up, Edgell and other top executives bought HBJ Publications themselves on Dec. 31, 1987, in a $334 million leveraged buyout. The division was renamed Edgell Communications, Inc., with Edgell as chairman and top executive.

Despite the large debt, Edgell said no layoffs or other cost-cutting measures would be implemented. He predicted that the company's revenues and profit would continue to grow at a rate of 12 percent a year. That would enable the company to make more acquisitions and start new publications, he said. "It will be business as usual, only better," Edgell told a reporter at the time.

Wall Street liked the deal, too. Ivan Obolensky, a publishing analyst with the New York brokerage house of Josephthal and Company, saw only sunny days ahead: "The future is a beautiful thing for Edgell. This is a fire sale," Obolensky was quoted as saying about the $334 million acquisition cost.

Despite the optimism, the company had problems from the start. The projections on paying off the debt were based on a robust growth in advertising lineage among the business publications. They did not factor in a downturn that began in 1988. The company lost $65 million that year. But the biggest problem was making debt payments. Interest costs were staggering—$42.1 million in 1988 and $38.5 million in 1989.

By contrast, interest charges had been less than $1 million in 1987, when the division was part of Harcourt Brace. To make those steep payments, Edgell Communications, for the first time, began eliminating jobs.

The company also sold publications to raise cash, a move that Robert Edgell found especially distressing.

By early 1990, the company was in grave financial condition. Edgell had recorded another large loss in 1989—$35.3 million. In March 1990, Standard & Poor's Corporation lowered the rating on Edgell's corporate bonds and said the company faced "potential violations of senior debt financial covenants."

All of this took a heavy toll on Robert Edgell. Not only was the company he had built coming apart, but the investments of many who worked for him and had joined him in the buyout were rapidly evaporating. On May 6, 1990, Edgell resigned and left the company. Richard B. Swank, a former executive with Dun and Bradstreet Corporation, was brought in as the new chairman.

Edgell tried to put the firm's troubles behind him. On Aug. 3, 1990, he and his wife, Yvonne, bought a luxury condominium on Florida's Gulf Coast, near Sarasota, seemingly far away from the troubled Edgell empire. The Edgells chose a corner apartment on the seventh floor of a new building on Longboat Key, overlooking the Gulf of Mexico. From the balcony, they could take in dazzling sunsets. The Longboat Key Club called the new development "Sanctuary."

But for Robert Edgell this idyllic setting was not a haven. The Edgell Communications debacle would not go away. When the company failed to make a $7 million interest payment, the default set off a frenzied effort to restructure the debt. Seven business magazines were put up for sale. Rumors were rife that the company might soon have to seek bankruptcy court protection. The company missed the deadline for a second $7 million interest payment on its debt.

On New Year's Day 1991, the Edgells had lunch in their condominium with old friends from out of town. After the two couples had finished the meal, Edgell excused himself from the table. At 2:00 P.M., while his wife and friends were in another part of the apartment, Edgell quietly stepped out to the balcony, climbed up on the railing and, in full view of several people, jumped seven floors to his death.

Edgell left tape recordings to his family and a suicide note. Although the contents of the note were not disclosed, the Longboat Key police chief said the note indicated Edgell was distraught over the reversal of the company's fortunes.

How a Tax Break Was Saved

Whatever the cause of Robert Edgell's suicide, there is no mistaking the cause of Harcourt's demise: excessive debt made possible by a tax code that provides for a nearly unlimited interest deduction. It was this deduction that the Alliance for Capital Access lobbied so intensely to preserve.

The Alliance, incorporated on Aug. 8, 1985, in Washington, was a trade association representing companies dedicated to blocking any changes in the rules on junk bonds. Its articles of incorporation spelled out the group's goal: "To prevent a negative impact on the free flow of capital due to unreasonable corporate or governmental restriction, interference, or regulation."

Its top officers had close ties to Michael Milken. Dozens of the companies that paid membership dues to the Alliance owed, if not their existence, at least their temporary prosperity, to Milken, who had peddled junk bonds on their behalf. Two of its three directors—Carl Lindner, president of American Financial Corporation in Cincinnati, and Richard Grassgreen, president of Kinder-Care Learning Centers in Montgomery, Alabama—headed companies that had been part of Milken's junk-bond network. The incorporation papers were filed by Craig Cogut, a lawyer with Cambrent Financial Group, an offshoot of Milken's financial empire, which had offices in the same Beverly Hills building where Milken ran Drexel Burnham's junk-bond operation.

Over the next five years, more than half of the 120 companies that contributed to the Alliance had ties to Milken. Like all successful Washington lobbies, the Alliance lined up a politically well-connected lawyer to do the actual lobbying. This was David Aylward, who as staff director of Timothy Wirth's House Energy and Commerce subcommittee had once helped organize congressional hearings to probe corporate takeovers and evaluate the role of junk bonds in refinancing them.

As executive director of the Alliance, Aylward began to sing the praises of junk bonds. "High-yield bonds . . . have become a critical financing source for some of the fastest-growing, most dynamic . . . companies," Aylward said in August 1987 when releasing a survey of high-yield bond financing. His main job for the Alliance was "combating misunderstandings" about high-yield bonds and educating the "media and government officials" about the types of companies that used such bonds, Aylward said.

To get this point across, Aylward said Alliance members often went to Washington to pay personal calls on members of Congress. "The messenger is as important as the message," he said. "The best thing was for these people to come to Washington and tell congressmen why they should be left alone. Very simple basic lobbying."

While the Alliance lobbied on a number of legislative issues, most of them were centered on efforts to scale back or limit the deduction for interest paid on corporate debt. "If you wanted to fool with junk bonds," said Aylward, "the way you did it was interest deduction."

At the start, the Alliance estimated "monthly expenses at nearly $11,000 per month to paid lobbyists." In fact, the organization raised and spent much more—$4.9 million from 1985 through 1990. With this war chest, the Alliance became a familiar organization on Capitol Hill. Lobby reports from 1985 to 1989 tell the story:

"Mayflower Hotel . . . Breakfast Meeting with members of Congress."

"Joe and Mo's . . . Lunch with Congressional Staff."

"Cafe Berlin . . . Lunch with Senate Staff."

"The Washington Palm . . . Lunch with Senate Staff."

"La Colline . . . Lunch with Congressional Staff."

"Hunan of Capitol Hill. Lunch with Senate Staff."

"Banquet Services. Congressmen and staff. Botanic Gardens."

"Joe and Mo's . . . meeting with Congressional staff to discuss corporate finance issues."

"U.S. Senate Restaurant . . . for Congressional staff luncheon."

"Refreshments for reception with Members of Congress and Congressional Staff."

"Gifts to Congressional and Senate Staff."

"Limousine services for members of Congress and staff."

"Bird's Florist . . . Floral arrangements for Congressional Dinner."

On May 20 and 21 of 1986, the Alliance catered two receptions at a cost of $1,115 in the House of Representatives restaurant in the Rayburn House Office Building. On the night of May 20, the Alliance sponsored a dinner at the Hyatt Regency Washington for members of Congress. The events came at a time of rejoicing for the organization and its members.

The tax-writing committees in both houses had just completed preliminary work on the massive Tax Reform Act of 1986. In that historic legislation, the tax writers repealed numerous tax breaks—from IRA accounts to the deduction for most consumer interest. But they left intact the deduction for corporate interest on debt.

The Alliance had been in the forefront of the drive to oppose limitations on the deductibility of interest or any other measure that might restrict mergers, acquisitions or takeovers.

When a House subcommittee weighed legislation in 1987, Alliance representatives urged lawmakers to leave the system intact. Nelson Peltz, chairman of Triangle Industries in New York, praised junk bonds before a House subcommittee on telecommunications and finance on June 11, 1987, and urged lawmakers to refrain from enacting any measures "limiting high-yield bond financing." He testified, "We can't have legislation that limits access to capital for certain companies that lack investment-grade ratings, that limits the use of debt in acquisitions, that restricts investment in high-yield securities or that imposes arbitrary limits on corporate debt levels."

Peltz went on to say that high-yield bonds were crucial to America's industrial future—that they would help finance companies to "rebuild our manufacturing base." "They are a vital source of financing for those firms that are creating and saving jobs and helping to push America back to prominence in all the world markets," Peltz said.

Two years later, on Feb. 2, 1989, Erwin Schulze, appearing on behalf of the Alliance at a House Ways and Means Committee hearing probing the tax aspects of mergers and acquisitions, urged lawmakers to preserve the unlimited deduction for corporate interest. "I believe that an interest cut-back will have a far-reaching and damaging effect on the ability of entrepreneurs and growth companies to build their businesses," testified Schulze, then chairman of CECO Corporation, a Chicago-based supplier of materials to the construction industry. "The Alliance believes that the big losers from a drop in the interest deduction would be these very companies."

Just what were these entrepreneurial companies that were "creating and saving jobs"? They were, it turns out, not exactly the kinds of enterprises likely to rebuild America's industrial base or to make products that could compete with goods from abroad.

They were companies such as SuperCuts, Inc. of San Rafael, California, the nation's first discount haircutting chain. And Fair Lanes, Inc. of Baltimore, the nation's largest independent operator of bowling alleys. And LivingWell, Inc. of Houston, the nation's largest owner and operator of fitness salons. And they were companies such as Public Storage, Inc. of Glendale, California.

Public Storage is the nation's largest owner of mini-warehouses. The company's orange "Public Storage" logo is a familiar sight along interstate highways. Of all the Alliance members who contributed to the lobbying effort that blocked rules changes, Public Storage best illustrates the fallacy that junk bonds created jobs. Founded in 1972, the company grew spectacularly in the 1980s with the help of Drexel Burnham Lambert, its investment adviser.

Drexel helped the privately held company raise millions of dollars through limited partnerships that acquired land and built mini-warehouses, then leased the facilities back to Public Storage. Today, the company and its partnerships have 233 installations in thirty-five states.

And virtually no employees. Once a mini-warehouse is built, staffing requirements are minimal, a Drexel Burnham report pointed out. Users get in with an ID code that opens a computer-locked door. Some of the facilities have caretakers, but as an investment report of Frederick Research Corporation stressed, those jobs are low-paying: "Usually the properties have a man-and-wife employee living free in the facility but at minimum-type wages to keep an eye on things."

Mr. and Mrs. Wallace Christina of Lincoln City, Oregon, were one such couple. In 1988 they took over as resident managers of a 546-unit Public Storage facility in Gresham, Oregon, near Portland, earning, ostensibly, $4.80 an hour.

Mrs. Christina was the manager and worked forty hours; her husband worked twenty hours. Together they grossed about $1,250 a month in hourly wages. From that was deducted $300 a month rent on a two-bedroom, 1,100-square-foot apartment adjoining the public storage lockers. By the time they went to work for Public Storage, the company was charging managers rent for their on-site living quarters.

That left them with about $950 in gross monthly earnings, meaning their hourly wage rate was about $3.65 an hour—or just slightly above the

United States minimum wage in 1988. "You can't live on the money those jobs pay," Christina explained. He and his wife were able to do so because they were retired and had outside income. But "anybody with small children or a family," Christina added, "just couldn't do it."

Consequently, there was a high turnover in managers, he said. Finally, the Christinas, weary of the low pay and working conditions, quit caretaking in 1991, when the United States minimum wage of $4.25 an hour exceeded their hourly take-home pay.

In addition to mini-warehouses, fitness salons, bowling alleys and haircutting salons, Alliance members sold tax shelters (Integrated Resources), bought junk bonds (Centrust, Columbia, Imperial and Lincoln Savings), sold annuities (Executive Life Insurance), provided day care (Kinder-Care), owned a professional hockey team (Delaware North Companies), leased computers (Comdisco), built retirement villages (Forum Group, Inc.), arranged retail displays (Action), operated ice cream shops (Brigham's, Inc.), managed investments (Shamrock Holdings Corporation), sold insurance (Zenith National Insurance) and leased medical equipment (American Shared Hospital Services).

Whatever their business, companies that had used junk bonds were regularly portrayed before Congress as successful ventures that were creating jobs and building for the future. They were, as Andrew G. Galef, chairman of MagneTek, described them in testimony before the House Ways and Means Committee on May 17, 1989, "the very companies leading America to economic renaissance."

So how goes the renaissance? Four savings and loan associations that contributed thousands of dollars to the Alliance lobbying blitz are insolvent and have been seized by federal regulators. The four—Centrust Savings Bank, Columbia Savings and Loan, Imperial Savings and Loan and Lincoln Savings and Loan—collapsed when the junk bonds that propelled their rise sank in value. The parent companies of Imperial and Lincoln in turn were forced to seek bankruptcy court protection. Now being run under federal supervision, the four thrifts will cost American taxpayers billions to bail out.

Another group of Alliance members—Doskocil Companies, First Executive Corporation, the Forum Group, Inc., Integrated Resources, Living-Well, Inc., Southmark Corporation and U.S. Home Corporation—have sought bankruptcy court protection. The reason: inability to generate sufficient profits to cover the high debt service of their junk bonds.

Yet another group of Alliance contributors has verged on collapse. Western Union is in such shaky financial condition that the board of directors changed the corporate name in 1991 to New Valley Corporation "to minimize any negative impact that its financial condition may have on its operating business."

Ingersoll Publications Company, which acquired a string of daily and weekly newspapers in this country and Europe with cash raised from junk-bond sales, was forced to sell all of its United States publications in 1991 to stave off default on its bonds. Kinder-Care, Inc., the nation's largest day-care center operator, used millions of dollars in junk bonds to diversify into fields other than day care. The company bought savings and loans and a hunting magazine as part of a strategy that left it saddled with so much debt that it had to be restructured.

So it is that many of the companies that bankrolled the lobbying of the Alliance for Capital Access have fallen victims of the very philosophy they embraced.

When David Aylward was asked how it had come to pass that Congress chose to preserve the interest deduction for junk bonds—a deduction that had resulted in the destruction of so many businesses, so much decline for America's middle class—he replied:

"There was not an organized constituency in favor of restrictions on these bonds."

EPILOGUE

REWRITING THE GOVERNMENT RULE BOOK

CAPITAL GAINS TAX CUT: WHO GAINS?

If Congress enacts a capital gains tax cut, the benefits will flow overwhelmingly to a tiny percentage of individuals and families.

72% of 1989 capital gains income — $108.2 billion — went to 1.3 million individuals and families earning $100,000 or more.

That's **1%** of all U.S. tax filers.

28% of 1989 capital gains income — $42.0 billion — went to 7.2 million individuals and families earning less than $100,000.

That's **6%** of all U.S. tax filers.

103.8 million individuals and families received no capital gains income.

They represent **93%** of all U.S. tax filers.

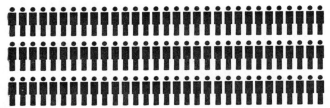

SOURCE: Internal Revenue Service

So What Is America to Do?

Once upon a time, Congress and the White House responded to the nation's needs by enacting sweeping legislative and regulatory reforms. More often than not, they acted only after events had pushed the country to the edge of crisis—or beyond. Even then, opposition was intense.

But at least they responded.

So it was in 1906. That was a time when Americans were routinely swindled—and often died—when they bought and consumed adulterated foods and drugs. Machine oil was canned and sold as "genuine olive oil." Glucose was colored with coal-tar dye and sold as plum preserves. Cocoa was diluted with starch.

Patent medicines were laced with opium, cocaine and other addictive or poisonous substances. A dose of any number of widely available cure-alls often proved fatal. A Fall River, Massachusetts, couple administered something called "Nurses and Mothers' Treasure" to their child. The medical examiner concluded that the child's death was caused by opium poisoning. A twenty-eight-year-old man in Chillicothe, Ohio, suffering from a cold, took a dose of Hardman's Magic Cure. He died twenty minutes later.

Stories abounded about the sale of rotten meat, foods packaged in poisoned preservatives and patent medicines spiked with narcotics that resulted in death to unsuspecting consumers. Nonetheless, many lawmakers vigorously opposed taking action—just as their predecessors had done on other issues, just as their successors would do for the rest of the century. In fact, just about every effort to enact legislation to correct social and economic injustices has first had to overcome powerful opposition within Congress.

In the case of proposed legislation to regulate food and drugs, opponents argued it would represent the first step toward a police state, that it was unconstitutional for the federal government to intrude in matters that were the province of the states. The states, they said, were better equipped to enforce such laws.

Representative Charles H. Grosvenor, an Ohio Republican, dismissed the notion that the federal government should protect the health of residents of one state from adulterated food or drugs produced in another. It was no more logical to do so, he said, than it would be for the federal government to close brothels in New York City because "that business is spreading disease into the states of New Jersey and Connecticut."

Nonetheless, Congress finally responded by passing the Pure Food and Drug Act of 1906. It did so only after substantial pressure by reform-minded citizens and lawmakers. As Representative William H. Ryan, a Democrat from New York, put it during debate, "There is a demand for this legislation. . . . The people are demanding pure food. They are demanding that articles of food shall be correctly labeled and that Congress prevent, by the enactment of this bill, the adulteration or misbranding of foods or drugs."

The most far-reaching food and drug legislation ever enacted, it made adulteration and misbranding criminal offenses. President Theodore Roosevelt, who signed it into law on June 30, 1906, later described its importance:

"The enactment of a pure food law was a recognition of the fact that the public welfare outweighs the right to private gain, and that no man may poison the people for his private profit."

Congress responded again in 1913. That was a time, not unlike our own, when working-class Americans were paying a disproportionate share of the cost of running the federal government, when living standards were declining. In those years, federal revenue was derived largely from the tariff—a tax added to imported goods—which, as the House Ways and Means Committee concluded, "is the principal cause of the unequal distribution of wealth. It is a system of taxation which makes the rich richer and the poor poorer."

The committee explained: "The amount each citizen contributes is governed, not by his ability to pay tax, but by his consumption of the articles taxed. It requires as many yards of cloth to clothe, and as many ounces of food to sustain, the day laborer, as the largest holder of invested wealth; yet each pays into the federal Treasury a like amount of taxes upon the food he eats, while the former at present pays a larger rate of tax upon his cheap suit of woolen clothing than the latter upon his costly suit."

To correct the growing imbalance in American society, Congress took up legislation calling for an income tax. Again there was intense opposition in Washington. Senator Henry Cabot Lodge, the patrician Massachusetts Republican, complained that it was an attempt "to punish a man simply because he has succeeded and has accumulated property by thrift and intelligence and character." Others charged that the income tax was a communist plot.

But once more, as a result of pressure by reform-minded citizens and politicians, Congress responded, this time by passing the Revenue Act of 1913. The most dramatic overhaul of the tax system in the nation's history, it provided the framework for the progressive income tax. President Woodrow Wilson signed the measure into law on Oct. 3, 1913. Clyde H. Tavenner, a Democratic congressman from Illinois, summed up the intent of the new law:

"Under this bill a man will be taxed according to his ability to pay. If he has a small income he will pay a small tax, and if he has a large income he will pay a large tax. John D. Rockefeller, for instance . . . would pay an annual tax of more than $2 million. Heretofore Mr. Rockefeller has paid little if any more toward defraying the expenses of the national government than the poor man with a large family."

Congress responded again in 1933. That was a time when many Americans, who had lost their life savings when banks folded, who had lost their jobs when companies collapsed, were struggling to survive the Great Depression. It was a time when public anger was rising over tales of wealthy and powerful citizens who peddled unsound stocks, engaged in rigged securities dealings, encouraged speculation with borrowed money and cut special stock deals for their friends.

That's what J.P. Morgan and Company, the Wall Street investment house, did when it offered to sell Alleghany Corporation common stock for $20 a share to one of the firm's clients. A J.P. Morgan partner had explained the deal in a letter to the client: "I believe that the stock is selling in the market around $35 to $37 a share. . . . We are reserving for you 1,000 shares at $20 a share, if you would like to have it." The Morgan client later became secretary of the United States Treasury.

Again, after years of such stories and pressure by reform-minded citizens and lawmakers, Congress finally responded by passing the Securities Act of 1933, the most sweeping overhaul of the securities system ever. When President Franklin D. Roosevelt signed it into law on May 27, 1933, he described its importance:

"This measure at last translates some elementary standards of right and wrong into law. Events have made it abundantly clear that the merchandising of securities is really traffic in the economic and social welfare of our people. . . . The act is thus intended to correct some of the evils which have been so glaringly revealed in the private exploitation of the public's money. This law and its effective administration are steps in a program to restore some old-fashioned standards of rectitude. Without such an ethical foundation, economic well-being cannot be achieved."

Throughout American history, whenever excesses within the economy resulted in private gain for the few and hardships for the many, Congress and the White House responded. Often reluctantly. Usually after interminable delays. But in the end they responded.

Until the 1980s and the 1990s.

Today, the two branches of government are in a legislative gridlock. Even worse, many in Washington insist there are no problems that require comprehensive legislative remedies. They say that a comparatively minor recession will pass and that all will be well. It is a timeless economic viewpoint. Consider this assessment:

"The fundamental business of the country, that is, the production and distribution of commodities, is on a very sound and prosperous basis. . . . There has been a tendency for wage increases and the output per worker has increased, all of which indicates a very healthy situation."

The date was Oct. 25, 1929.

The speaker was President Herbert Hoover.

So it is in 1992. In addition to those lawmakers who see only a bright future for America's shrinking middle class, others are busily proposing legislation that would continue to serve special interests. They can be found in both political parties. President Bush wants to cut the capital gains tax. Representative Dan Rostenkowski, the Illinois Democrat who heads the tax-writing Ways and Means Committee, wants to give corporations a tax deduction for their "goodwill."

First, the proposed tax cut for capital gains—income derived from the sale of stocks, bonds, commodities and other assets. According to IRS statistics, capital gains reported on 1989 tax returns totaled $150.2 billion. Of that sum, $108.2 billion—or 72 percent of the total—went to 1.3 million individuals and families who earned more than $100,000. Those people represented 1 percent of the 112.3 million people who filed tax returns.

The remaining $42 billion in capital gains income was reported by 7.2 million individuals and families with incomes under $100,000. They represented 6 percent of all tax filers. That left 103.8 million individuals and families—93 percent of tax filers—without any capital gains income.

Now look at the numbers on a more personal level. People in the $500,000 to $1 million income bracket averaged $185,000 in capital gains income. That was nearly six times the average salary of people earning $30,000 to $40,000. More than 90 percent of the latter group had no capital gains income.

So, a cut in the capital gains taxes would produce a tax savings for 7 percent of all persons filing tax returns. Most of the money would go to 1 percent of the tax filers. The remaining 93 percent would receive no benefit.

Next, the proposed corporate tax deduction for "goodwill," which means the value assigned to a company's name and its products. For decades, corporations have been prohibited from taking a writeoff for goodwill. And for good reason, since the valuations are often whimsical. Imagine placing a value on your family name, and then deducting that value on your personal tax return over a period of years.

But in the summer of 1991, Rostenkowski introduced legislation to simplify the tax code that included a deduction for goodwill. Financial analysts have predicted that it will be part of any tax package enacted in 1992. If so, the goodwill deduction will give a boost to another round of corporate takeovers and result in the further elimination of jobs and additional lost tax revenue running into the billions of dollars.

The government rule book has become a catalogue of special-interest provisions like the proposed capital gains tax cut and the corporate write-off for goodwill. That's why America's middle class finds itself in a downward spiral. And it is why that spiral won't be reversed with narrow measures such as a onetime, limited tax cut that would mean $200 or $300 in savings per family. It will only be reversed with enactment of broad legislative programs that are designed to correct the structural imbalances built into the economy over many years and to address the emerging problems of a global economy. Even then, to be fully effective, the legislative action would have to be accompanied by other social and educational reforms. But changes in the rule book are a starting point.

The possibilities are limitless. One is to craft legislation that would encourage the creation of jobs that actually pay middle-class wages—rather than rewarding short-term investments that lead to the elimination of jobs. This would include creating—rather than abolishing—manufacturing jobs.

Another would be legislation to reward corporations for investing in research and development—which would lead to new jobs over the long term—rather than actually penalizing companies for making such investments, as the current tax code inadvertently does.

Yet another would be to develop legislation to assure that residents of foreign countries who invest in the United States pay income taxes on those earnings at the same rates paid by United States residents with comparable incomes.

And yet another possibility would be to require that Congress identify the beneficiaries of all proposed legislation, as well as the lawmakers responsible for the bills.

It is, of course, easy to come up with a list of potential legislative initiatives that would create a level economic playing field for everyone and thereby reverse the decline of the middle class. It is even easy to put forth legislative goals that would attract universal support, such as providing a basic level of health care for all Americans.

But while there may be widespread agreement on guaranteeing that everyone has access to medical care, there are widely disparate views on how to pay for it. Some believe the cost should be absorbed by employers—this even though corporations have been systematically shifting such costs to their employees. Some believe taxes should be increased across the board. Some believe that taxes should be increased only on upper-income individuals and families.

On still other issues, a majority of the population may support a particular legislative change, but their efforts are thwarted by a powerful and influential minority. So it is with proposals to restore the progressive income tax. In 1968 the bottom tax rate was 14 percent, the top 75 percent. That was a spread of 61 percentage points. In 1992, the bottom rate is 15 percent, the top rate 31 percent. That's a spread of just 16 percentage points. In reality, many members of the middle class pay taxes on at least part of their income at a 28 percent rate. That means the spread between middle-class taxpayers and millionaires—even billionaires—is 3 percentage points.

The story would be much the same—a majority would support, but a powerful minority would oppose—if efforts were made to enact legislation that would repeal the virtually unlimited deduction for interest on corporate debt. Or to end tax subsidies for companies that eliminate jobs in the United States and create jobs offshore. Or to more severely restrict the use of the net operating loss deduction. Or to reduce the tax deduction granted to banks for bad loans. Or to impose a capital gains tax on the wealthy at death. Or to prohibit corporate takeover specialists from using the assets of the company they buy to pay for the acquisition.

At the same time, most people undoubtedly would endorse legislation that would put an end to a system that allows members of Congress and other public employees to draw larger pensions than their final salaries. Or legislation that would end, once and for all, a variety of practices that allow profit-making companies and wealthy individuals to pay taxes at a lower rate than middle-class families. Or legislation that would halt the federal government's use of Social Security tax revenue to fund its other programs.

Other potential legislative changes would require study and debate. For example, legislation might be considered to mandate an end to large trade imbalances with other countries. Or to make Social Security taxes more progressive. Or to limit or end the payment of Social Security benefits to the wealthiest recipients. Or to more closely regulate the sale of stocks, bonds, commodities and other securities in a global marketplace. Or to require corporations to secure a federal charter to stop companies from playing one state against another. Or to require all corporations—public and private—to disclose the amount and type of taxes they pay in the United States and in other countries—country by country.

In some cases, achieving desired goals would require a reversal of decades-old policies or thinking. In other cases, it would require fresh approaches to old practices that only recently have become problems.

Consider the tax exemption for bonds sold by state and local governments, which has existed for most of this century. The exemption is rooted in a long-outdated concept. It is the same concept that for years held that employees of state and local governments were exempt from paying federal income taxes. Which they were, until the government rule book was amended to end the practice. The major beneficiaries of the exemption for interest on state and local bonds are investors who buy the bonds, mostly wealthy individuals and businesses. Claims by local and state government officials that borrowing costs would go up if the exemption was eliminated could be dealt with in other ways—if the claims proved true.

At the same time, new laws could be enacted to reward state and local governments that establish progressive tax structures. With few exceptions, state and local taxes—sales taxes, flat-rate income taxes and per capita taxes—are even more regressive than the current federal tax system. That is, the taxes fall most heavily on middle-class individuals and families as well as on those at the bottom of the income ladder.

The Internal Revenue Code is riddled with inequities that result in favored treatment of some individuals at the expense of everyone else. One example is the deduction of corporate executive pay. In years gone by, when corporate compensation was more modest, the fairness issue was of little concern. But in a day when corporate executives routinely receive multi-million-dollar compensation packages, the deduction effectively shifts the costs of that compensation from the company's stockholders to taxpayers. One solution would be to cap the deduction at a multiple of the wage or salary received by the lowest-paid worker. Thus, if workers at the bottom end of the company pay scale received $15,000 a year, the tax deductibility of corporate executive pay could be limited to, say, fifteen times that amount, or $225,000. Any compensation above that figure could not be deducted on the company's tax return.

With the transition to a global economy, the criminal statutes relating to securities and other economic-related offenses have to be overhauled. Practices deemed unlawful need to be spelled out more clearly. New penalties could be experimented with. One possibility might be to apply provisions of the drug-forfeiture law to economic crimes. Under the existing system, a Michael Milken, whose activities led to the collapse of companies and the elimination of thousands of jobs, will serve time in prison but retain the hundreds of millions of dollars that he made. Under a forfeiture system, Milken's assets—his cars, his houses, his investments—would be seized by the federal government.

These are just some of the revisions of the government rule book that would help restore balance to the system. In each case, there are powerful lobbies that oppose any change, or support change that will benefit their constituents at the expense of everyone else. Unlike the lobbies, which have paid agents and political action committees to hand out money to lawmakers or to fund initiatives they support, the average citizen has no such outlet.

This, too, has always been so. When lobbyists in 1913 mounted an intense campaign to block enactment of the progressive income tax, President Wilson observed that "it is of serious interest to the country that the people at large should have no lobby and be voiceless in these matters, while great bodies of astute men seek to create an artificial opinion and to overcome the interests of the public for their private profit. . . . Only public opinion can check and destroy it."

Indeed so.

In 1991, after the *Philadelphia Inquirer* published "America: What Went Wrong?"—the series on which this book is based—more than 20,000 people wrote or called the newspaper. Some wrote to offer their observations on the plight of the middle class and the American condition in the waning days of the twentieth century. Some wrote to suggest solutions. Many displayed a clearer grasp of the problems confronting the country than the rule-makers in Washington. And many saw reason for hope, rather than despair. As one reader concluded:

"To the extent that federal policy, rather than impersonal economic factors, is responsible for the hardships our citizens are suffering, there is reason to hope for the better. . . . *We* make those policies through our elected representatives. What we make, we can unmake."

NOTE ON SOURCES

This book is based on interviews and public records and data drawn from a wide variety of federal, state and local agencies in fifty cities in sixteen states and Mexico.

During the course of the project, we extracted more than seventy years of tax data from reports compiled by the United States Internal Revenue Service (IRS), as well as information concerning scores of corporations that was drawn from a variety of reports filed with the United States Securities and Exchange Commission (SEC) over several decades.

In addition to IRS and SEC records, material also came from the Treasury Department, Federal Reserve Board, Interstate Commerce Commission, Federal Election Commission, Senate Records Office, House Clerk's Office, Social Security Administration, Bureau of Labor Statistics, Japan Economic Institute, Pension Benefit Guaranty Corporation, Patent and Trademark Office, Resolution Trust Corporation, Congressional Budget Office, Department of Education, Census Bureau, Administrative Office of the U.S. Courts, Embassy of Japan, Bureau of Economic Analysis and the Business Development Office of the State of Tamaulipas, Mexico.

State and federal courts as well as bankruptcy courts also proved to be invaluable sources of information to document the story of what happened in corporate America in the 1980s. We drew on bankruptcy filings in many jurisdictions, including New York; Boston; Los Angeles; Miami; Cincinnati; Pittsburgh; San Diego; Washington, D.C.; Charleston, West Virginia; Topeka, Kansas; Rockville, Maryland; Dallas; Jacksonville; Phoenix; and Akron, Ohio.

To fill out the stories that emerged from the research, two years were spent crisscrossing the country—interviewing men and women who worked in glass plants and department stores, shoe factories and packing houses, trucking terminals and brokerage houses, lumber mills and airlines, as well as government officials and corporate managers. In tracing the operations of scores of these once-thriving companies, more than 100,000 pages of documents were gathered.

HOW TO WRITE OR TELEPHONE RULE-MAKERS

Following is a list of government rule-makers, who write the rules under which the economy operates.

PRESIDENT GEORGE BUSH
THE WHITE HOUSE
1600 Pennsylvania Avenue, NW
Washington, DC 20500
202-456-1414

House and Senate members have offices in five office buildings in Washington, the addresses for which are listed below. All phone numbers are area code 202.

DSOB:
Dirksen Senate Office Building
Washington, DC 20510

RSOB:
Russell Senate Office Building
Washington, DC 20510

LHOB:
Longworth House Office Building
Washington, DC 20515

HSOB:
Hart Senate Office Building
Washington, DC 20510

CHOB:
Cannon House Office Building
Washington, DC 20515

RHOB:
Rayburn House Office Building
Washington, DC 20515

Name Party	Dist.	Room	Bldg.	Tele.
ALABAMA				
Senators				
Howell T. Heflin (D)		728	HSOB	224-4124
Richard Shelby (D)		313	HSOB	224-5744
Representatives				
Tom Bevill (D)	4th	2302	RHOB	225-4876
Glen Browder (D)	3rd	1221	LHOB	225-3261
Sonny Callahan (R)	1st	1330	LHOB	225-4931
Robert E. 'Bud' Cramer (D)	5th	1431	LHOB	225-4801
William L. Dickinson (R)	2nd	2406	RHOB	225-2901
Ben Erdreich (D)	6th	439	CHOB	225-4921
Claude Harris (D)	7th	1009	LHOB	225-2665
ALASKA				
Senators				
Frank H. Murkowski (R)		709	HSOB	224-6665
Ted Stevens (R)		522	HSOB	224-3004
Representative				
Don Young (R)		2331	RHOB	225-5765
ARIZONA				
Senators				
Dennis DeConcini (D)		328	HSOB	224-4521
John McCain (R)		111	RSOB	224-2235
Representatives				
Jim Kolbe (R)	5th	410	CHOB	225-2542
Jon Kyl (R)	4th	336	CHOB	225-3361
Ed Pastor (D)	2nd	234	CHOB	225-4065
John J. Rhodes (R)	1st	326	CHOB	225-2635
Bob Stump (R)	3rd	211	CHOB	225-4576
ARKANSAS				
Senators				
Dale Bumpers (D)		229	DSOB	224-4843
David Pryor (D)		267	RSOB	224-2353
Representatives				
Bill Alexander (D)	1st	233	CHOB	225-4076
Beryl F. Anthony (D)	4th	1212	LHOB	225-3772
John P. Hammerschmidt (R)	3rd	2110	RHOB	225-4301
Ray Thornton (D)	2nd	1214	LHOB	225-2506

Name Party	Dist.	Room	Bldg.	Tele.
CALIFORNIA				
Senators				
Alan Cranston (D)		112	HSOB	224-3553
John Seymour (R)		367	DSOB	224-3841
Representatives				
Glenn M. Anderson (D)	32nd	2329	RHOB	225-6676
Anthony C. Beilenson (D)	23rd	1025	LHOB	225-5911
Howard L. Berman (D)	26th	137	CHOB	225-4695
Barbara Boxer (D)	6th	307	CHOB	225-5161
George E. Brown (D)	36th	2300	RHOB	225-6161
Thomas Campbell (R)	12th	313	CHOB	225-5411
Gary Condit (D)	15th	1529	LHOB	225-6131
Christopher Cox (R)	40th	412	CHOB	225-5611
Randy 'Duke' Cunningham (R)	44th	1017	LHOB	225-5452
William E. Dannemeyer (R)	39th	2234	RHOB	225-4111
Ronald V. Dellums (D)	8th	2136	RHOB	225-2661
Julian C. Dixon (D)	28th	2400	RHOB	225-7084
Calvin M. Dooley (D)	17th	1022	LHOB	225-3341
John T. Doolittle (R)	14th	1524	LHOB	225-2511
Robert K. Dornan (R)	38th	301	CHOB	225-2965
David Dreier (R)	33rd	411	CHOB	225-2305
Mervyn M. Dymally (D)	31st	1717	LHOB	225-5425
Don Edwards (D)	10th	2307	RHOB	225-3072
Vic Fazio (D)	4th	2113	RHOB	225-5716
Elton Gallegly (R)	21st	107	CHOB	225-5811
Wally Herger (R)	2nd	1108	LHOB	225-3076
Duncan L. Hunter (R)	45th	133	CHOB	225-5672
Robert J. Lagomarsino (R)	19th	2332	RHOB	225-3601
Tom Lantos (D)	11th	1526	LHOB	225-3531
Richard H. Lehman (D)	18th	1319	LHOB	225-4540
Meldon E. Levine (D)	27th	2443	RHOB	225-6451
Jerry Lewis (R)	35th	2312	RHOB	225-5861
William D. Lowery (R)	41st	2433	RHOB	225-3201
Matthew G. Martinez (D)	30th	2446	RHOB	225-5464
Robert T. Matsui (D)	3rd	2353	RHOB	225-7163
Alfred A. McCandless (R)	37th	2422	RHOB	225-5330
George Miller (D)	7th	2228	RHOB	225-2095
Norman Y. Mineta (D)	13th	2350	RHOB	225-2631
Carlos J. Moorhead (R)	22nd	2346	RHOB	225-4176

Name Party	Dist.	Room	Bldg.	Tele.
Ronald C. Packard (R)	43rd	434	CHOB	225-3906
Leon E. Panetta (D)	16th	339	CHOB	225-2861
Nancy Pelosi (D)	5th	109	CHOB	225-4965
Frank D. Riggs (R)	1st	1517	LHOB	225-3311
Dana Rohrabacher (R)	42nd	1039	LHOB	225-2415
Edward R. Roybal (D)	25th	2211	RHOB	225-6235
Pete Stark (D)	9th	239	CHOB	225-5065
William M. Thomas (R)	20th	2402	RHOB	225-2915
Esteban Torres (D)	34th	1740	LHOB	225-5256
Maxine Waters (D)	29th	1207	LHOB	225-2201
Henry A. Waxman (D)	24th	2418	RHOB	225-3976

COLORADO
Senators

Name Party	Dist.	Room	Bldg.	Tele.
Hank Brown (R)		717	HSOB	224-5941
Timothy E. Wirth (D)		380	RSOB	224-5852

Representatives

Name Party	Dist.	Room	Bldg.	Tele.
Wayne Allard (R)	4th	513	CHOB	225-4676
Ben Nighthorse Campbell (D)	3rd	1530	LHOB	225-4761
Joel Hefley (R)	5th	222	CHOB	225-4422
Patricia Schroeder (D)	1st	2208	RHOB	225-1955
David Skaggs (D)	2nd	1507	LHOB	225-2161
Dan Schaefer (R)	6th	1007	LHOB	225-7882

CONNECTICUT
Senators

Name Party	Dist.	Room	Bldg.	Tele.
Christopher J. Dodd (D)		444	RSOB	224-2823
Joseph L. Lieberman (D)		502	HSOB	224-4041

Representatives

Name Party	Dist.	Room	Bldg.	Tele.
Rosa L. DeLauro (D)	3rd	327	CHOB	225-3661
Gary A. Franks (R)	5th	1609	LHOB	225-3822
Samuel Gejdenson (D)	2nd	2416	RHOB	225-2076
Nancy L. Johnson (R)	6th	227	CHOB	225-4476
Barbara B. Kennelly (D)	1st	204	CHOB	225-2265
Christopher Shays (R)	4th	1531	LHOB	225-5541

DISTRICT OF COLUMBIA
Representative

Name Party	Dist.	Room	Bldg.	Tele.
Eleanor Holmes Norton (D)		1631	LHOB	225-8050

DELAWARE
Senators

Name Party	Dist.	Room	Bldg.	Tele.
Joseph R. Biden (D)		221	RSOB	224-5042
William V. Roth (R)		104	HSOB	224-2441

Representative

Name Party	Dist.	Room	Bldg.	Tele.
Thomas R. Carper (D)		131	CHOB	225-4165

FLORIDA
Senators

Name Party	Dist.	Room	Bldg.	Tele.
Bob Graham (D)		241	DSOB	224-3041
Connie Mack III (R)		517	HSOB	224-5274

Representatives

Name Party	Dist.	Room	Bldg.	Tele.
Jim Bacchus (D)	11th	431	CHOB	225-3671
Charles E. Bennett (D)	3rd	2107	RHOB	225-2501
Michael Bilirakis (R)	9th	2432	RHOB	225-5755
Dante B. Fascell (D)	19th	2354	RHOB	225-4506
Sam M. Gibbons (D)	7th	2204	RHOB	225-3376
Porter J. Goss (R)	13th	224	CHOB	225-2536
Earl D. Hutto (D)	1st	2435	RHOB	225-4136
Andy Ireland (R)	10th	2466	RHOB	225-5015
Craig James (R)	4th	1408	LHOB	225-4035

Name Party	Dist.	Room	Bldg.	Tele.
Harry A. Johnston II (D)	14th	1028	LHOB	225-3001
William Lehman (D)	17th	2347	RHOB	225-4211
Tom F. Lewis (R)	12th	2351	RHOB	225-5792
Bill McCollum (R)	5th	2453	RHOB	225-2176
Douglas 'Pete' Peterson (D)	2nd	1415	LHOB	225-5235
Ileana Ros-Lehtinen (R)	18th	416	CHOB	225-3931
E. Clay Shaw (R)	15th	2338	RHOB	225-3026
Lawrence Smith (D)	16th	113	CHOB	225-7931
Clifford B. Stearns (R)	6th	1123	LHOB	225-5744
C.W. Bill Young (R)	8th	2407	RHOB	225-5961

GEORGIA
Senators

Name Party	Dist.	Room	Bldg.	Tele.
Wyche Fowler, Jr. (D)		204	RSOB	224-3643
Sam Nunn (D)		303	DSOB	224-3521

Representatives

Name Party	Dist.	Room	Bldg.	Tele.
Douglas Barnard (D)	10th	2227	RHOB	225-4101
George Darden (D)	7th	228	CHOB	225-2931
Newt Gingrich (R)	6th	2438	RHOB	225-4501
Charles F. Hatcher (D)	2nd	2434	RHOB	225-3631
Ed Jenkins (D)	9th	2427	RHOB	225-5211
Benjamin L. Jones (D)	4th	514	CHOB	225-4272
John Lewis (D)	5th	329	CHOB	225-3801
Richard Ray (D)	3rd	225	CHOB	225-5901
J. Roy Rowland (D)	8th	423	CHOB	225-6531
Lindsay Thomas (D)	1st	240	CHOB	225-5831

HAWAII
Senators

Name Party	Dist.	Room	Bldg.	Tele.
Daniel K. Akaka (D)		720	HSOB	224-6361
Daniel K. Inouye (D)		722	HSOB	224-3934

Representatives

Name Party	Dist.	Room	Bldg.	Tele.
Neil Abercrombie (D)	1st	1440	LHOB	225-2726
Patsy Mink (D)	2nd	2135	RHOB	225-4906

IDAHO
Senators

Name Party	Dist.	Room	Bldg.	Tele.
Larry Craig (R)		302	HSOB	224-2752
Steven D. Symms (R)		509	HSOB	224-6142

Representatives

Name Party	Dist.	Room	Bldg.	Tele.
Larry LaRocco (D)	1st	1117	LHOB	225-6611
Richard Stallings (D)	2nd	1221	LHOB	225-5531

ILLINOIS
Senators

Name Party	Dist.	Room	Bldg.	Tele.
Alan J. Dixon (D)		331	HSOB	224-2854
Paul Simon (D)		462	DSOB	224-2152

Representatives

Name Party	Dist.	Room	Bldg.	Tele.
Frank Annunzio (D)	11th	2303	RHOB	225-6661
Terry Bruce (D)	19th	419	CHOB	225-5001
Cardiss Collins (D)	7th	2264	RHOB	225-5006
Jerry Costello (D)	21st	119	CHOB	225-5661
John W. Cox, Jr. (D)	16th	501	CHOB	225-5676
Philip M. Crane (R)	12th	1035	LHOB	225-3711
Richard T. Durbin (D)	20th	129	CHOB	225-5271
Lane Evans (D)	17th	1121	LHOB	225-5905
Thomas W. Ewing (R)	15th	1632	LHOB	225-2371
Harris W. Fawell (R)	13th	435	CHOB	225-3515
J. Dennis Hastert (R)	14th	515	CHOB	225-2976

Name Party	Dist.	Room	Bldg.	Tele.
Charles A. Hayes (D)	1st	1131	LHOB	225-4372
Henry J. Hyde (R)	6th	2262	RHOB	225-4561
William O. Lipinski (D)	5th	1501	LHOB	225-5701
Robert H. Michel (R)	18th	2112	RHOB	225-6201
John E. Porter (R)	10th	1026	LHOB	225-4835
Glenn Poshard (D)	22nd	314	CHOB	225-5201
Dan Rostenkowski (D)	8th	2111	RHOB	225-4061
Marty Russo (D)	3rd	2233	RHOB	225-5736
George E. Sangmeister (D)	4th	1032	LHOB	225-3635
Gus Savage (D)	2nd	2419	RHOB	225-0773
Sidney R. Yates (D)	9th	2109	RHOB	225-2111

INDIANA
Senators

Name Party	Dist.	Room	Bldg.	Tele.
Daniel R. Coats (R)		411	RSOB	224-5623
Richard G. Lugar (R)		306	HSOB	224-4814

Representatives

Name Party	Dist.	Room	Bldg.	Tele.
Dan L. Burton (R)	6th	120	CHOB	225-2276
Lee H. Hamilton (D)	9th	2187	RHOB	225-5315
Andrew Jacobs (D)	10th	2313	RHOB	225-4011
James Jontz (D)	5th	1317	LHOB	225-5037
Jill Long (D)	4th	1513	LHOB	225-4436
Frank McCloskey (D)	8th	127	CHOB	225-4636
John T. Myers (R)	7th	2372	RHOB	225-5805
Tim Roemer (D)	3rd	415	CHOB	225-3915
Philip R. Sharp (D)	2nd	2217	RHOB	225-3021
Peter Visclosky (D)	1st	330	CHOB	225-2461

IOWA
Senators

Name Party	Dist.	Room	Bldg.	Tele.
Charles Grassley (R)		135	HSOB	224-3744
Tom Harkin (D)		531	HSOB	224-3254

Representatives

Name Party	Dist.	Room	Bldg.	Tele.
Fred Grandy (R)	6th	418	CHOB	225-5476
Jim Leach (R)	1st	1514	LHOB	225-6576
Jim R. Lightfoot (R)	5th	1222	LHOB	225-3806
David R. Nagle (D)	3rd	214	CHOB	225-3301
Jim Nussle (R)	2nd	507	CHOB	225-2911
Neal Smith (D)	4th	2373	RHOB	225-4426

KANSAS
Senators

Name Party	Dist.	Room	Bldg.	Tele.
Robert Dole (R)		141	HSOB	224-6521
Nancy Kassebaum (R)		302	RSOB	224-4774

Representatives

Name Party	Dist.	Room	Bldg.	Tele.
Dan Glickman (D)	4th	2311	RHOB	225-6216
Jan Meyers (R)	3rd	1230	LHOB	225-2865
Dick Nichols (R)	5th	1605	LHOB	225-3911
Pat Roberts (R)	1st	1110	LHOB	225-2715
James C. Slattery (D)	2nd	1512	LHOB	225-6601

KENTUCKY
Senators

Name Party	Dist.	Room	Bldg.	Tele.
Wendell Ford (D)		173A	RSOB	224-4343
Mitch McConnell (R)		120	RSOB	224-2541

Representatives

Name Party	Dist.	Room	Bldg.	Tele.
Jim Bunning (R)	4th	116	CHOB	225-3465
Larry J. Hopkins (R)	6th	2437	RHOB	225-4706
Carroll Hubbard (D)	1st	2268	RHOB	225-3115
Romano L. Mazzoli (D)	3rd	2246	RHOB	225-5401
William H. Natcher (D)	2nd	2333	RHOB	225-3501

Name Party	Dist.	Room	Bldg.	Tele.
Carl C. Perkins (D)	7th	1004	LHOB	225-4935
Harold Rogers (R)	5th	343	CHOB	225-4601

LOUISIANA
Senators

Name Party	Dist.	Room	Bldg.	Tele.
John Breaux (D)		516	HSOB	224-4623
J. Bennett Johnston (D)		136	HSOB	224-5824

Representatives

Name Party	Dist.	Room	Bldg.	Tele.
Richard H. Baker (R)	6th	404	CHOB	225-3901
James A. Hayes (D)	7th	503	CHOB	225-2031
Clyde C. Holloway (R)	8th	1206	LHOB	225-4926
Jerry Huckaby (D)	5th	2182	RHOB	225-2376
William J. Jefferson (D)	2nd	506	CHOB	225-6636
Robert L. Livingston (R)	1st	2368	RHOB	225-3015
Jim McCrery (R)	4th	429	CHOB	225-2777
W. J. Tauzin (D)	3rd	2342	RHOB	225-4031

MAINE
Senators

Name Party	Dist.	Room	Bldg.	Tele.
William S. Cohen (R)		322	HSOB	224-2523
George J. Mitchell (D)		176	RSOB	224-5344

Representatives

Name Party	Dist.	Room	Bldg.	Tele.
Thomas H. Andrews (D)	1st	1724	LHOB	225-6116
Olympia J. Snowe (R)	2nd	2464	RHOB	225-6306

MARYLAND
Senators

Name Party	Dist.	Room	Bldg.	Tele.
Barbara A. Mikulski (D)		320	HSOB	224-4654
Paul S. Sarbanes (D)		309	HSOB	224-4524

Representatives

Name Party	Dist.	Room	Bldg.	Tele.
Helen D. Bentley (R)	2nd	1610	LHOB	225-3061
Beverly B. Byron (D)	6th	2430	RHOB	225-2721
Benjamin L. Cardin (D)	3rd	117	CHOB	225-4016
Wayne T. Gilchrest (R)	1st	502	CHOB	225-5311
Steny H. Hoyer (D)	5th	1705	LHOB	225-4131
Thomas McMillen (D)	4th	420	CHOB	225-8090
Kweisi Mfume (D)	7th	217	CHOB	225-4741
Constance Morella (R)	8th	1024	LHOB	225-5341

MASSACHUSETTS
Senators

Name Party	Dist.	Room	Bldg.	Tele.
Edward M. Kennedy (D)		315	RSOB	224-4543
John F. Kerry (D)		421	RSOB	224-2742

Representatives

Name Party	Dist.	Room	Bldg.	Tele.
Chet Atkins (D)	5th	123	CHOB	225-3411
Brian Donnelly (D)	11th	2229	RHOB	225-3215
Joseph D. Early (D)	3rd	2349	RHOB	225-6101
Barney Frank (D)	4th	2404	RHOB	225-5931
Joseph P. Kennedy II (D)	8th	1208	LHOB	225-5111
Edward J. Markey (D)	7th	2133	RHOB	225-2836
Nicholas Mavroules (D)	6th	2334	RHOB	225-8020
Joe Moakley (D)	9th	235	CHOB	225-8273
Richard E. Neal (D)	2nd	437	CHOB	225-5601
John Oliver (D)	1st	1116	LHOB	225-5335
Gerry E. Studds (D)	10th	237	CHOB	225-3111

MICHIGAN
Senators

Name Party	Dist.	Room	Bldg.	Tele.
Carl M. Levin (D)		459	RSOB	224-6221
Donald W. Riegle (D)		105	DSOB	224-4822

Name Party	Dist.	Room	Bldg.	Tele.
Representatives				
David E. Bonior (D)	12th	2242	RHOB	225-2106
William S. Broomfield (R)	18th	2306	RHOB	225-6135
Dave Camp (R)	10th	511	CHOB	225-3561
Bob Carr (D)	6th	2439	RHOB	225-4872
Barbara-Rose Collins (D)	13th	1541	LHOB	225-2261
John Conyers (D)	1st	2426	RHOB	225-5126
Robert W. Davis (R)	11th	2417	RHOB	225-4735
John D. Dingell (D)	16th	2328	RHOB	225-4071
William D. Ford (D)	15th	2371	RHOB	225-6261
Paul B. Henry (R)	5th	215	CHOB	225-3831
Dennis M. Hertel (D)	14th	2442	RHOB	225-6276
Dale E. Kildee (D)	7th	2239	RHOB	225-3611
Sander Levin (D)	17th	323	CHOB	225-4961
Carl D. Pursell (R)	2nd	1414	LHOB	225-4401
Bob Traxler (D)	8th	2366	RHOB	225-2806
Fred Upton (R)	4th	1713	LHOB	225-3761
Guy Vander Jagt (R)	9th	2409	RHOB	225-3511
Howard Wolpe (D)	3rd	1535	LHOB	225-5011
MINNESOTA				
Senators				
David Durenberger (R)		154	RSOB	224-3244
Paul Wellstone (D)		702	HSOB	224-5641
Representatives				
James L. Oberstar (D)	8th	2209	RHOB	225-6211
Timothy J. Penny (D)	1st	436	CHOB	225-2472
Collin Peterson (D)	7th	1725	LHOB	225-2165
Jim Ramstad (R)	3rd	504	CHOB	225-2871
Martin Olav Sabo (D)	5th	2201	RHOB	225-4755
Gerry Sikorski (D)	6th	403	CHOB	225-2271
Bruce F. Vento (D)	4th	2304	RHOB	225-6631
Vin Weber (R)	2nd	106	CHOB	225-2331
MISSISSIPPI				
Senators				
Thad Cochran (R)		326	RSOB	224-5054
Trent Lott (R)		487	RSOB	224-6253
Representatives				
Mike Espy (D)	2nd	216	CHOB	225-5876
G.V. Montgomery (D)	3rd	2184	RHOB	225-5031
Mike Parker (D)	4th	1504	LHOB	225-5865
Gene Taylor (D)	5th	1429	LHOB	225-5772
Jamie L. Whitten (D)	1st	2314	RHOB	225-4306
MISSOURI				
Senators				
Christopher S. Bond (R)		293	RSOB	224-5721
John C. Danforth (R)		249A	RSOB	224-6154
Representatives				
William L. Clay (D)	1st	2470	RHOB	225-2406
E. Thomas Coleman (R)	6th	2468	RHOB	225-7041
Bill Emerson (R)	8th	438	CHOB	225-4404
Richard A. Gephardt (D)	3rd	1432	LHOB	225-2671
Melton Hancock (R)	7th	318	CHOB	225-6536
Joan Kelly Horn (D)	2nd	1008	LHOB	225-2561
Ike Skelton (D)	4th	2134	RHOB	225-2876
Harold L. Volkmer (D)	9th	2411	RHOB	225-2956
Alan Wheat (D)	5th	1210	LHOB	225-4535

Name Party	Dist.	Room	Bldg.	Tele.
MONTANA				
Senators				
Max Baucus (D)		706	HSOB	224-2651
Conrad Burns (R)		183	DSOB	224-2644
Representatives				
Ron Marlenee (R)	2nd	2465	RHOB	225-1555
Pat Williams (D)	1st	2457	RHOB	225-3211
NEBRASKA				
Senators				
J. James Exon (D)		528	HSOB	224-4224
J. Robert Kerrey (D)		316	HSOB	224-6551
Representatives				
Bill Barrett (R)	3rd	1607	LHOB	225-6435
Douglas K. Bereuter (R)	1st	2348	RHOB	225-4806
Peter Hoagland (D)	2nd	1710	LHOB	225-4155
NEVADA				
Senators				
Richard H. Bryan (D)		364	RSOB	224-6244
Harry Reid (D)		324	HSOB	224-3542
Representatives				
James H. Bilbray (D)	1st	319	CHOB	225-5965
Barbara Vucanovich (R)	2nd	206	CHOB	225-6155
NEW HAMPSHIRE				
Senators				
Warren B. Rudman (R)		530	HSOB	224-3324
Robert C. Smith (R)		332	DSOB	224-2841
Representatives				
Dick Swett (D)	2nd	128	CHOB	225-5206
William H. Zeliff (R)	1st	512	CHOB	225-5456
NEW JERSEY				
Senators				
Bill Bradley (D)		731	HSOB	224-3224
Frank R. Lautenberg (D)		506	HSOB	224-4744
Representatives				
Robert E. Andrews (D)	1st	1005	LHOB	225-6501
Bernard J. Dwyer (D)	6th	2428	RHOB	225-6301
Dean A. Gallo (R)	11th	1318	LHOB	225-5035
Frank J. Guarini (D)	14th	2458	RHOB	225-2765
William J. Hughes (D)	2nd	341	CHOB	225-6572
Frank Pallone (D)	3rd	213	CHOB	225-4671
Donald Payne (D)	10th	417	CHOB	225-3436
Matthew J. Rinaldo (R)	7th	2469	RHOB	225-5361
Robert A. Roe (D)	8th	2243	RHOB	225-5751
Marge Roukema (R)	5th	2244	RHOB	225-4465
H. James Saxton (R)	13th	324	CHOB	225-4765
Chris Smith (R)	4th	2440	RHOB	225-3765
Robert G. Torricelli (D)	9th	317	CHOB	225-5061
Dick Zimmer (R)	12th	510	CHOB	225-5801
NEW MEXICO				
Senators				
Jeff Bingaman (D)		524	HSOB	224-5521
Pete V. Domenici (R)		427	DSOB	224-6621
Representatives				
William B. Richardson (D)	3rd	204	CHOB	225-6190
Steven Schiff (R)	1st	1427	LHOB	225-6316
Joe Skeen (R)	2nd	2447	RHOB	225-2365

Name Party	Dist.	Room	Bldg.	Tele.
NEW YORK				
Senators				
Alfonse M. D'Amato (R)		520	HSOB	224-6542
Daniel Patrick Moynihan (D)		464	RSOB	224-4451
Representatives				
Gary Ackerman (D)	7th	238	CHOB	225-2601
Sherwood Boehlert (R)	25th	1127	LHOB	225-3665
Thomas J. Downey (D)	2nd	2232	RHOB	225-3335
Eliot L. Engel (D)	19th	1213	LHOB	225-2464
Hamilton Fish (R)	21st	2269	RHOB	225-5441
Floyd H. Flake (D)	6th	1034	LHOB	225-3461
Benjamin A. Gilman (R)	22nd	2185	RHOB	225-3776
Bill Green (R)	15th	2301	RHOB	225-2436
George J. Hochbrueckner (D)	1st	124	CHOB	225-3826
Frank Horton (R)	29th	2108	RHOB	225-4916
Amory Houghton, Jr. (R)	34th	1216	LHOB	225-3161
John J. LaFalce (D)	32nd	2367	RHOB	225-3231
Norman F. Lent (R)	4th	2408	RHOB	225-7896
Nita M. Lowey (D)	20th	1313	LHOB	225-6506
Tom Manton (D)	9th	331	CHOB	225-3965
David O'B. Martin (R)	26th	442	CHOB	225-4611
Raymond J. McGrath (R)	5th	205	CHOB	225-5516
Matthew F. McHugh (D)	28th	2335	RHOB	225-6335
Michael R. McNulty (D)	23rd	414	CHOB	225-5076
Susan K. Molinari (R)	14th	315	CHOB	225-3371
Robert J. Mrazek (D)	3rd	306	CHOB	225-5956
Henry J. Nowak (D)	33rd	2240	RHOB	225-3306
Major R. Owens (D)	12th	114	CHOB	225-6231
Bill Paxon (R)	31st	1314	LHOB	225-5265
Charles B. Rangel (D)	16th	2252	RHOB	225-4365
James H. Scheuer (D)	8th	2221	RHOB	225-5471
Charles E. Schumer (D)	10th	126	CHOB	225-6616
Jose E. Serrano (D)	18th	1217	LHOB	225-4361
Louise M. Slaughter (D)	30th	1424	LHOB	225-3615
Stephen J. Solarz (D)	13th	1536	LHOB	225-2361
Gerald B. Solomon (R)	24th	2265	RHOB	225-5614
Edolphus Towns (D)	11th	1726	LHOB	225-5936
James T. Walsh (R)	27th	1238	LHOB	225-3701
Ted Weiss (D)	17th	2467	RHOB	225-5635
NORTH CAROLINA				
Senators				
Jesse Helms (R)		403	DSOB	224-6342
Terry Sanford (D)		716	HSOB	224-3154
Representatives				
Cass Ballenger (R)	10th	328	CHOB	225-2576
Howard Coble (R)	6th	430	CHOB	225-3065
W. G. Hefner (D)	8th	2161	RHOB	225-3715
Walter B. Jones (D)	1st	241	CHOB	225-3101
Martin Lancaster (D)	3rd	1417	LHOB	225-3415
Alex McMillan (R)	9th	401	CHOB	225-1976
Stephen L. Neal (D)	5th	2463	RHOB	225-2071
David E. Price (D)	4th	1406	LHOB	225-1784
Charlie Rose (D)	7th	2230	RHOB	225-2731
Charles H. Taylor (R)	11th	516	CHOB	225-6401
Tim T. Valentine (D)	2nd	1510	LHOB	225-4531
NORTH DAKOTA				
Senators				
Quentin N. Burdick (D)		511	HSOB	224-2551
Kent Conrad (D)		724	HSOB	224-2043

Name Party	Dist.	Room	Bldg.	Tele.
Representative				
Byron L. Dorgan (D)		210	CHOB	225-2611
OHIO				
Senators				
John H. Glenn (D)		503	HSOB	224-3353
Howard M. Metzenbaum (D)		140	RSOB	224-2315
Representatives				
Douglas Applegate (D)	18th	2183	RHOB	225-6265
John A. Boehner (R)	8th	1020	LHOB	225-6205
Dennis E. Eckart (D)	11th	1111	LHOB	225-6331
Edward F. Feighan (D)	19th	1124	LHOB	225-5731
Paul E. Gillmor (R)	5th	1203	LHOB	225-6405
Bill Gradison (R)	2nd	1125	LHOB	225-3164
Tony P. Hall (D)	3rd	2162	RHOB	225-6465
David L. Hobson (R)	7th	1338	LHOB	225-4324
Marcy Kaptur (D)	9th	1228	LHOB	225-4146
John R. Kasich (R)	12th	1133	LHOB	225-5355
Charles J. Luken (D)	1st	1107	LHOB	225-2216
Bob McEwen (R)	6th	2431	RHOB	225-5705
Clarence Miller (R)	10th	2308	RHOB	225-5131
Mary Rose Oakar (D)	20th	2231	RHOB	225-5871
Michael G. Oxley (R)	4th	2448	RHOB	225-2676
Donald J. Pease (D)	13th	2410	RHOB	225-3401
Ralph S. Regula (R)	16th	2207	RHOB	225-3876
Thomas C. Sawyer (D)	14th	1518	LHOB	225-5231
Louis Stokes (D)	21st	2365	RHOB	225-7032
James A. Traficant (D)	17th	312	CHOB	225-5261
Chalmers P. Wylie (R)	15th	2310	RHOB	225-2015
OKLAHOMA				
Senators				
David L. Boren (D)		453	RSOB	224-4721
Don Nickles (R)		713	HSOB	224-5754
Representatives				
Bill K. Brewster (D)	3rd	1407	LHOB	225-4565
Mickey Edwards (R)	5th	2330	RHOB	225-2132
Glenn English (D)	6th	2206	RHOB	225-5565
James M. Inhofe (R)	1st	408	CHOB	225-2211
Dave McCurdy (D)	4th	2344	RHOB	225-6165
Mike Synar (D)	2nd	2441	RHOB	225-2701
OREGON				
Senators				
Mark O. Hatfield (R)		711	HSOB	224-3753
Bob Packwood (R)		259	RSOB	224-5244
Representatives				
Les AuCoin (D)	1st	2159	RHOB	225-0855
Peter A. DeFazio (D)	4th	1233	LHOB	225-6416
Michael J. Kopetski (D)	5th	1520	LHOB	225-5711
Robert F. Smith (R)	2nd	118	CHOB	225-6730
Ron Wyden (D)	3rd	2452	RHOB	225-4811
PENNSYLVANIA				
Senators				
Arlen Specter (R)		303	HSOB	224-4254
Harris Wofford (D)		283	RSOB	224-6324
Representatives				
Lucien E. Blackwell (D)	2nd	1725	LHOB	225-4001
Robert A. Borski (D)	3rd	407	CHOB	225-8251
William F. Clinger (R)	23rd	2160	RHOB	225-5121

Name Party	Dist.	Room	Bldg.	Tele.
Lawrence Coughlin (R)	13th	2309	RHOB	225-6111
William J. Coyne (D)	14th	2455	RHOB	225-2301
Thomas M. Foglietta (D)	1st	231	CHOB	225-4731
Joseph M. Gaydos (D)	20th	2186	RHOB	225-4631
George W. Gekas (R)	17th	1519	LHOB	225-4315
William F. Goodling (R)	19th	2263	RHOB	225-5836
Paul E. Kanjorski (D)	11th	424	CHOB	225-6511
Joseph P. Kolter (D)	4th	212	CHOB	225-2565
Peter H. Kostmayer (D)	8th	2436	RHOB	225-4276
Joseph M. McDade (R)	10th	2370	RHOB	225-3731
Austin J. Murphy (D)	22nd	2210	RHOB	225-4665
John P. Murtha (D)	12th	2423	RHOB	225-2065
Thomas J. Ridge (R)	21st	1714	LHOB	225-5406
Don Ritter (R)	15th	2202	RHOB	225-6411
Richard John Santorum (R)	18th	1708	LHOB	225-2135
Richard T. Schulze (R)	5th	2267	RHOB	225-5761
Bud Shuster (R)	9th	2188	RHOB	225-2431
Robert S. Walker (R)	16th	2369	RHOB	225-2411
Curt Weldon (R)	7th	316	CHOB	225-2011
Gus Yatron (D)	6th	2205	RHOB	225-5546

RHODE ISLAND
Senators

Name Party	Dist.	Room	Bldg.	Tele.
John H. Chafee (R)		567	DSOB	224-2921
Claiborne Pell (D)		335	RSOB	224-4642

Representatives

Ronald K. Machtley (R)	1st	132	CHOB	225-4911
John F. Reed (D)	2nd	1229	LHOB	225-2735

SOUTH CAROLINA
Senators

Ernest F. Hollings (D)		125	RSOB	224-6121
Strom Thurmond (R)		217	RSOB	224-5972

Representatives

Butler Derrick (D)	3rd	221	CHOB	225-5301
Liz J. Patterson (D)	4th	1641	LHOB	225-6030
Arthur Ravenel, Jr. (R)	1st	508	CHOB	225-3176
Floyd Spence (R)	2nd	2405	RHOB	225-2452
John Spratt (D)	5th	1533	LHOB	225-5501
Robin Tallon (D)	6th	432	CHOB	225-3315

SOUTH DAKOTA
Senators

Thomas A. Daschle (D)		317	HSOB	224-2321
Larry Pressler (R)		133	HSOB	224-5842

Representative

Tim Johnson (D)		428	CHOB	225-2801

TENNESSEE
Senators

Albert Gore, Jr.(D)		393	RSOB	224-4944
James R. Sasser (D)		363	RSOB	224-3344

Representatives

Bob Clement (D)	5th	325	CHOB	225-4311
James H. Cooper (D)	4th	125	CHOB	225-6831
John Duncan, Jr. (R)	2nd	115	CHOB	225-5435
Harold E. Ford (D)	9th	2305	RHOB	225-3265
Bart Gordon (D)	6th	103	CHOB	225-4231
Marilyn Lloyd (D)	3rd	2266	RHOB	225-3271
James H. Quillen (R)	1st	102	CHOB	225-6356
Donald K. Sundquist (R)	7th	230	CHOB	225-2811

Name Party	Dist.	Room	Bldg.	Tele.
John S. Tanner (D)	8th	1232	LHOB	225-4714

TEXAS
Senators

Lloyd Bentsen (D)		703	HSOB	224-5922
Phil Gramm (R)		370	RSOB	224-2934

Representatives

Thomas Andrews (D)	25th	303	CHOB	225-7508
Bill Archer (R)	7th	1236	LHOB	225-2571
Richard Armey (R)	26th	130	CHOB	225-7772
Joe L. Barton (R)	6th	1225	LHOB	225-2002
Jack Brooks (D)	9th	2449	RHOB	225-6565
John Bryant (D)	5th	208	CHOB	225-2231
Albert Bustamante (D)	23rd	1133	LHOB	225-4511
Jim Chapman (D)	1st	236	CHOB	225-3035
Ronald D. Coleman (D)	16th	440	CHOB	225-4831
Larry Combest (R)	19th	1527	LHOB	225-4005
E. (Kika) de la Garza (D)	15th	1401	LHOB	225-2531
Tom DeLay (R)	22nd	308	CHOB	225-5951
Chet Edwards (D)	11th	425	CHOB	225-6105
Jack Fields (R)	8th	108	CHOB	225-4901
Martin Frost (D)	24th	2459	RHOB	225-3605
Preston Pete Geren (D)	12th	1730	LHOB	225-5071
Henry B. Gonzalez (D)	20th	2413	RHOB	225-3236
Ralph M. Hall (D)	4th	2236	RHOB	225-6673
Sam Johnson (R)	3rd	1223	LHOB	225-4201
Greg Laughlin (D)	14th	218	CHOB	225-2831
Solomon P. Ortiz (D)	27th	2445	RHOB	225-7742
J.J. Pickle (D)	10th	242	CHOB	225-4865
Bill Sarpalius (D)	13th	126	CHOB	225-3706
Lamar Smith (R)	21st	422	CHOB	225-4236
Charles W. Stenholm (D)	17th	1226	LHOB	225-6605
Craig A. Washington (D)	18th	1711	LHOB	225-3816
Charles Wilson (D)	2nd	2256	RHOB	225-2401

UTAH
Senators

Jake Garn (R)		505	DSOB	224-5444
Orrin G. Hatch (R)		135	RSOB	224-5251

Representatives

James V. Hansen (R)	1st	2421	RHOB	225-0453
Bill Orton (D)	3rd	1723	LHOB	225-7751
Wayne Owens (D)	2nd	1728	LHOB	225-3011

VERMONT
Senators

James Jeffords (R)		530	DSOB	224-5141
Patrick J. Leahy (D)		433	RSOB	224-4242

Representative

Bernard Sanders (I)		509	CHOB	225-4115

VIRGINIA
Senators

Charles Robb (D)		493	RSOB	224-4024
John W. Warner (R)		225	RSOB	224-2023

Representatives

Herbert H. Bateman (R)	1st	1030	LHOB	225-4261
Thomas J. Bliley (R)	3rd	2241	RHOB	225-2815
Rick Boucher (D)	9th	405	CHOB	225-3861
James P. Moran (D)	8th	1523	LHOB	225-4376
James R. Olin (D)	6th	1410	LHOB	225-5431

Name Party	Dist.	Room	Bldg.	Tele.
L.F. Payne (D)	5th	1118	LHOB	225-4711
Owen B. Pickett (D)	2nd	1204	LHOB	225-4215
Norman Sisisky (D)	4th	426	CHOB	225-6365
George F. Allen (R)	7th	1404	LHOB	225-6561
Frank Wolf (R)	10th	104	CHOB	225-5136

WASHINGTON
Senators

		Room	Bldg.	Tele.
Brock Adams (D)		513	HSOB	224-2621
Slade Gorton (R)		730	HSOB	224-3441

Representatives

Name Party	Dist.	Room	Bldg.	Tele.
Rod Chandler (R)	8th	223	CHOB	225-7761
Norman D. Dicks (D)	6th	2429	RHOB	225-5916
Thomas S. Foley (D)	5th	1201	LHOB	225-2006
James A. McDermott (D)	7th	1707	LHOB	225-3106
John Miller (R)	1st	322	CHOB	225-6311
Sid Morrison (R)	4th	1434	LHOB	225-5816
Al Swift (D)	2nd	1502	LHOB	225-2605
Jolene Unsoeld (D)	3rd	1508	LHOB	225-3536

WEST VIRGINIA
Senators

		Room	Bldg.	Tele.
Robert C. Byrd (D)		311	HSOB	224-3954
John D. Rockefeller IV (D)		109	HSOB	224-6472

Name Party	Dist.	Room	Bldg.	Tele.
Representatives				
Alan B. Mollohan (D)	1st	229	CHOB	225-4172
Nick J. Rahall (D)	4th	2104	RHOB	225-3452
Harley O. Staggers, Jr. (D)	2nd	1323	LHOB	225-4331
Robert Wise (D)	3rd	1421	LHOB	225-2711

WISCONSIN
Senators

		Room	Bldg.	Tele.
Robert W. Kasten (R)		110	HSOB	224-5323
Herbert Kohl (D)		330	HSOB	224-5653

Representatives

Name Party	Dist.	Room	Bldg.	Tele.
Les Aspin (D)	1st	2336	RHOB	225-3031
Steven Gunderson (R)	3rd	2235	RHOB	225-5506
Gerald D. Kleczka (D)	4th	226	CHOB	225-4572
Scott L. Klug (R)	2nd	1224	LHOB	225-2906
James P. Moody (D)	5th	1019	LHOB	225-3571
David Obey (D)	7th	2462	RHOB	225-3365
Thomas E. Petri (R)	6th	2245	RHOB	225-2476
Tobias Roth (R)	8th	2352	RHOB	225-5665
F. James Sensenbrenner (R)	9th	2444	RHOB	225-5101

WYOMING
Senators

		Room	Bldg.	Tele.
Alan K. Simpson (R)		261	DSOB	224-3424
Malcolm Wallop (R)		237	RSOB	224-6441

Representative

Name Party	Dist.	Room	Bldg.	Tele.
Craig Thomas (R)		1721	LHOB	225-2311

INDEX

229